Victims of Progress

THIRD EDITION

JOHN H. BODLEY

Washington State University

Mayfield Publishing Company
Mountain View, California

Library of Congress Cataloging-in-Publication Data

Bodley, John H.
    Victims of progress / John H. Bodley. — 3rd ed.
        p.   cm.
    Bibliography: p.
    Includes index.
    ISBN 0–87484–945–4
    1. Indigenous peoples. 2. Culture conflict. 3. Social change.
I. Title.
GN380.B63   1990
306—dc20
                                                                89-33782
                                                                CIP

Manufactured in the United States of America

10   9   8   7   6   5   4   3

Mayfield Publishing Company
1240 Villa Street
Mountain View, California 94041

Sponsoring editor, Janet M. Beatty; *managing editor*, Linda Toy; *production editor*, Sondra Glider; *manuscript editor*, Margaret Moore; *text designer*, Wendy Calmenson, The Book Company; *cover designer*, David Toy; *cover photographer*, Belinda Wright; *map illustrator*, Salinda Tyson. The text was set in 10/12 Janson by G & S Typesetters and printed on 50# Finch Opaque by Banta Company.

Preface

Victims of Progress will appeal to students in courses that stress culture change, modernization, and economic development as they relate to tribal cultures. Over the years, the book has also been widely used in introductory general and cultural anthropology courses when the instructor wished to present these topics in depth. Because this book continues to present a particular viewpoint on controversial issues, it often serves as a stimulus for debate. Clear arguments, abundant case material, and ample documentation provide a solid basis for classroom discussion and encourage further reading.

This work assumes that government policies and attitudes are the basic determinants of the fate of tribal cultures and that governments throughout the world care most about the increasingly efficient exploitation of the human and natural resources of the areas under their control. The chapters examine and document the worldwide regularities characterizing interaction between industrial nations and tribal cultures since 1830. It is an unfortunate record of wholesale cultural imperialism, aggression, and exploitation that has involved every major nation, regardless of differences in political, religious, or social philosophies. While blatant extermination policies have become relatively infrequent, basic native policies and the motives underlying them have changed little since the industrial powers began to expand more than 150 years ago. Today, however, many hopeful signs are appearing, especially at the international level.

The first edition of this book was based largely on conditions existing in the iv · PREFACE

early 70s. Since then a dramatic shift toward the political mobilization of indigenous peoples has occurred throughout the world. Federations of indigenous peoples have been formed in several regions, and a World Council of Indigenous Peoples now exists. We've seen a proliferation of new, nonindigenous organizations designed to support various native efforts to maintain traditional ways of life. Conditions today are certainly much more dynamic, and the outlook for genuine cultural diversity seems more promising than it did in the 70s.

This third edition reflects developments over the past eight years. I've made clarifications in several cases to emphasize that I am *not* arguing that tribals were perfect human beings, who enjoyed perfect health and existed in complete harmony with their natural environments. While tribal communities have been victimized by progress, tribal individuals have sometimes benefited by and even encouraged the process, as Eder (1987) has noted in his *On the Road to Tribal Extinction.* My primary concern is with the larger political decisions that have encouraged the invasion of tribal lands by outsiders in the first place.

I have completely rewritten the final chapter as "Human Rights and the Politics of Ethnocide" to make this emphasis even clearer. This chapter reinterprets the historical development of tribal policy in terms of a split between those arguing for and against tribal autonomy. Ultimately, the future of indigenous peoples is a human rights issue. This view has emerged only recently and is now promoted by both indigenous political organizations and a variety of support organizations. If inordinate attention seems to be devoted to an analysis of "realists" in Chapter 10 and proportionately less space to the modern "idealist" organizations such as Cultural Survival, IWGIA, and Survival International, it is not because I feel these latter organizations are less important. It is the indigenous organizations themselves that should be the center of attention; they should have the primary role in defining their interests and the terms of the struggle.

Acknowledgments

The first edition of this work was supported in part by a summer research stipend awarded to me by Washington State University for research during the summer of 1972. In 1980 I was on professional leave at the International Work Group for Indigenous Affairs (IWGIA) in Copenhagen, Denmark, to gather new material for the second edition. In London, I benefited from discussion with Stephen Corry of Survival International. I am grateful for the many kindnesses extended to me by the IWGIA staff, but I would like to especially acknowledge my debt to the late Helge Kleivan, former director of IWGIA and one of its original founders. His total dedication to the human rights struggle on behalf of indigenous peoples is a continuing source of inspiration.

This third edition has benefited from the many readers who have kindly sent me useful materials and comments over the years, and who are too numerous to thank individually. I gained valuable insights during a five-week seminar I attended at the University of Uppsala, Sweden in 1985, where Kaj Arhem,

Hugh Beach, Claes Corlin, and Jan Ovesen were my hosts. In 1986, Ray Barnhardt of the University of Alaska invited me to present a special course on Native Peoples in Fairbanks and Bethel, which gave me a close view of Alaskan issues. Jerome Bailen of the University of the Philippines in Manila was my host for a brief 1986 visit to the Philippines, and he helped arrange contacts with indigenous leaders in the Cordillera.

Special thanks go to Napoleon Chagnon, University of California, Santa Barbara; Michael Howard, Simon Fraser University, British Columbia; and Susan Lees of Hunter College for their critical reviews of the first draft of the third edition. At Mayfield, Janet Beatty was the sponsoring editor who encouraged me to prepare this edition and she directed it throughout. Sondra Glider served as production editor. Margaret Moore, who copyedited the first edition, also gave this manuscript a careful reading.

Contents

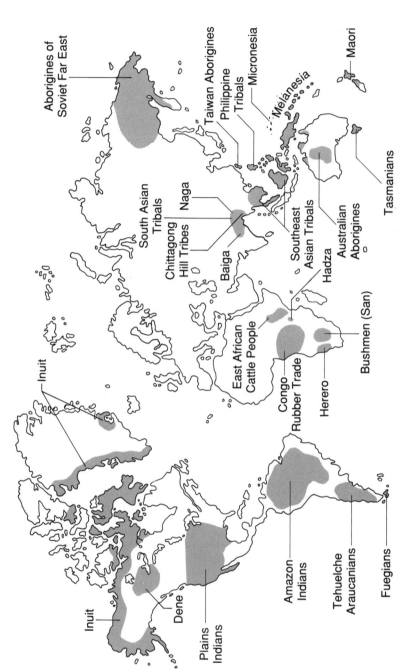

Cultural Areas and Case Studies Featured in This Book

Introduction

INDUSTRIAL CIVILIZATION IS NOW completing the process of transformation and absorption or extermination of the world's tribal peoples and cultures that politically organized states have been carrying out for 6,000 years. According to many authorities within industrial civilization, this disappearance or drastic modification of these cultures is necessary for the "progress" of civilization and is inevitable, natural, and, in the long run, beneficial for the peoples involved. However, ironically, now that we foresee the imminent possibility of the total disappearance of free tribal peoples, we are just beginning to realize the staggering worldwide costs of industrialization. It is increasingly apparent that civilization's "progress" destroys the environment as well as other peoples and cultures and that modern civilization may become a victim of its own progress. In view of this situation, we might question the wisdom of endorsing and encouraging the final disappearance of peoples who reject our "advances" and instead find satisfaction in small-scale, relatively egalitarian ways of life, which are geared more to the sustained use of natural resources.

The impact of modern civilization on tribal peoples has been a dominant research theme in anthropology, but in the past anthropologists often viewed it from the same ethnocentric premises accepted by government officials, developers, missionaries, and the general public. Surprisingly, anthropologists, who discovered ethnocentrism and built their profession by scientifically documenting and analyzing tribal cultures and the process of their "modernization," too

1

often took positions facilitating their destruction. Applied anthropologists attempted to reconcile the natives to the "inevitable" loss of their "maladaptive" cultures and often worked to speed the process while perhaps easing some of the detrimental side effects. Unfortunately, many anthropologists disregarded their own humanistic admonitions concerning ethnocentrism, cultural relativism, and the fundamental right of different life styles to coexist. They developed theoretical concepts and advanced seemingly "scientific" arguments masking the political realities of civilization's systematic destruction of tribal cultures.

However, since 1968 the situation has changed dramatically and is now in many ways more hopeful. Surviving tribals have not remained passive as states have enveloped them; instead, they have redefined themselves as "indigenous peoples" and have struggled with some success to retain their distinctive features. At the same time, many observers now recognize that the survival of tribal and indigenous peoples is in fact an international human rights issue. Safeguarding the rights of tribal and indigenous peoples to maintain their independent existence and manage their own natural resources represents genuine "progress" that in the long run will benefit the entire international community.

· I ·

Progress and Tribal Peoples

The Industrial Revolution disrupts and transforms all preceding cultures in West and East alike, and at the same time throws their resources into a common pool.

Graham, 1971:193

TRIBAL PEOPLES ARE BEING drastically affected by civilization, and their cultural patterns and, in many cases, the peoples themselves are disappearing as civilization advances. For many years anthropologists have made this topic a special field of study, but many seem to have missed its larger significance by failing to stress that the ecological irresponsibility of modern industrial nations and the reckless pursuit of progress are the basic causes of the continuing destruction of tribal peoples. This book is an attempt to dispel some of the widely held ethnocentric misconceptions concerning the disappearance of tribal cultures and to focus attention on the basic causes, because these causes reveal serious problems within industrial culture itself and must be understood before the world will be safe for cultural diversity.

At the outset the problem must be viewed in long-term perspective as a struggle between two incompatible cultural systems—tribes and states. For the purpose of understanding the interaction between these two systems, the most critical features of tribal groups are their political independence, reliance on local natural resources, and relative internal social equality. Tribes are small-scale sovereign nations that tend to manage local ecosystems for long-term sustained use. In comparison with states, and especially industrial states, tribal systems tend to expand more slowly and have been environmentally less destructive.

Maintaining a greater internal social equality translates into less incentive for tribes to elevate economic production and consumption beyond local subsistence demands and more uniformly satisfies basic human needs. These differences explain why territories still controlled by tribal groups are so attractive to "developing nations"—because tribal territories contain "underutilized" resources.

The struggle between tribes and states has been over conflicting systems of resource management and internal social organization. Tribes represent small-scale, classless societies, with decentralized, communal, long-term resource management strategies, whereas states are class-based societies, with centralized management systems that extract resources for the short-term profit of special interest groups. Understandably, then, the political conquest of tribal areas often brings rapid environmental deterioration and may impoverish tribal peoples.

I am speaking here in global terms about a generalized tribal system for the purpose of understanding the causes and consequences of the incorporation and conquest of tribes by states. There are many exceptions to this ideal tribal model, and any specific culture exists at some point along a continuum between tribal and state organization. I am not assuming that tribes were ever isolated or completely self-sufficient, or existed in perfect equality, harmony, and absolute "balance" with nature. Nor would I argue that tribes are inherently good and states inherently evil. Both systems have advantages and disadvantages. However, given this disclaimer, significant qualitative differences between tribes and states remain, and these differences illuminate the recent fate of tribals along the frontiers of national expansion. The most advantageous unique qualities of tribal systems will need to be acknowledged and safeguarded by national governments if the future of indigenous peoples is to be secured.

People have led a tribal existence for at least the past half million years, and only for the past 10,000 years or so have any people lived in cities or states. Since the first appearance of urban life and state organization, the earlier tribal cultures were gradually displaced from the world's most productive agricultural lands and were relegated to marginal areas. Tribal peoples persisted for thousands of years in a dynamic equilibrium or symbiotic relationship with civilizations that had reached and remained within their own ecological boundaries. But this situation shifted abruptly a mere 500 years ago as Europeans began to expand beyond the long-established frontiers separating tribal peoples from states. However, by 1750, after 250 years of preindustrial European expansion, tribal peoples still seemed secure and successfully adapted to their economically "marginal" refuges—but industrialization suddenly reduced the possibilities for the continued existence of politically independent tribal groups.

PROGRESS: THE INDUSTRIAL EXPLOSION

In the mid-eighteenth century the industrial revolution launched the developing Western nations on an explosive growth in population and consumption called "progress," which led to an unprecedented assault on the world's tribal peoples

FIGURE I.I

Traditional tribal cultures and industrial civilization are contrasting and incompatible systems. This contrast is obvious in this scene from highland New Guinea where a tribal group is observing the presence of modern technology suddenly thrust upon them. (Patricia K. Littlewood.)

and their resources. Within the 250 years since then the world has been totally transformed, many self-sufficient tribal cultures have disappeared, and dramatic resource shortages and environmental disasters have materialized. Now that many researchers are struggling to explain why industrial civilization seems to be floundering in its own success, anthropologists are beginning to realize that the first and most ominous victims of industrial progress were the several million tribal people who still controlled over half the globe in 1820 and who shared a relatively stable, satisfying, and proven cultural adaptation. It is highly significant and somewhat unsettling to realize that the cultural systems of these first victims of progress present a striking contrast to the characteristics of industrial civilization (see Bodley, 1985).

The industrial revolution is nothing less than an *explosion* because of the unparalleled scope and the catastrophic nature of the transformations that it has initiated. Phenomenal increases in both population and per capita consumption rates were the two most critical correlates of industrialization because they quickly led to overwhelming pressure on natural resources.

The acceleration in world population growth rates and their relationship to industrial progress have been well documented. Immediately prior to the industrial revolution, for example, the doubling time of the world's population was approximately 250 years. However, after industrialization was under way, the

European population of 1850 doubled in just over eighty years, and the European populations of the United States, Canada, Australia, and Argentina tripled between 1851 and 1900 (Woodruff, 1966). The doubling time of the world's population reached its lowest point of about thirty-three years (an annual growth rate of over 2 percent) during the period 1965–1973. By 1986 the global rate of population growth had declined only slightly to 1.8 percent a year. In contrast, clear anthropological evidence shows that tribal populations grow slowly and use their natural resources conservatively. The relative stability of tribal populations is due only partly to higher mortality rates; it is also attributed to social, economic, and religious controls on fertility, the significance of which is still not fully understood. Although tribal populations have the capacity for growth, and may expand rapidly into empty lands, they are politically and economically designed to operate most effectively at low densities and low absolute size.

THE CULTURE OF CONSUMPTION

The increased rates of resource consumption accompanying industrialization have been even more critical than mere population increase. Above all else, industrial civilization is a culture of *consumption*, and in this respect it differs most strikingly from tribal cultures. Industrial economies are founded on the principle that consumption must be ever expanded, and complex systems of mass marketing and advertising have been developed for that specific purpose. Social stratification in industrial societies is based primarily on inequalities in material wealth and is both supported and reflected by differential access to resources. Industrial ideological systems stress belief in continual economic growth and progress and characteristically measure "standard of living" in terms of levels of material consumption.

Tribal cultures contrast strikingly in all of these aspects. Their economies are geared to the satisfaction of basic subsistence needs, which are assumed to be fixed, while a variety of cultural mechanisms serve to limit material acquisitiveness and to redistribute wealth. Wealth itself is rarely the basis of social stratification, and there is generally free access to natural resources for all. These contrasts are the basis for the incompatibility between tribal and industrial cultures and are the traits that are the sources of particular problems when tribals are conquered by industrial societies.

The most obvious consequences of tribal consumption patterns are that these cultures tend to be highly stable, make light demands on their environments, and can easily support themselves within their own boundaries. The opposite situation prevails for the culture of consumption. Almost overnight the industrialized nations literally ate up their own local resources and outgrew their boundaries. This was dramatically apparent in England, where local resources comfortably supported tribal cultures for thousands of years, but after 100 years of industrial progress the area was unable to meet its basic needs for grain, wood, fibers, and hides. Between 1851 and 1900 Europe was forced to export 35 million people because it could no longer support them (Woodruff, 1966). In the United States, where industrial progress has gone the furthest, since 1970 Americans have been consuming per capita some fifteen times more energy than neolithic agriculturalists and seven times the world average in non-renewable resources. They are also importing vast tonnages of food, fuels, and other resources to support themselves.

Indeed few, if any, industrial nations can now supply from within their own boundaries the resources needed to support further growth or even to maintain current consumption levels. It should not be surprising, then, that the "under-developed" resources controlled by the world's self-sufficient tribal peoples were quickly appropriated by outsiders to support their own industrial progress.

RESOURCE APPROPRIATION AND ACCULTURATION

In case after case, government programs for the progress of tribal peoples directly or indirectly force culture change, and these programs in turn are linked invariably to the extraction of tribal resources to benefit the national economy. From the strength of this relationship between tribal "progress" and the exploitation of tribal resources, we might even infer that tribal peoples would not be asked to surrender their resources and independence if industrial societies learned to control their own culture of consumption. This point must be made explicit, because considerable confusion exists in the enormous culture change literature regarding the basic question of why tribal cultures seem inevitably to be acculturated or modernized by industrial civilization. The consensus, at least among economic development writers (and the view often expressed in introductory textbooks), is the ethnocentric view that contact with superior industrial culture causes tribal peoples to voluntarily reject their own cultures in order to obtain a better life. Other writers, however, have seemed curiously mystified by the entire process. An example of this latter position can be seen in Julian Steward's summary of a monumental study of change in traditional cultures in eleven countries. Steward (1967:20–21) concluded that while many startling parallels could be identified, the causal factors involved in the modernization process were still "not well conceptualized."

This inability to conceptualize the causes of the transformation process in simple, nonethnocentric terms—or indeed the inability to conceptualize the causes at all—may be due to the fact that the analysts are members of the culture of consumption that today is the dominant world culture type. The most powerful cultures have always assumed a natural right to exploit the world's resources wherever they find them, regardless of the prior claims of indigenous populations. Arguing for efficiency and survival of the fittest, early colonialists elevated this "right" to the level of an ethical and legal principle that could be invoked to justify the elimination of any cultures that were not making "effective" use of their resources.

Members of the expanding culture rationalized as "natural" evolutionary

FIGURE 1.2

A Campa Indian of the Peruvian Amazon pre-
pares wild rubber for sale. The ever-increasing
need of the industrial nations for resources has
been a primary cause of the transformation of
tribal cultures. (Author.)

processes that eliminated groups considered to be either culturally or racially
inferior. They thought this "selection" process was so natural and "inevitable"
that nothing could prevent it. For example, in 1915 Paul Popenoe told the scientists assembled in Washington, D.C., for the 19th International Congress of
Americanists that the mass destruction of native Americans following the European invasion was "a process of racial purification of weak stocks." The Indian
was "killed off by natural selection." Popenoe declared: "The native succumbed
to the process of evolution, and no conceivable kindnesses from their conquerors
could have prevented this elimination" (1915:620). Certainly, disease was a
major factor in New World depopulation, but it was accompanied by conquest
and colonization, which were political processes for which people were responsible. Treating ethnocide and genocide as scientific law is to mask their underlying political causes.

    These old attitudes of social darwinism are embedded in our ideological
system and still occur in the professional literature on culture change. In fact,
one development writer declared: "Perhaps entire societies will lack survival

value and vanish before the onslaught of industrialization" (Goulet 1971:266). This viewpoint also appears in modern theories of cultural evolution, where it is expressed as the "Law of Cultural Dominance":

That cultural system which more effectively exploits the energy resources of a given environment will tend to spread in that environment at the expense of less effective systems.

Kaplan, 1960:75

Apart from the obvious ethical implications involved here, upon close inspection all of these theories expounding the greater adaptability, efficiency, and survival value of the dominant industrial culture prove to be misleading. Of course, as a culture of consumption, industrial civilization is uniquely capable of consuming resources at tremendous rates, but this does not make it a more *effective* culture than low-energy tribal cultures, if stability or long-run ecological success is taken as the criterion for "effectiveness." Likewise, the assumption that a given environment is not being exploited effectively by a traditional culture may merely reflect the unwillingness of national political authorities to allow local tribal groups to manage their own resources for their own interests. We should expect, then, that members of the culture of consumption would probably consider another culture's resources to be underexploited and to use this as a justification for appropriating them.

"Optimum" Land Use for Hill Tribes

The experience of the Chittagong Hills peoples of East Pakistan (Bangladesh since 1972) provides an excellent example of the process by which industrialization leads to a shortage of resources at the national level and ultimately results in the political conquest and dispossession of tribal peoples who have preserved their resources more effectively. Along with other parts of the world—thanks to the intervention of the industrial nations—East Pakistan had such a severe population explosion that by 1965 population densities reached an average of 470 people per square kilometer and the soil resources of the country were being pushed to the limits. As the crunch on resources worsened, the government made dramatic efforts to emulate the industrialization-economic development route of the developed nations and soon directed special attention to the still largely self-sufficient Chittagong Hills tribal areas, which had managed to remain outside of the cash economy and had avoided major disruptions due to industrial intrusion. The French anthropologist Claude Levi-Strauss (1951), who visited the area in 1950, found the hill tribes flourishing and observed that the Chittagong Hills "form a kind of anthropological sanctuary." Although the twelve ethnic groups making up the hill tribes were not totally isolated, they had enjoyed considerable political autonomy, especially under British control. However, the tribal areas were beginning to show population growth and subsequent pressure on their own resources due to shortening swidden cycles. But with only thirty-five people per square kilometer, they remained an island of low population density and "underdeveloped" resources in what had suddenly become an impoverished and overpopulated country.

External exploitation of tribal resources in the interests of the national economy initially focused on the forests of the Chittagong Hills. Twenty-two percent of the district was declared a forest "reserve," a "Forest Industries Development Corporation" was organized by the provincial government, and in 1953 lumber and paper mills were in operation to facilitate the modern commercial utilization of the region's bamboo and tropical hardwoods. In 1962 the largest river in the tribal area was dammed to supply hydroelectric power to help feed the rising energy demands of East Pakistan's urban affluent. In the process, however, 673 square kilometers of the best tribal agricultural land were converted into a lake, further aggravating the land scarcity that was already developing because of earlier disruptions of the population-resources balance and requiring the resettlement and "rehabilitation" of many hill people.

Still dissatisfied with the level of resource exploitation in the Chittagong Hills, in 1964 the Pakistani government enlisted an eleven-member international team of geologists, soil scientists, biologists, foresters, economists, and agricultural engineers to devise a master plan for the integrated development of the area based on what they considered to be optimum land-use possibilities. The team worked for two years with helicopters, aerial photographs, and computers. They concluded that regardless of how well the traditional economic system of shifting cultivation and subsistence production may have been attuned to its environment in the past, today it "can no longer be tolerated" (Webb, 1966:3232). The research team decided that the hill tribes should allow their land to be used primarily for the production of forest products for the benefit of the national economy because it was not well suited for large-scale cash cropping. The report left no alternative to the tribal peoples, as a member of the research team observes:

> More of the Hill tribesmen will have to become wage earners in the forest or other developing industries, and purchase their food from farmers practicing permanent agriculture on an intensive basis on the limited better land classes. It is realized that a whole system of culture and an age-old way of life cannot be changed overnight, but change it must, and quickly. The time is opportune. The maps and the basic data have been collected for an integrated development toward optimum land use.
>
> Webb, 1966:3232

The government policy of "optimum" land use brought immediate disaster for the hill tribes (Mey, 1983; Nietschmann, 1985; Zaman, 1985). The USAID-funded Kaptai Dam inundated 253 square miles of tribal land, including much of the best cultivable land, and displaced 100,000 tribal people. At the same time, the government allowed large-scale entry by Bengali settlers, who practiced plow agriculture and began to further displace the tribals. In 1977 the Bangladeshi military initiated a genocidal extermination policy against the hill tribes. By 1982 some 400,000 Bengali settlers held tribal lands and were supported by 30,000 government troops. Two years later international organizations reported that 185,000 tribals had been killed. The Shanti Bahini, a guerrilla organization formed to defend tribal interests, proved unable to prevent the slaughter (IWGIA Newsletter, 1984, 37:15–17).

The Role of Ethnocentrism

Although resource exploitation is clearly the basic cause of the destruction of tribal peoples and cultures, it is important to identify the underlying ethnocentric attitudes that are often used to justify exploitative policies. *Ethnocentrism*, the belief in the superiority of one's own culture, is vital to the integrity of any culture, but it can threaten the well-being of other peoples when it becomes the basis for forcing irrelevant standards upon tribal cultures. Anthropologists may justifiably take credit for exposing the ethnocentrism of nineteenth-century writers who described tribal peoples as badly in need of improvement, but they often overlook the ethnocentrism that occurs in the modern professional literature on economic development. Ironically, ethnocentrism threatens tribal peoples even today through its support of culturally insensitive government policies.

Ethnocentrism and Ethnocide

Anthropologists have been quick to stress the presumed deficiencies of tribal cultures as a justification for externally imposed change or a rejection of proposals that tribals be granted political autonomy. For example, in 1940 British anthropologist Lord Fitzroy Raglan, who later became president of the Royal Anthropological Institute, declared that tribal beliefs in magic were a chief cause of "folly and unhappiness" and the "worst evils of the day." He argued that, as long as tribals persist in such beliefs, the rest of the world cannot be considered civilized. In his view, existing tribes constituted "plague spots" that threatened to reinfect civilized areas, and the rapid imposition of civilization was the only solution. He declared:

> We should bring to them our justice, our education, and our science. Few will deny that these are better than anything which savages have got.
>
> Raglan, 1940:62

More recently, American anthropologist Arthur Hippler (1979) echoed Raglan's remarks. In a debate with Gerald Weiss over the merits of tribal autonomy, Hippler argued that national religions are superior to the "terrors of shamanism." He found "our own culture" more exciting, interesting, and varied, and better at promoting human potential than are "backward" tribal cultures, and he assumed that all tribals would inevitably be drawn to it. Hippler suggested that only internal oppression from tribal elders prevents tribals from improving their culture. Not surprisingly, Hippler specifically opposed autonomy proposals for the defense of tribal groups because autonomy would keep people "backward" against their will. Furthermore, he argued that "culture" is an abstraction, not something that can be defended or "saved" from extinction. Thus, ethnocide, the destruction of a cultural or an ethnic group, could not occur. In his response, Weiss (1988) exposed the ethnocentrism of Hippler's position point by point.

Crude Customs and Traditions

Ethnocentrism by culture change professionals, as illustrated in the following example from India, has often been a powerful support for coercive government policies directed against tribal peoples. A group of Indian scholars and administrators presented an unsympathetic view of tribal culture in a series of papers and speeches at a seminar on new policy directions for the hill tribes of North East India, which was held at Calcutta in 1966 (Mittra & Das Gupta, 1967). Some participants in the seminar complained that prior British administrators had committed the fundamental error of placing tribal culture above the "basic need for human progress" (Moasosang, 1967:51), because for a time they had attempted to prevent the economic exploitation of the region by nontribal peoples. Throughout the seminar, participants attacked the entire range of traditional culture on ethnocentric grounds. They called the tribal economic system backward, wasteful, and in need of "scientific permanent farming" (Nag, 1967: 90); an Indian professor complained of "crude customs and traditions" and characterized the tribal Garo peoples as being steeped in "primitive ignorance," "tradition-bound," and "static." Participants called for more thorough research to determine whether or not Garo society could be lifted out of its "morass of backwardness, traditionalism, and pseudo-modernism" (Kar, 1967:80–90).

In one paper curiously entitled "An Outlook for a Better Understanding of Tribal People" (Thiek, 1967:103–109), an enlightened tribal member characterized his tribal kin as backward, lacking in culture, and living in darkness. Not only were these people described as cultureless, but according to an educated official they also lacked language:

> You see, unfortunately here they do not have a language, what they speak is an illiterate dialect, lacking grammar and orthography.
>
> Chatterjee, 1967:20

A few years earlier, an Indian sociologist supported the conclusion that tribal languages are "merely corruptions of good speech and unworthy of survival." He wanted to see these people adopt the "more highly evolved" Indo-Aryan languages, because he considered the tribal peoples to be nothing more than backward Hindus (Ghurye, 1963:187–190).

Technological Ethnocentrism

Development writers with tractors and chemicals to sell have expressed more ethnocentrism in their treatment of traditional economic systems than for any other aspect of tribal culture. These writers automatically assume that tribal economies must be unproductive and technologically inadequate and therefore consistently disregard the abundant evidence to the contrary. It has long been fashionable to attack the supposed inefficiency of shifting cultivation and pastoral nomadism and the precariousness of subsistence economies in general. But it could be argued that it is industrial subsistence techniques that are inefficient and precarious. Mono-crop agriculture, with its hybrid grains and dependence on chemical fertilizers, pesticides, and costly machinery, is extremely expensive in terms of energy demands and is highly unstable because of its susceptibility to disease, insects, and the depletion of critical minerals and fuels. The complexity of the food distribution system in industrial society also makes it vulnerable to collapse because of the breakdowns in the long chain from producer to consumer. In contrast, tribal systems are highly productive in terms of energy flow and are ecologically much stabler, while they enjoy efficient and reliable food distribution systems.

Cultural reformers almost unanimously agree that all people share our desire for what we define as material wealth, prosperity, and progress and that others have different cultures only because they have not yet been exposed to the superior technological alternatives offered by industrial civilization. Supporters of this view seem to minimize the difficulties of creating new wants in a culture and at the same time make the following questionable and ethnocentric assumptions.

1. The materialistic values of industrial civilization are cultural universals.
2. Tribal cultures are unable to satisfy the material needs of their peoples.
3. Industrial goods are, in fact, always superior to their handcrafted counterparts.

Unquestionably, tribal cultures represent a rejection of the materialistic values of industrial civilization, yet tribal individuals can be made to reject their traditional values if outside interests create the necessary conditions for this rejection. Far more is involved here than a mere demonstration of the superiority of industrial civilization.

The ethnocentrism of the second assumption is obvious. Clearly, tribal cultures could not have survived for half a million years if they did not do a reasonable job of satisfying basic human needs.

The third assumption—the superiority of industrial goods and techniques—deserves special comment because abundant evidence indicates that many of the material accouterments of industrial civilization may not be worth their real costs regardless of how appealing they may seem initially. To cite a specific example, it could be argued that the bow is superior to a gun in certain cultural and environmental contexts, because it is far more versatile and more efficient to manufacture and maintain. A single bow can be used for both fishing and hunting a variety of animals. Furthermore, bow users are not dependent on an unpredictable external economy, because bows can be constructed of local materials and do not require expensive ammunition. At the same time, use of the bow places some limits on game harvesting and demands a closer relationship between humans and animals, which may have great adaptive significance. Hames (1979) has shown that Amazon Indians who have adopted shotguns have dramatically increased their hunting yields, but these gains do not entirely offset the extra labor that must go into raising the money to support the new technology. Furthermore, the increased hunting efficiency also means that certain vulnerable species are more likely to be depleted.

Many of the ethnocentric interpretations of tribal cultures are understandable when we realize that development writers often mistakenly attribute to them the conditions of starvation, ill health, and poverty, which are actually related to civilization and industrialization. Self-sufficient tribal peoples do not belong in the underdeveloped category. "Poverty" is an irrelevant concept in tribal societies, and poverty conditions do not result from subsistence economies per se.

Tribal Wards of the State

Writers on international law and colonial experts often called on the *wardship principle* in an effort to justify harsh government programs of culture change directed against tribal peoples. This so-called legal principle reflects the grossest ethnocentrism in that it considers tribal peoples to be incompetent or even retarded children. It defines the relationship between tribal peoples and the state as that of a benevolent parent-guardian and a ward who must be protected from his or her own degrading culture and gradually reformed or corrected. According to the wardship principle, the state is under a moral obligation to make all tribal peoples share in the benefits of civilization—that is, in health, happiness, and prosperity as defined primarily in terms of consumption.

This legal inferiority of tribal peoples has contributed significantly to the speed with which their acculturation or "reform" can occur and has worked marvelously to satisfy both the conscience and the economic needs of modern states.

Placing tribal peoples in the legal category of incompetent children reflects a tendency to view tribal culture as abnormal, sick, and mentally retarded. This obviously ethnocentric theme runs throughout the colonial literature, in which the civilization process is often described as *mental* correction, but this same theme has continued to appear in the modern literature: Some economic development writers have lumped tribal peoples indiscriminately with underdeveloped peoples, referred explicitly to economic underdevelopment as a "sickness," spoken of the "medicine of social change," and compared change agents to brain surgeons (Arensberg & Niehoff, 1964:4–6). It appears that the attitudes of some modern cultural reformers were unaffected by the discovery of ethnocentrism.

A Sacred Trust of Civilization

As we have seen, the modern civilizing mission undertaken by governments against tribal peoples was supported by a variety of ethnocentric assumptions, some of which were recognized as principles of international law. Not surprisingly, therefore, prestigious international organizations such as the United Nations also threw their support behind official attempts to bring civilization to all peoples—whether or not they desired it.

During the second half of the nineteenth century the colonizing industrial nations began to justify their scramble for foreign territories as a fulfillment of a sacred duty to spread their form of civilization to the world. When the major imperialist powers met in 1884–1885 at Berlin to set guidelines for the partitioning of Africa, they pledged support for the civilizing crusade and promised to assist missionaries and all institutions "calculated to educate the natives and to teach them to understand and appreciate the benefits of civilization" (General Act of the 1884–1885 Berlin Africa Conference). This position was reiterated and took on a more militant tone in Article Two of the Brussels Act of 1892, which called on the colonial powers to raise African tribal peoples to civilization and to "bring about the extinction of barbarous customs." This constituted an internationally approved mandate for ethnocide in the interests of progress.

Whereas such attitudes are perhaps to be expected from colonial nations at the height of their power, they seem inappropriate when expressed by world organizations dedicated to peace and self-determination of peoples. Nevertheless, the 1919 League of Nations Covenant in Article 22 gave "advanced nations" responsibility for "peoples not yet able to stand by themselves under the strenuous conditions of the modern world," thereby placing many tribal peoples officially under tutelage as "a sacred trust of civilization." In fact, this sacred trust proved to be a profitable colonial booty for the trust powers because it gave them the internationally recognized right to exploit the resources of thousands of square kilometers of formerly nonstate territory while making only token allowance for the wishes of the native peoples involved. Under the 1945 United Nations Charter, many of these same tribal peoples were identified as "peoples who have not yet attained a full measure of self-government," and their continued advancement was to be promoted by their guardians "by constructive measures of development" (Articles 73 and 76, UN Charter). Here again, responsibility for deciding what constitutes tribal peoples' welfare is effectively taken from them and is legally placed in the hands of outside interests. The carefully worded and seemingly nonderogatory phrases "peoples not yet able to stand by themselves" and "nonself-governing" are glaringly ethnocentric and derogatory because these peoples have governed themselves for thousands of years without the support of civilization. Of course, they were unable to defend themselves against the incursions of militant, resource-hungry states. But many modern nations exist only at the discretion of more powerful nations, and the UN Charter would not advocate making all militarily weak nations surrender their political autonomy to their stronger neighbors.

CIVILIZATION'S UNWILLING CONSCRIPTS

It now seems appropriate to ask the obvious question: How do autonomous tribal peoples themselves feel about becoming participants in the progress of industrial civilization? Because of the power at their disposal, industrial peoples have become so aggressively ethnocentric that they have difficulty even imagining that another life style—particularly one based on fundamentally different premises—could possibly have value and personal satisfaction for the peoples following it. Happily arrogant in their own supposed cultural superiority, many industrial peoples assume that those in other cultures perhaps realize their obsolescence and inferiority and eagerly desire progress toward the better life. This belief persists in the face of abundant evidence that independent tribal peoples are not anxious to scrap their cultures and would rather pursue their own form of the good life undisturbed. Peoples who have already chosen their major cultural patterns and who have spent generations tailoring them to local conditions are probably not even concerned that another culture might be superior to theirs. Indeed, it can perhaps be assumed that people in any autonomous, self-reliant culture would prefer to be left alone. Left to their own devices, tribal peoples are unlikely to volunteer for civilization or acculturation. Instead:

> *Acculturation has always been a matter of conquest . . . refugees from the foundering groups may adopt the standards of the more potent society in order to survive as individuals. But these are conscripts of civilization, not volunteers.*

> Diamond, 1960: vi

Free and Informed Choice

The question of choice is a critical point because many development authorities have stressed that tribal peoples should be allowed to choose progress. This view was obvious at a 1936 conference of administrators, educators, and social scientists concerning education in Pacific colonial dependencies, where it was stated that choices regarding cultural directions "must lie with the indigenous peoples themselves" (cited Keesing, 1941:84). Anthropologists at a more recent international conference in Tokyo took the same position when they called for "just and scientifically enlightened programs of acculturation which allow the peoples concerned a free and informed basis for choice" (Eighth International Congress of Anthropological and Ethnological Sciences, Resolution on Forced Acculturation, 1968, cited Sturtevant, 1970:160). Apparently, no one noticed the obvious contradiction between a scientific culture change program and free choice, or even the possible conflict between free and informed. The official position of the Australian government on free choice for the Aborigine in 1970 indicates the absurdities to which such thinking can lead:

> *The Commonwealth and State governments have adopted a common policy of assimilation which seeks that all persons of Aboriginal descent will choose to attain a similar*

manner and standard of living to that of other Australians and live as members of a
single Australian community.

Australia, Commonwealth Bureau of Census and Statistics, 1970:967

Those who so glibly demand choice for tribal peoples do not seem to realize
the problems of directly instituting such a choice, and at the same time they
refuse to acknowledge the numerous indicators that tribal peoples have already
chosen their own cultures instead of the progress of civilization. In fact, the
question of choice itself is probably ethnocentric and irrelevant to the peoples
concerned. Do we choose civilization? is not a question that tribal peoples
would ask, because they in effect have already answered it. They might consider the concept of choosing a way of life to be as irrelevant in their own cultural context as asking a person if he or she would choose to be a tree.

It is also difficult to ask whether tribal peoples desire civilization or economic development because affirmative responses will undoubtedly be from individuals already alienated from their own cultures by culture modification
programs, and their views may not be representative of their still autonomous
tribal kin.

Other problems are inherent in the concept of free and informed choice.
Even when free to choose, tribal peoples would not generally be in a position to
know what they were choosing and would certainly not be given a clear picture
of the possible outcomes of their choice, because the present members of industrial cultures do not know what their own futures will be. Even if tribal peoples
could be given a full and unbiased picture of what they were choosing, obtaining that information could destroy their freedom to choose, because participation in such an "educational" program might destroy their self-reliance and
effectively deny them their right to choose their own tribal culture. An obvious
contradiction exists in calling for culture change in order to allow people to
choose or not to choose culture change. The authorities at the 1936 conference
referred to earlier were caught in just such Alice-in-Wonderland double talk
when they recommended the promotion of formal education programs (which
would disrupt native culture) so that the people could freely decide whether
they wanted their cultures disrupted:

> *It is the responsibility of the governing people, through schools and other means, to*
> *make available to the native an adequate understanding of non-native systems of life*
> *so that these can be ranged alongside his own in order that his choices may be made.*

cited Keesing, 1941:84

Such a program of education might sound like a sort of "cultural smorgasbord,"
but in fact there is only one correct choice allowed—tribal peoples must choose
progress.

One further problem overlooked in the "free choice" approach is that of the
appropriateness of industrial progress or of any foreign cultural system in a
given cultural and environmental context—even if freely chosen. Should Eski-
mos be encouraged to become nomadic camel herders or to develop a taste for

bananas? Does the American "car complex" belong on a Micronesian coral atoll of four square kilometers? What will be the long-term effects of a shift from a self-reliant subsistence economy to a cash economy based on the sale of a single product on the uncertain world market? There are inescapable limits to what can constitute a successful human adaptation in a given cultural and environmental setting.

We Ask to Be Left Alone

At this point we will again ask the question posed earlier regarding whether tribal people freely choose progress. This question has actually been answered many times by independent tribal peoples who, in confrontations with industrial civilization, have (1) ignored it, (2) avoided it, or (3) responded with defiant arrogance. Any one of these responses could be interpreted as a rejection of further involvement with progress.

Many of the Australian Aborigines reportedly chose the first response in their early contacts with members of Western civilization. According to Captain Cook's account of his first landing on the Australian mainland, Aborigines on the beach ignored both his ship and his men until they became obnoxious. Elkin (1951) confirmed that this complete lack of interest in white people's habits, material possessions, and beliefs was characteristic of Aborigines in a variety of contact settings. In many cases, tribal peoples have shown little interest in initial contacts with civilized visitors because they simply assumed that the visitors would soon leave and they would again be free to pursue their own way of life undisturbed.

Among contemporary tribal peoples who still retain their cultural autonomy, rejection of outside interference is a general phenomenon that cannot be ignored. The Pygmies of the Congo represent a classic case of determined resistance to the incursions of civilization. Turnbull (1963), who studied the Pygmies intensively in their forest environment, was impressed with the fact that in spite of long contact with outsiders they had successfully rejected foreign cultural domination for hundreds of years. Attempts of Belgian colonial authorities to settle them on plantations ended in complete failure, basically because the Pygmies were unwilling to sacrifice their way of life for one patterned for them by outsiders whose values were irrelevant to their environment and culture. According to Turnbull, the Pygmies deliberated over the changes proposed by the government and opted to remain within their traditional territory and pursue their own way of life. Their decision was clear:

> So for the Pygmies, in a sense, there is no problem. They have seen enough of the outside world to feel able to make their choice, and their choice is to preserve the sanctity of their own world up to the very end. Being what they are, they will doubtless play a masterful game of hide-and-seek, but they will not easily sacrifice their integrity.

> Turnbull, 1963

Anthropologist Cavalli-Sforza (1986), who coordinated a long-term series of multidisciplinary field studies of Pygmies throughout Africa beginning in 1966, confirmed Turnbull's basic conclusion about the Pygmy rejection of directed change. He attributes the remarkable 2,000-year persistence of Pygmies as a distinct people to the attractiveness of their way of life and the effectiveness of their enculturation practices. But like Turnbull, he also cites the importance of the forest itself and the Pygmies' successful symbiosis with their village-farmer neighbors. The most critical threat to Pygmies is now deforestation and disruption of their exchange relationships caused by the invasion of new colonists and the development of large-scale coffee plantations (Bailey, 1982; Hart & Hart, 1984; Peacock, 1984). As the forest shrinks, there simply will be no place for Pygmies as forest peoples. Bailey warns: "Unless sufficient areas of forest are set aside, a unique subsistence culture based on hunting and gathering forest resources will be lost in the Ituri [rain forest] and throughout central Africa forever" (1982:25).

Avoiding Progress: Those Who Run Away

Direct avoidance of progress represents what is a widespread, long-established pattern of cultural survival whose implications should not be ignored by those who promote culture change.

Throughout South America and many other parts of the world, many nonhostile tribal peoples have made their attitudes toward progress clear by choosing to follow the Pygmies' game of hide-and-seek and actively avoiding all contact with outsiders. In the Philippines, a term meaning "those who run away" has been applied to tribal peoples who have chosen to flee in order to preserve their cultures from government influence (Keesing & Keesing, 1934:87).

Many little-known tribal peoples scattered in isolated areas around the world have, in fact, managed to retain their cultural integrity and autonomy until recently by quietly retreating farther and farther into more isolated refuge areas. As the exploitative frontier has gradually engulfed these stubborn tribes, the outside world periodically has been surprised by the discovery of small pockets of unknown "Stone Age" peoples who have clung tenaciously to their cultures up to the last possible moment. The extent and significance of this phenomenon have seldom been recognized by the public at large and certainly not by professional agents of culture change. In South America throughout this century, many different groups, including the Xeta, the Kreen-a-kore in Brazil, various Panoan speakers such as the Amarakaeri and Amahuaka in headwater areas of the Peruvian Amazon, and the Akuriyo of Surinam, have been found using stone tools and deliberately avoiding contact with outsiders. These determined people are generally peaceful, except when harassed too severely. To avoid contact they prefer to desert their homes and gardens and thrust arrows point-up in their paths, rather than resort to violence. All that even the most persistent civilized visitors usually find—if they do manage to locate the natives' well-hidden villages—are empty houses and perhaps smoldering cooking fires.

FIGURE I.3

A Batangan man from the interior of Mindoro,
Philippines. This tribe is only one of the many
that prefer to flee and hide as civilization advances. (Pennoyer.)

If a village is disturbed too often, the people abandon the site and relocate in a
more isolated place. When, after continuous encroachment, their resource base
shrinks to the point that it will no longer support their population and there is
no place to retreat to, or when violent attacks by civilized raiders and introduced
illnesses reduce their numbers to the point that they are no longer a viable society, then they must surrender to progress. Most of the groups that we know
about have stopped hiding. The most successful groups would have remained
completely hidden, and it seems likely that a few remain in that category.

How successfully some of these groups have managed to avoid contact can
be seen in the case of the Akuriyo Indians of Surinam. These foraging people
were first seen by outsiders in 1937, when a Dutch expedition discovered them
while surveying the Surinam-Brazil border. After this brief encounter the Akuriyo remained out of sight for nearly thirty years until American missionaries
began to find traces of their camps. The missionaries were determined to make

contact with them in order to win them for Christianity, but it was three years before they finally succeeded with the assistance of ten missionized Indians, shortwave radios, and airplanes. They tracked the Akuriyo along their concealed trails through a succession of hastily abandoned camps until they caught up with a few women and children and an old man who, with obvious displeasure, asked the first man who greeted them, "Are you a tiger that you smelled me out?" This small group had been left behind by others who had gone in search of arrow canes to defend themselves against the intruders. The Indians allowed the missionary party to remain with them only one night. Refusing to reveal either their tribal or their personal identities, they fed and traded with the intruders and then insisted that they leave. The mission Indians sang hymns and tried to tell them about God, but the Akuriyo were unimpressed. According to the missionaries:

> *The old chief commented that God must really be good. He said he knew nothing about Him, and that he had to leave now to get arrow cane.*
>
> Schoen, 1969

Obviously these people were expressing their desire to be left alone in the most dignified and elegant terms. But the missionaries proceeded to make plans for placing Christianized Indian workers among them and requested "for the sake of this tribe" that the Surinam government grant their mission exclusive permission to supervise further contacts with the Akuriyo. Within a short time, contact was reestablished, and the mission was able to encourage about fifty Akuriyo to settle in mission villages. Tragically, in barely two years 25 percent of the group had died and only about a dozen people still remained in the forest (Kloos, 1977).

Whereas the Akuriyo are an example of a group avoiding contact in a remote area, many other examples can be cited of small tribes that have survived successfully on the fringes of civilized areas. One of the most outstanding of such cases was the discovery in 1970 that unknown bands of Indians were secretly living within the boundaries of the Iguazú Falls national park in Argentina (Bartolomé, 1972).

Some observers argue that these cases do not represent real rejections of civilization and progress because these people were given no choice by their hostile neighbors, who refused to share the benefits of civilization, and so they were forced to pretend that they didn't desire these benefits. Critics point out that such people often eagerly steal or trade for steel tools. This argument misses the real point and represents a misunderstanding of the nature of culture change. Stability and ethnocentrism are fundamental characteristics of all cultures that have established a satisfactory relationship with their environment. Some degree of change, such as adopting steel tools, may well occur to enhance an ongoing adaptation and to prevent greater change from occurring.

CULTURAL PRIDE VERSUS PROGRESS

The pride and defiance of numerous tribal peoples in the face of forced culture change are unmistakable and have often been commented upon by outsiders. The ability of these cultures to withstand external intrusion is related to their degree of ethnocentrism, or to the extent to which tribal individuals feel self-reliant and confident that their own culture is best for them. The hallmark of such ethnocentrism is the stubborn unwillingness to feel inferior even in the presence of overwhelming enemy force.

A case of calm but defiant self-assurance of this sort is offered by a warrior-chief of the undefeated Xavante (Shavante) of central Brazil, who had personally participated in the 1941 slaying of seven men of a "pacification" mission sent by the Brazilian government to end the Xavante's bitter fifty-year resistance to civilization. As further evidence of their disdain for intruders, the Xavante shot arrows into an air force plane and burned the gifts it dropped (*Life*, 1945, 18:70–72). After one Xavante community finally accepted the government's peace offers in 1953, the air force flew the chief to Rio de Janeiro in order to impress him with the superiority of the Brazilian state and the futility of further resistance. To everyone's amazement, he observed Rio, even from the air, with absolute calm. He was then led into the center of a soccer field to be surrounded by thousands of applauding fans, and it was pointed out to him how powerful the Brazilian state was and how unwise it was for the Xavante to be at war with it. The chief remained unmoved and responded simply: "This is the white man's land, mine is Xavante land" (Fabre, 1963:34–35). The Xavante have been militant in defense of their lands since "pacification" and have forcibly expelled settlers and occupied government offices to force the authorities to fulfill their promise of legal protections (Maybury-Lewis, 1983). A Xavante leader, Mario Juruna, carried the struggle further into the political arena by winning election to Brazil's House of Representatives in 1982. Juruna has campaigned effectively for the land rights of Brazilian Indians at both the national and international level.

THE PRINCIPLE OF STABILIZATION

According to theories of cultural evolution, adaptation, and integration, resistance to change is understandable as a natural cultural process. If the technological, social, and ideological systems of a culture gradually specialize to fit the requirements of successful adaptation to a specific environment, other cultural arrangements become increasingly difficult, if not impossible, to accommodate without setting in motion major disruptive changes that have unforeseen consequences. Resistance to change—whether it be direct avoidance of new cultural patterns, overt ethnocentrism, or open hostility to foreigners—may thus be seen to be a significant means of adaptation because it operates as a "cultural isolating mechanism" (Meggers, 1971:166) to protect successfully established cultures from the disruptive effects of foreign cultural elements. The resulting "stability" refers to a relative lack of change in the major cultural patterns and does not imply complete changelessness in all the nuances of culture because minor changes probably occur constantly in all cultures. Stability is such a fundamental characteristic of cultures that it has been formulated as a general principle: "A culture at rest tends to remain at rest" (Harding, 1960:54). A corollary of this so-called principle of stabilization states:

When acted upon by external forces a culture will, if necessary, undergo specific changes only to the extent of and with the effect of preserving *unchanged its fundamental structure and character.*

Harding, 1960:54

As change agents are well aware, resistance to change is based not only on the natural resistance or inertia of already established cultural patterns, but also on the realization by the people concerned of the risks of experimenting with unproven cultural patterns. Either the rewards of adopting new ways must appear to be worth the risks, or some form of coercion must be applied. However, change agents convinced of their own cultural superiority tend to overlook the fact that native fears about the dangers of untested innovations may be justified. Peoples that reject such unproven cultural complexes as miracle grains, pesticides, and chemical fertilizers may prove in the long run to be wiser and better adapted to their natural environments.

For peoples in relatively stable, self-reliant cultures, resistance to change is a positive value. It is only in industrial cultures that such emphasis is placed on change for its own sake, and among those who make a profession of promoting change, that cultural stability is given a negative connotation and is identified as backwardness and stagnation.

· 2 ·

The Uncontrolled Frontier

The history of the European settlements in America, Africa, and Australia, presents everywhere the same general features—a wide and sweeping destruction of native races by the uncontrolled violence of individuals, if not of colonial authorities, followed by tardy attempts on the part of governments to repair the acknowledged crime. . . . Desolation goes before us, and civilization lags slowly and lamely behind.

Herman Merivale, 1861

IF, AS HAS BEEN argued in Chapter 1, tribal peoples are not eager to exchange their basically satisfying cultures for the dubious benefits of civilization, we are faced with the problem of explaining how their unwillingness has been overcome. Little "progress" can be made as long as tribal peoples remain autonomous, sovereign societies that are both politically and economically self-sufficient. Therefore, the problem is to explain how this autonomy has been broken. In general it appears that three processes have been weakening tribal resistance and preparing the way for further transformations:

The uncontrolled frontier

Military force

The peaceful extension of administrative control

For analytic purposes, I will distinguish these processes arbitrarily and treat them in separate chapters, even though frequently they may overlap in a given area.

24

THE FRONTIER PROCESS

The initial breakdown of tribal autonomy was accomplished in many areas of the world by the direct action of the countless individual traders, settlers, missionaries, and labor recruiters who, in seeking their own self-interest, dealt directly with native peoples in frontier areas beyond government control.

Many definitions have been proposed for the term *frontier*, but for our purposes those concerned with resource exploitation and the role of the state will be most useful. Billington, for example, defines the frontier as:

> *the geographic area adjacent to the unsettled portions of the continent in which a low man-land ratio and abundant natural resources provide an unusual opportunity for the individual to better himself economically and socially without external aid.*
>
> Billington, 1963:7

In this definition, the significant point is that frontier resources are considered to be freely available for exploitation by outsiders. Webb (1952:2) speaks of the frontier as "an area inviting entrance" with its gifts of land and minerals, and, along with many other historians, he explicitly disregards the aboriginal population. Indeed, a common aspect of the frontier process is the fact that the prior ownership rights and interests of aboriginal inhabitants are considered irrelevant by both the state and the invading individuals. Another aspect of the above definition is that in frontier areas individuals are given the opportunity to better themselves without external aid, that is, without any effective legal restraint by the state. This combination of free resources and free enterprise distinguishes the frontier process from the use of military force and from formal native administration, both of which involve direct and effective government control.

Without the restraints of law, individuals used force or deception to ruthlessly and profitably obtain the land, labor, minerals, and other resources they sought. In the process, tribal societies were disrupted, weakened, and embittered, or simply exterminated. There is certainly no mystery to be explained here. It has long been recognized that frontier violence, the dispossession of tribal peoples from their homelands, the destruction of their subsistence bases, the introduction of foreign diseases, the availability of guns and alcohol, and numerous forms of economic exploitation have all directly led to depopulation, apathy, dependence, and detribalization. What *is* remarkable is the extent of the destruction and the fact that this familiar and uniform pattern has been repeated over the years throughout the world and still continues in some areas today with the implicit approval of the governments involved.

The main features of the frontier process have been understood at least since the 1836–1837 publication of the thousand-page "Official Report and Minutes of Evidence of the British House of Commons Select Committee on Aborigines." The fifteen-member committee was commissioned by Parliament to consider measures for the protection of native rights in frontier areas and spent ten months interviewing more than forty settlers, soldiers, politicians, missionaries, and natives from South Africa, Canada, Australia, New Zealand, the South Seas, and British Guiana (now Guyana). Their cautious general conclusion was that frontier contacts had been "a source of many calamities to uncivilized nations."

> *Too often, their territory has been usurped; their property seized; their numbers diminished; their character debased; . . . European vices and diseases have been introduced amongst them, and they have been familiarized with the use of our most potent instruments for the subtle or the violent destruction of human life, viz. brandy and gunpowder.*
>
> British Parliamentary Papers, 1837:5

Furthermore:

> *From very large tracts we have, it appears, succeeded in eradicating them; and though from some parts their ejection has not been so apparently violent as from others, it has been equally complete, through our taking possession of their hunting-grounds, whereby we have despoiled them of the means of existence.*
>
> British Parliamentary Papers, 1837:6

This committee called on Britain in the strongest terms to end this unnecessary oppression of natives. They did not of course reject colonialism itself; rather, they felt that it would be more efficient economically if the process were carried out more humanely. They suggested several specific measures to bring order to the frontier by regulating the use of native labor, prohibiting the provision of alcohol to natives, and the direct purchasing of native lands from natives by individual colonists. Apparently, however, their evidence and recommendations were not widely accepted, because since that time similar official investigations have been independently repeated in several countries, the same list of problems has been drawn up, and more suggestions made, but frontier abuses have not stopped. Considering this fact, it seems appropriate to risk "overemphasis" and review here some of the more outstanding regularities characteristic of the uncontrolled frontier since about 1820.

I Didn't Know It Was Wrong to Kill Indians

The 1836–1837 Select Committee on Aborigines noted in its report that in frontier areas indigenous peoples were being classed as "savages," and it warned ominously that this could result in their being treated as less than human. It is clear from the committee's own published findings that in frontier areas around the world in the 1830s, tribal peoples were indeed being considered less than human and were being treated accordingly. For example, it was reported that in Canada it was long considered a "meritorious" act to kill an Indian. Significantly, the Dutch Boers in South Africa felt the same way toward natives, according to a letter received by the committee stating, "A farmer thinks he cannot proclaim a more meritorious action than the murder of one of these people." Reportedly, in South Africa it was customary for settlers to speak of killing natives with the same indifference applied to shooting partridge, and in fact one settler boasted proudly of personally killing 300 natives. At the same time, the tattooed heads of New Zealand Maori were being offered for sale as curiosities in Australia (British Parliamentary Papers, 1837:3–15).

The committee reported that "many deeds of murder and violence" had been committed by the settlers in Australia, and, in fact, the same violence had continued on the Australian frontier for at least 100 years, sometimes taking remarkably treacherous forms. In Victoria, Aborigines were known to have been poisoned by arsenic mixed with flour (Corris, 1968:153–157), while strichnine was reportedly used to eliminate Aborigines in western Australia in 1861. In the Northern Territory in 1901, "It was notorious, that the blackfellows were shot down like crows and that no notice was taken" (Price, 1950:107–108). As recently as 1928, thirty-two Aborigines were killed in that area in reprisal for the death of a Dingo hunter (Price, 1950:106–114). Violent anti-Aborigine slogans were again heard in Australia's Northern Territory in the late 1970s as the Aborigines successfully pressed for legal recognition of their land rights (see Figure 2.1).

The frequent attitude of settlers on the American frontier can be summarized by Sheridan's famous statement, "The only good Indian is a dead Indian," and hardly need be elaborated upon here. However, it is not always remembered that in South American frontier areas the same approach is still being taken, as demonstrated by the reported killing of eleven Pai Tavytere Indians in Paraguay in 1988 (IWGIA Newsletter 1988 (55/56):77–78). In southern Brazil professional Indian hunters were killing the Xokleng Indians until their final pacification in 1914 (Henry, 1941). In São Paulo, one man claimed to have killed 2,000 Kaingang Indians in 1888 by poisoning their drinking wells with strichnine (Moreira Neto, 1972:312). In the northeast, the Brazilian ethnologist Curt Nimuendaju reports that an entire village of 150 Timbira Indians was wiped out by a band of settlers in 1913. In this case the murderers were brought to trial, but all were acquitted (Nimuendaju, 1946:30). In nearby Paraguay in 1903, settlers were killing Guayaki Indians and using their bodies to bait jaguar traps (Münzel, 1973). In 1941 it was reported that local settlers still felt that killing Guayaki was not a crime, but rather "a praiseworthy action, like killing a jaguar." The rationalization for such violence was that because the Guayaki were not baptized Catholics, they were not human beings (Chase-Sardi, 1972:195).

By 1962, after decades of continual harassment, a Guayaki band of fifty people finally surrendered. It was discovered that every man in the Guayaki group carried bullet wounds received in clashes with the local German colonists, many of whom proudly displayed Guayaki "trophies" in their homes (Chase-Sardi, 1972:197–199). During the early 1970s German anthropologist Mark Münzel found indications that indiscriminate killings of the Guayaki (now called Aché) were continuing on a scale that he labeled "genocidal" (Münzel,

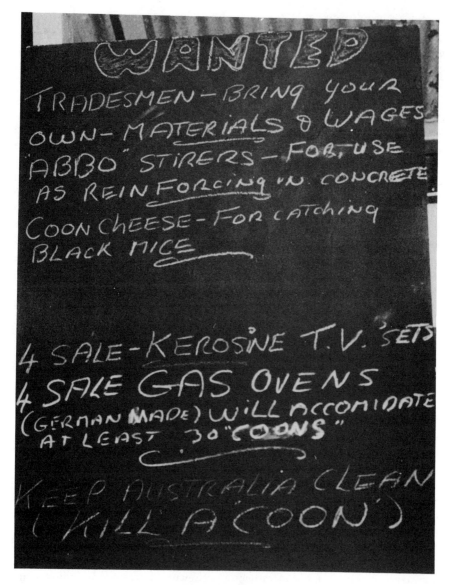

FIGURE 2.1

A sign in the Daly Waters Pub indicating the degree of European backlash to the granting of aboriginal land rights in the Northern Territory in 1978. (Arthur B. Palmer, Northern Land Council, Darwin, Australia.)

FIGURE 2.2

A Cuiva Indian of the llanos of Colombia relaxes in a hammock. The Cuiva are among the tribal groups that have been repeatedly attacked by settlers invading their traditional territories. (Bernard Arcand.)

1973). Further investigations carried out in 1978 and 1979, following widespread international protests over the Indian situation in Paraguay, found that the worst abuses had ended (Maybury-Lewis & Howe, 1980).

The Guayaki situation has close parallels in other South American countries. In 1968 shocking news reports came from Brazil of the massacre of several Indian groups, including the Cinta-Larga, and others in Rondonia and Mato Grosso. In these cases hired killers used arsenic, and dropped dynamite and fired machine guns from light planes. In Colombia, anthropologist Bernard Arcand (1972) has reported that the Cuiva Indians in the llanos are constantly subject to attacks from neighboring cattlemen. He found many Indians bearing bullet scars and was himself fired upon while accompanying them. In 1967, in the same area of Colombia, settlers massacred fifteen Indians and were acquitted in a jury trial because it was considered customary to kill Indians. In his own defense one of the admitted killers stated, "I didn't believe it was wrong since they were Indians." Even more significantly, another stated:

I killed those Indians because I knew that the government would not reprimand us nor make us pay for the crime that was committed.

Akwesasne Notes, summer 1972:26

This statement raises an interesting question about the role of the government in the uncontrolled frontier process. Local officials frequently claim that atrocities committed by settlers are beyond the control of any government to prevent, but a closer look at the facts casts doubt upon such claims. Even in 1837, the Select Committee on Aborigines refused to accept this explanation and condemned the indifference and slackness of local authorities, which the committee felt had allowed entire tribes to be exterminated. The committee specifically pointed out that white settlers were seldom punished for their crimes against natives, but that courts were thorough in meting out punishment to natives for attempting to defend themselves against settlers. In frontier Australia throughout the nineteenth century, a simple legal mechanism was used to protect whites who openly killed Aborigines: The testimony of surviving aboriginal witnesses was not admitted because they were "ignorant of the existence of a God or a future state" (Corris, 1968:105). When the authorities finally took action against known offenders and ordered the hanging of seven whites for massacring twenty-eight aboriginal men, women, and children in New South Wales in 1838, the murderers protested with a familiar excuse that demonstrated official connivance at such crimes:

> We were not aware that in killing blacks we were violating the law or that it could take any notice of our doing so, as it has (according to our belief) been so frequently done before.

> cited Price, 1950:108

Undoubtedly, many of these crimes against tribal peoples would not have been committed, and certainly not as openly, if local officials had not cooperated in them. In Brazil in 1968, the evidence for large-scale involvement in Indian massacres by many public officials of the Indian Protectorate Service was so overwhelming that the organization was abolished. In 1971 in Paraguay, officials of the Native Affairs Department refused to take any action against known Indian hunters or even to conduct investigations into the well-known crimes being committed against the Guayaki (Münzel, 1973). Such official ignorance of frontier crimes, and the general failure of legal processes to protect tribal peoples, suggests that lack of control has been a deliberate policy on many frontiers.

Dispossession

Generally the primary purpose of the killing of tribal peoples has been to remove them from the land. In many cases less violent, but equally effective, methods have been used to accomplish this purpose.

In South Africa in the 1830s, the Select Committee reported that the Boers were in the habit of extending their territory by simply herding their cattle into native territory, destroying native gardens, and taking over natives' houses. The Boers informed protesting natives that complaining would not help them because the government would be unconcerned (British Parliamentary Papers, 1837:29). One hundred years later white farmers were still actively dispossessing natives as squatters in the frontier areas of South Africa. The justification for this action was the familiar argument that the natives were merely subsistence farmers and deserved to be treated as squatters because they were not engaged in any systematic forms of agriculture. The twentieth-century version of the dispossession process has been described in detail by a South African education professor:

> When the new owner of the land enters into possession he generally summons a meeting of the squatters, informs them that he is the new owner of the land, announces how many native families he proposes to retain on his property, selects those he desires, and gives the remainder notice to quit at a certain date after they have reaped their crops. The dispossessed natives have the alternative of seeking a new landlord who will receive them as "labor tenants" or of attempting to find a place in a near-by Native Reserve or of gravitating towards an urban area.
>
> Loram, 1932:170

In South America, settlers and ranchers have also applied remarkably similar processes in the twentieth century. Nimuendaju (1946:60) reported that in the Brazilian northeast in the 1930s it was common practice for ranchers to deliberately break down fences and drive their cattle through Timbira gardens in order to force the Indians to abandon their village sites. Dispossessed Indians appealed to the Indian Protectorate Service and petitioned state and federal government officials for help, but their pleas were ignored. Fifty years later cattlemen were still driving out the Timbira and even burning their villages with impunity (Moreira Neto, 1972:321). The continuous construction of Brazil's Transamazon highway system, under way since 1970, has opened Indian territory to ever-increasing frontier pressures driven by the country's enormous social inequality and a national population that grew by nearly 50 percent between 1970 and 1986. The killing of ten Nambiquara Indians in Rôndonia by settlers in 1986 is just one example of the ongoing process of destruction (IWGIA Yearbook, 1986:27).

Other modern examples could be cited from throughout South America, colonial Africa, and the American frontier, but the important point is that all of these cases illustrate that the unwillingness of governments to protect the rights of tribal peoples against the interests of intruding settlers has resulted in the natives' dispossession. The problem of land policies is examined in more detail in a later chapter, but at this point it must be emphasized that one primary impact of frontier dispossession has been the disturbance of traditional subsistence patterns, forcing tribal people into participation in the market economy. Dispossessed Aborigines on the Australian frontier and Indians in the American West were unable to feed themselves by hunting and were forced either to beg food from the missions and government welfare posts or to work for settlers at menial tasks in order to stay alive. African farmers and herders also experienced severe subsistence hardships when they were pushed off their lands, and, as Loram indicated above, few alternatives were open to them but to labor for whites.

Certainly, direct physical violence has been a prominent frontier process, but it must also be emphasized that the *economic* exploitation of tribal peoples in an uncontrolled frontier situation has been just as destructive of traditional culture. In the following sections, brief case studies are presented that demonstrate the impact of the rubber trade in the Amazon and the Congo and the labor trade in the Pacific. Finally, the patron system of debt slavery is examined, and an assessment is made of the demographic impact of the frontier on tribal populations.

Atrocities of the Putumayo

World demand for rubber began to rise in the 1870s after the development of vulcanization, and particularly after 1900, when the automotive industry began to become important. As a result, the price of rubber soared, and the Amazon regions of Brazil and Peru, which were the primary sources of natural rubber, became major new frontier areas as thousands of outsiders arrived to share in the wealth. This initiated a period of frantic economic activity called the rubber boom, which continued until about 1915, when East Indian plantation rubber captured the world market. Regular labor was scarce in the Amazon, but because tribal Indians were numerous in many of the rubber zones, they quickly became the backbone of the new extractive industry. The Indians were especially useful because they could be induced to work for cheap trade goods, were largely self-sufficient and knew the rubber forests perfectly. Best of all, however, the prevailing attitudes of the local government and military officials were highly favorable toward allowing relatively uncontrolled economic exploitation of the Indians, who were considered to be savages in need of civilization.

Given this setting, serious abuses were almost certain to occur. In fact, what followed was the ruthless exploitation and incredibly violent destruction of thousands of people, which must have fully equaled the cruelest periods of the Spanish conquest. The need for Indian laborers in the rubber zones became so great that merely luring them to work with trade goods was not enough, and undisguised slaving activities became institutionalized. Slave raids, popularly known as *correrías*, were commonly reported occurrences even outside the rubber zones and involved armed gangs assaulting isolated Indian settlements, killing the resisting men, and capturing the women and children to be sold as slaves. Not surprisingly, these activities were widely approved as economically advantageous and necessary civilizing measures, as the following commentary by a contemporary Peruvian writer indicates:

> *It is not strange, then, that, there exists the cruel procedure known as* correrías, *which consists of surprising the habitations of some tribe and taking the members of it prisoner. These prisoners are taken to far territories and are dedicated to work. . . . This catechization has the advantage that the individual soon obtains precise concepts of the importance that his personal work has in the commerce of civilized people. . . . In our century, the procedure is cruel and wounds all the fibers of our sensibility;* but one must recognize the powerful and rapid help that it lends to civilization.
>
> Palacios i Mendiburu, 1892:289–290, my translation, emphasis supplied

Under the direction of large corporations such as the British-owned Peruvian Amazon Company, Ltd., a highly profitable system of rubber production was formulated in which a number of regional company officials controlled managers who organized the scattered tribal populations into local sections and directed the actual rubber-gathering activities. Section managers kept records of their Indian laborers and assigned them specific rubber quotas, which had to be carried to the regional administrators at regular intervals. Many of these lower-level company officials, or rubber barons, wielded enormous power and lived lavishly in great houses surrounded by Indian servants and concubines and armed bodyguards. In the Putumayo district of Peru, where some 12,000 Indians were reported to be working in 1905 (Fuentes, 1908), it was common knowledge that rubber barons regularly used direct physical violence to increase production. Indians who failed to meet their assigned quotas or who attempted to escape were flogged and tortured or simply shot. Even though these actions occurred openly and were widely reported, the government refused to take any action against known offenders.

Finally, in 1907 an outraged Peruvian as a private citizen presented the local court and newspapers with a carefully documented formal denunciation of unspeakable atrocities committed against the Putumayo Indians. The denunciation, which named twenty prominent individuals as responsible, detailed specific crimes of rape, slavery, torture by flogging and mutilation, and mass murder by shooting, poisoning, starvation, and burning—all of which reportedly resulted in the deaths of thousands of Indians. These reports shocked the nation, and the president of Peru called on local officials to make investigations. Because of the involvement of a British company, the matter was even debated in the British Parliament and Sir Roger Casement was sent to investigate. A local Peruvian judge, Carlos Valcarcel, also conducted his own investigation; soon the testimony of eyewitnesses and the discovery of mass burials and other physical evidence left no doubt that crimes of immense proportion had occurred (Valcarcel, 1915). The scale of the atrocities is made evident by comparing the estimated 50,000 pre-1886 Indian population of the Putumayo district with the estimated population of only 10,000 by about 1910 (Casement in Hardenburg, 1912:336–337; Steward, 1948). The precise figure will never be known, but it is certain that thousands of Indians died.

The attitude of the local government officials toward these crimes was continued denial and inaction. The judge who had pursued the case was suspended, and the most prominent of the accused company officials was praised for his talent and capital with which he had brought economic progress to the department (Fuentes, 1908:113). In this case the frontier was being left deliberately uncontrolled.

Heart of Darkness

We have now to record the operations of a System which Conan Doyle has described as the "greatest crime in all history." . . . And it is undeniable that all the misdeeds of Europeans in Africa since the abolition of the over-sea slave trade, pale into insignificance when compared with the tragedy of the Congo. Indeed, no comparison is possible as regards scale, motive, and duration of time alike.

Morel, 1969:105

Events in the Congo closely paralleled and occurred at the same time as the situation in the Amazon. But in the Congo, government involvement was more direct and the scale of the atrocities committed even greater. The Congo Free State, under King Leopold of Belgium from 1885 to 1908, and the adjacent French Congo were based on a system of economic exploitation under which local company officials and government servants were urged to obtain maximum production of rubber and ivory by using whatever means they found most profitable. This exploitation was carried out by government officials under the guise of taxation and by concessionaire companies that were given complete freedom of operation. Officially, of course, murder and slavery were illegal, but in fact they were employed on a massive scale by individuals eager to increase their profits, and here as in the Amazon, the courts seemed unwilling to punish known offenders. Local officials employed government troops to terrorize villagers into greater production, and the concessionaire companies hired undisciplined private armies for the same purpose. Women and children were held captive in special hostage houses to force the men to greater exertions, or were themselves forced to labor in the rubber forests. Villages were burned and looted and entire districts were devastated because, if production declined, the population was said to be in a state of rebellion.

As a result of such oppression, disastrous rebellions did occur, subsistence pursuits came to a halt, and disease and starvation became widespread. Although there is no certain estimate of the depopulation occurring as a consequence of all of these conditions, there is no doubt that it was enormous. Morel, who founded the Congo Reform Movement in England to fight the abusive system, estimated that 8 million people died in the nearly twenty-five years of Free State exploitation alone (Morel in Louis & Stengers, 1968:7). He cites an estimate that in one district 6,000 natives were killed and mutilated every six months (Morel, 1969:123). Whatever the actual figures, the Congo must have been the scene of some of the worst frontier violence in modern times.

The atrocities set off an outcry in Europe after they were publicized by the Congo Reform Movement and in such books as Morel's *Red Rubber* (1906) and Conrad's novel *Heart of Darkness* (1971). Eventually a number of official inquiries were conducted, resulting in the annexation of the Congo Free State by Belgium in 1908, which brought the establishment of more normal forms of colonial administration.

"Blackbirding" in the South Seas

It would be difficult to exaggerate the evil influence of the process by which the natives of Melanesia were taken to Australia and elsewhere to labour for the white man. It forms one of the blackest of civilization's crimes.

Rivers, 1922

From approximately 1860 to 1910 the South Pacific became the scene of frontier violence and exploitation similar to that occurring in the Amazon and Congo. Certainly frontierlike disturbances had arisen earlier in connection with the sandalwood trade, but widespread threats to tribal autonomy did not occur until the American Civil War brought British cotton imports to a halt and stimulated the development of plantations in Queensland, Australia, and Fiji. Unfortunately for the planters, labor was scarce in these areas because white Australians were considered unsuitable for tropical labor, and the native Fijians refused plantation work. Consequently, in 1863 the Queensland planters began sending ships into Melanesia to recruit cheap tribal labor, and the profitable but outrageously exploitative operation known as "blackbirding" became established.

The completely uncontrolled recruiting during the early years relied heavily on deception and often amounted to kidnapping. It was often impossible, for lack of interpreters, to explain the purpose of recruitment to the islanders. Frequently, the islanders were led to believe that they would be away for three months of fun, when actually they were being induced to sign a three-year indentured labor contract. Shrewd captains devised a variety of ingenious means to fill the holds of their ships with recruits. In order to lure wary natives close enough to be pulled into their boats, they employed the famous "missionary trick," in which they masqueraded as missionaries and even passed out Bible tracts that were actually pages from old almanacs. The most direct methods involved ramming canoes to spill their occupants into the sea, or the "eye drop" trick, which consisted of luring native canoes to the stern of the ship for trade and then dropping heavy pieces of metal to sink them (Docker, 1970:47). It is true that islanders sometimes deliberately boarded the recruiting ships in order to obtain trade goods or because they were looking for adventure, but force and deception were the prime means of recruitment.

Unwilling natives were often killed accidentally before they could be dragged aboard ship, and it was not uncommon for them to jump overboard and drown while attempting to escape. Further deaths resulted from fighting between recruits when enemies from different islands were thrown together or when mutinous recruits were shot and thrown overboard by the crews. In one case, seventy recruits were killed in this manner (Docker, 1970:82–84). Disease on board ship also took many lives because of overcrowding, poor food, and inadequate medical attention, and, in some cases, up to half of the cargo died before reaching the plantations (Scarr, 1968:16). Once on the plantations, the recruits might be sold—rather, their "passage" would be paid by the highest bidder—and they could then look forward to three years of labor, ten to twelve hours a day, six days a week, at an annual wage that was only 5 percent of what low-paid government officials earned at that time. Health conditions were little better on the plantations than aboard ship, and annual mortality rates for new recruits sometimes ran as high as 18 percent (Docker, 1970:205). Despite all of these outrages, the recruiting continued for more than forty years, during which over 60,000 natives were legally imported to Queensland alone, and the recruiters and plantation owners stoutly defended the process against critics who called it slavery.

However, the open abuses finally became too obvious for the government to ignore completely, and various Select Committees and Royal Commissions met in 1869, 1876, 1885, 1889, and 1906 to suggest means of regulating the recruiting process. Strict measures were enacted requiring the licensing of re-cruiters for specific shipments, assigning government inspectors to accompany each ship, and specifying how passengers were to be treated and informed what their contracts really meant. In practice, of course, the regulations were often openly defied by the recruiters, and the government inspectors were often in-competent and underpaid political appointees who retired to their cabins when irregularities occurred. The failure of the many regulations to achieve their pur-pose was well illustrated by the 1885 Royal Commission, which interviewed 480 natives in Queensland and found that virtually none had been legally re-cruited (Docker, 1970: 223–224).

As usual in frontier situations, the courts tended to move slowly to punish known offenders. This was certainly true with the case of the *Daphne*, a recruit-ing ship arrested on suspicion of slavery in 1869 off Fiji by Captain Palmer of the British Navy. The ship's bare hold was jammed with a hundred naked, un-derfed natives who were about to be sold to Fijian planters. It was peculiar that no interpreter was available to question the natives and that the ship's captain was authorized only to carry fifty natives to Queensland and not a hundred to Fiji. The circumstances looked suspicious to Captain Palmer, who was familiar with the African slave trade and under orders to investigate illegal recruiting activities in the islands. But the Australian courts felt differently: The natives themselves were not allowed to testify, because, as non-Christians, they would not be able to take the oath. It was ruled that as long as *contracts* were involved, whatever occurred could not be considered slavery, and the case had to be thrown out (Palmer, 1871).

Whatever the effects of the unrestricted recruiting in the South Pacific may have been for the individual tribesmen involved, the impact on the home villages was devastating. As in the Congo and the Amazon, normal village economic, ritual, and social life was disrupted with a significant proportion of the economi-cally active male population absent, and depopulation resulted from the new diseases introduced and from the increased violence aggravated by the guns and alcohol received from the labor recruiters. Depopulation caused by unrestricted recruiting was recognized as a threat to the labor supply that could not be allowed to continue indefinitely, and colonial governments set strict limits that specified which islands were open for recruiting during which years or seasons.

The Patron System of Debt Peonage

In many of the world's frontier areas, unregulated contacts between isolated tribal peoples and civilized traders have been conducted on the basis of an ex-ploitative system of debt peonage, which has certainly been less violent than the types of intrusions previously described, but which has also resulted in pro-found tribal disorganization. In many parts of North and South America, Sibe-ria, and India, traders concerned primarily with their own advancement have taken advantage of tribal peoples in their unfamiliarity with money and their desire for certain kinds of trade goods. Following a remarkably uniform pattern

FIGURE 2.3

Campa Indians from the Peruvian Amazon. Like many forest
Indians in South America, the Campa have been exploited un-
mercifully by outsiders. (K. M. Bodley.)

everywhere, traders advance goods to the natives on credit in exchange for furs,
rubber, lumber, fish, nuts, labor, or crops, to be delivered in the future. The
trick is that by continually advancing more goods, the trader or patron manages
the transactions so that the debt is never fully paid, and an extravagant profit is
reaped by overcharging for the goods he advances and grossly undercrediting
for the articles he takes in exchange. The tribal individual is gradually drawn
into a relationship of total dependence on the trader and is forced to work harder
as he finds himself further in debt and more attracted by increasingly more expensive goods. His difficulties are often complicated by other rules of the system by which debts are inherited and rules that discourage the use of cash or
prohibit a debtor from dealing with other traders. All of these features of the
system open it to flagrant exploitation, and in many cases the result is a situation
resembling slavery.

Comparative research has shown that the long-term effects of the debt
peonage system have followed a regular pattern even in widely separated areas
of the world and generally involve the gradual abandonment of traditional subsistence activities and the weakening of tribal sociopolitical organization, until
the basic autonomy of tribal culture is destroyed. These regularities were demonstrated clearly by Murphy and Steward (1956:353) in their comparison of the
impact of the Amazon rubber trade and the North American fur trade on native
peoples.

In other contexts and with minor modifications, debt peonage can destroy tribal autonomy by dispossession. This has happened widely in India, where the system known as agrestic serfdom has been used—in spite of government attempts at legislative control—as a means of robbing tribal peoples of their land.

In the Amazon today, the *patron* himself is often completely dependent on his Indian debtors for their labor and the forest products they supply. However, he still pushes his profits to the limit, because laws limiting the amount of indebtedness for which an Indian can be held responsible are not enforced. In recent years in the Peruvian Amazon it was common practice for patrons to charge Indians double for trade goods and credit them with half of the value of their products. Greedier patrons have been known to shift decimal points in their account books and charge up to twenty times the fair market value for certain articles. In one case a Campa Indian spent two years cutting valuable mahogany logs for his patron to pay for a twenty-five–dollar shotgun (Bodley, 1970:108). It is not surprising that such practices undermine both traditional social systems and economic patterns.

Demographic Impact of the Frontier

Wherever the European has trod, death seems to pursue the aboriginal.

Charles Darwin, cited Merivale, 1861:541

Severe depopulation of tribal peoples is a characteristic feature of the frontier process and has been reported by observers from all parts of the world over the past 150 years. As early as 1837 the members of the Select Committee on Aborigines found tribal populations to be declining at alarming rates in areas invaded by British colonists. They noted that the Indians of Newfoundland had been exterminated by 1823 and that the Canadian Cree had declined from 10,000 to 200 since 1800. They also found "fearful" depopulation in the Pacific where reportedly the Tasmanians would soon be extinct, and they found that the Australian Aborigines were vanishing from the earth.

In retrospect, it is clear that what the Select Committee was reporting on at that time was only the beginning of a catastrophic decline in tribal populations that continued in most areas of the world for another 100 years. Table 2.1 indicates the scale of some of this depopulation. According to these figures, tribal populations in lowland South America (east of the Andes and exclusive of the Caribbean) and North America (north of Mexico) were reduced by 95 percent or by nearly 15 million by 1930. It is noteworthy that in these areas much of this reduction has occurred *since* 1800 and can be only partly attributed to the Spanish and Portuguese conquests, which decimated large populations in the Orinoco, the lower Amazon, and eastern Brazil and Bolivia prior to 1800. Certainly in North America, with the exception of some portions of the southwest and California, and the eastern seaboard, most of the depopulation was again after

TABLE 2.1

World Survey of Tribal Depopulation

	PRECONTACT POPULATION	POPULATION LOWPOINT	DEPOPULATION
North America (U.S. and Canada)	7,000,000[a]	390,000[b]	6,610,000
Lowland South America	8,500,000[c]	450,000[d]	8,050,000
Oceania			
Polynesia[e]	1,100,000	180,000	920,000
Micronesia[f]	200,000	83,000	117,000
Melanesia			
Fiji[f,g]	300,000	85,000	215,000
New Caledonia[h]	100,000	27,000	73,000
Australia[i]	300,000	60,500	239,500
Africa			
Congo[j]			8,000,000
		Estimated Total Depopulation	24,224,500

[a,b] Thornton, 1987:30, 32.
[c] Denevan, 1976:291.
[d] Dobyns, 1966:415.
[e,f] Keesing, 1941.
[g,h] Roberts, 1969.
[i] Rowley, 1970:384. More recent estimates place the precontact population at as high as a million, but such a figure is not yet widely accepted.
[j] Morel in Louis and Stengers, 1968:123. (Suret-Canale, 1971:36–37, gives a more liberal estimate of 12 million for the depopulation of the French Congo alone between 1900 and 1921.)

1800. In Polynesia, Micronesia, and Australia, the population has been reduced by approximately 80 percent, or more than 1.25 million, since 1800. If allowances are made for further depopulation in areas not included in Table 2.1, such as Siberia, southern Asia, island Southeast Asia, southern Africa, and Melanesia, and if Morel's estimate for the Congo is accepted, it might be estimated that during the 150 years between 1780 and 1930 world tribal populations were reduced by at least 30 million as a result of the spread of industrial civilization. A more realistic estimate would place the figure at perhaps 50 million. Such an incredible loss has no parallel in modern times and must have been a major factor in the "acculturation" of tribal peoples. This was genocide on a grand scale and was widely recognized as such at the time as will be shown in Chapter 10.

The "population reduction" as discussed here is not strictly a record of "deaths," because in theory a population could experience increased mortality and show no population decline if fertility rates also increased. There could be many more deaths than those indicated by the "reduction" figures. However, in the case of many tribal groups it is likely that frontier disturbances caused a decline in fertility.

These population losses have greater meaning when their impact on specific tribal groups is examined, because countless groups were never able to recover from such massive depopulation and simply became extinct while those that did survive were seriously weakened. The speed with which many groups were engulfed by the frontier was a critical factor in the ultimate outcome. The Tasmanians, for example, were reduced by almost 98 percent from a population of 5,000 to 111 within thirty years. In western Victoria the aboriginal population of perhaps 4,000 was reduced to 213 full bloods after less than forty years of settlement, and within fifty years anthropologists could find no one who could reliably describe their traditional culture (Corris, 1968). In California, 75 percent of an estimated 85,000 Yokut and Wintun Indians were swept away by epidemic diseases in 1830–1833 (Cook, 1955).

In more recent times there have been reports of rapid rates of decline for many South American tribal groups. In Tierra del Fuego, for example, the nomadic Indians such as the Ona and Yahgan, who may have numbered more than 8,000 as recently as 1870, were effectively extinct by 1950. In Brazil alone an estimated 87 of 230 groups known to be in existence in 1900 were extinct by 1957 (Ribeiro, 1957), while many other surviving groups experienced drastic declines following white contacts. Among the most dramatic cases recorded for Brazil are the Caraja, estimated to number 100,000 in 1845, 10,000 in 1908, and 1,510 in 1939 (Lipkind, 1948: 180). The Araguaia Kayapo, who numbered 8,000 in 1903, were reduced to 27 by 1929 (Dobyns, 1966). More recently, the Kreen-a-kore were reduced from 300 to 35 in 1979, just six years after agreeing to establish permanent contact with the national society (Davis, 1977: 69–73; Latin America Political Report, 1979, 13[3]: 19). Depopulation of this magnitude clearly constitutes a major source of stress for any culture, particularly when it occurs in the context of conquest and economic exploitation.

The causes of tribal depopulation have been well understood, at least since the Select Committee's 1837 Report designated frontier violence, disease, alcohol, firearms, and demoralization as the principal causes. Ultimately, all of these causes can be reduced to the political decisions of national governments to encourage the invasion of tribal territories. However, there have been some ethnocentric attempts to attribute depopulation to inherent tribal decadence and racial inferiority and to suggest that civilization merely accelerated a decline that was already occurring. This view has been supported by some missionaries and government inquiries and by not a few scholars, such as the historian Roberts, who spoke vaguely of "a general racial decline, an indefinable *malaise* of the stock itself" (Roberts, 1969: 59). This explanation is no longer regarded seriously by anthropologists and was vigorously rejected years ago by the British anthropologists Rivers (1922) and Pitt-Rivers (1927), who showed how culture contact was responsible for the depopulation of the Pacific.

The only problem remaining for more recent writers to debate has been the difficulty of assessing *which* contact factors are the most critical. Some place special emphasis on the role of disease; others stress the importance of physical violence. Certainly both of these factors were important, but they should not detract attention from other indirect factors, because complex interrelationships and feedback mechanisms are operating among all of the variables leading to depopulation. For example, dispossession often forced enemy groups into intense competition for greatly reduced resources, and the availability of firearms made the resulting conflicts far more destructive than previous conflicts. These increased conflicts, combined with other new disturbances in economic and social patterns (such as those related to debt peonage), often placed new stresses on tribal societies and weakened them to the point that they willingly accepted outside control and welfare. Even depopulation itself is a form of stress that can lead to further depopulation by threatening the subsistence base. Rivers (1922) speculated that the sudden total transformation experienced by many tribes caused a form of shock that made people stop producing or desiring children, while in some cases they simply died because life was no longer worth living. Although this explanation is now in disrepute, it seems difficult to disprove.

Increased mortality alone does not account for the complete disappearance of so many tribal peoples: Other cultural variables are involved. Ironically, the special adaptive mechanisms of primitive cultures designed to prevent *overpopulation*, such as abortion, infanticide, and the ideal of a small family, may have actually contributed to *depopulation* and even extinction when frontier conditions drastically elevated mortality rates. There is little reliable data on this point because the importance of these population-regulating devices has only recently been recognized, but anthropologists have cited these factors to explain the depopulation of the Tapirape in Brazil (Wagley, 1951) and the Yap in Micronesia (Schneider, 1955).

· 3 ·

We Fought with Spears

Nothing much is said about the sufferings on our side. Yet we fought with spears, clubs, bows and arrows. The foreigners fought with cannons, guns and bullets.

F. Bugotu, 1968, Solomon Islands

THE EARLY ANTHROPOLOGISTS WHO studied the culture change process did not generally place sufficient emphasis on the role of military force in bringing about the initial breakdown of tribal autonomy. According to the "Memorandum for the Study of Acculturation" (Redfield, Linton, & Herskovits, 1936), *acculturation* is the result of groups with different cultures entering into "continuous firsthand contact, with subsequent changes in the original cultural patterns of either or both groups." The memorandum indicated that the contact situation could be friendly or hostile, but it gave no hint that force might be a major cause of acculturation. Even some modern anthropology textbooks continue to stress that acculturation often results from demands for change coming from tribal peoples themselves, due to their exposure to higher standards of living or the idea of progress—almost as if such "demonstration effects" were the basic cause of culture change (Starr, 1971:514, 516). Considered in a different light, giving full credibility to the historical record, ethnocide can in many cases be seen as the direct outcome of the defeat of individual tribes in separate engagements in a long war fought between all tribal peoples and industrial civilization throughout the world.

Although it is not appropriate here to present a full review of the history of military actions against tribal peoples, this chapter does emphasize the extent

42

and nature of this military pressure and shows how such pressure has frequently initiated culture change and ethnocide by destroying tribal autonomy.

In many parts of the world, tribal peoples fought back fiercely when their traditional cultures were threatened by outsiders and when they realized that those outsiders intended to impose their will on them. Often tribal peoples were forced into one-sided battles to defend their lives against militarily superior enemies, and in most cases the outcome was never long in doubt when natives were fighting against troops armed with modern weapons. Defeat on the battlefield was invariably followed by the surrender of cultural autonomy and the imposition of government administrative control leading ultimately to further culture change.

In general, two major varieties of military action against tribal peoples can be distinguished: punitive raids and wars. The difference between these categories is that punitive raids tend to be short-term punishments for specific offenses committed by the natives and the intent is merely to establish administrative control. Wars, however, may involve protracted campaigns, often for the purpose of extermination or the forced removal of native populations that are not in themselves of direct economic value. Both approaches have been widely applied and have had profound impacts on tribal culture, as is discussed in the following sections.

THE PUNITIVE RAID

The basic purpose of a punitive raid is to impress a tribal population with the overwhelming force at the government's disposal and to thereby gain their "cooperation." It is simply a form of intimidation, always with the threat of greater force in the background, and it normally does not aim at the total annihilation of a people.

The punitive raid has been used widely in New Guinea and throughout the Pacific, where the native population was too valuable as a source of labor to risk its extermination. The Germans conducted frequent raids in their New Guinea colony and often carried them to excessive lengths. When two white men and eight native laborers were killed by unpacified natives, the government responded by sending an expedition that killed eighty-one people, destroyed houses and canoes, and carried off women and children as prisoners (Reed, 1943:136–137). Such overreaction was a common feature of punitive raids. In 1928, when two native policemen in Australian New Guinea were killed by the Kwoma in a dispute over the rape of a village woman, the government massacred seventeen villagers in retaliation (Reed, 1943:154–155). By coincidence, in the same year Australian police killed seventeen Aborigines near Alice Springs (Rowley, 1967:73). Even if these raids were considered a necessary form of retribution for specific "crimes" committed by the natives, the police seldom made any effort to determine who the guilty parties were or to balance the punishment to fit the crime, let alone understand the real motives for the hostilities.

The French, Germans, British, and Americans often used naval battleships and cruisers in the Pacific to impress recalcitrant natives. This occurred as late as 1920, when the Americans stopped a revolt in Samoa with naval guns (Keesing, 1941:173). The Germans regularly used their warships in New Guinea but did not always gain the intended result. The natives may have been impressed with the noise, but often merely returned to their villages when the barrage was over and planted taro in the shell holes (Reed, 1943:136).

Punitive raids were also institutionalized in colonial Africa. In South Africa they were known as *commandos* and were often conducted by detachments of armed settlers whose leaders were officially acknowledged by both the government and the military. The usual excuse for a raid was to regain "stolen" cattle, but they often resulted in the indiscriminant destruction of tribal life and property.

Perhaps the most raided tribal group in Africa were the Nuer of the Sudan, who Evans-Pritchard found to be arrogant and suspicious in 1930. The British usually sent expeditions or patrols against tribes in the Sudan that refused to submit to government administration or that were fighting among themselves. The Nuer were one of the most difficult of such groups to subdue because they refused to be humbled and had abundant empty land in which to hide. According to the count of one historian, armed force was used against the Nuer and related tribes sixteen times between 1902 and 1932 (Beshir, 1968:19).

Such raids caused loss of life, which was a significant disruption of tribal society in itself, and they seriously disturbed the subsistence economy when stored food or gardens were destroyed. Further, the psychological impact of such displays of overwhelming force undermined native morale and the self-confidence necessary for tribal autonomy. When these disturbances were combined with the other difficulties characteristic of the uncontrolled frontier, the surrender of tribal peoples to the government becomes understandable.

Punitive raids are not a thing of the past and were never restricted to colonial governments. Such raids were a common tactic of the U.S. Army in the Indian Wars, especially during the 1870s, and were widely applied in Latin America. In Brazil, organized irregular troops, known as *bandeiras*, often punished Indian tribes in the nineteenth century. Thanks to modern technology, punitive raids can now be conducted more easily and much more effectively. In 1965 newspapers reported that Brazilian air, naval, and ground forces were used against the Marubo, a small Indian tribe in Amazonas that attacked settlers who had invaded their territory (Bowman, 1965). At about the same time in the Peruvian Amazon, the Peruvian air force used napalm to punish Campa Indians who were thought to be in support of leftist rebels. The Indonesian government in 1965–1966 used bombing raids and armed patrols to control 4,000 "disaffected" Arfak people in West Irian (Indonesian New Guinea), reportedly leaving 1,200 dead (Hastings, 1968:17).

WARS OF EXTERMINATION

Major campaigns and wars of extermination waged against tribal peoples have usually been for the purpose of removing the population so that their territory could be utilized by outsiders to benefit the national economy. The immediate justification for such action, as with punitive raids, has often been the need to protect settlers or colonists from "marauding savages," or to quell tribal rebellions, or it has simply been viewed as a quick means of spreading civilization and progress. In most cases rebellions and raids by tribal peoples were the direct result of pressures exerted against them by outsiders and could have been prevented if they had been left alone—but that policy was not often economically advantageous to outsiders.

Wars against tribal peoples became extremely frequent throughout the world as European expansion began and probably reached a high point in the period between 1850 and 1910. It is well known that the Indian Wars in the United States continued almost without respite from 1820 to 1890, but it is not often realized that similar wars were occurring in South America at the same time, sometimes on just as large a scale as in North America. Africa, particularly the southern and eastern regions, was also the scene of almost continual military action during the same period. In Asia, campaigns were conducted against tribal peoples in Formosa by the Japanese; in the Philippines by the Spanish and then by the Americans; in Indochina by the French; and in Burma and Assam by the British. In the Pacific, the Maori Wars of 1860–1872 and the New Caledonia revolt of 1878–1879 were the most significant major military actions. These tribal wars have received relatively little attention in history texts because they were overshadowed by other political and economic events occurring in Europe and America at the same time, but they were nevertheless critical struggles for the peoples most directly involved.

GUNS AGAINST SPEARS

Half measures do not answer with natives. They must be thoroughly crushed to make them believe in our superiority. . . . I shall strive to be in a position to show them how hopelessly inferior they are to us in fighting power although numerically stronger.

Lord Chelmsford, British Commander in the
Zulu Campaign, cited Furneaux, 1963:32

Modern weapons gave government forces a distinct advantage in conflicts with tribal peoples, particularly in large-scale battles between troops and natives still unfamiliar with the effects of firearms. Conventional forms of tribal resistance were usually futile and often ended tragically, like the Matabele rebellion in Rhodesia in 1896, which was decisively ended when machine gun fire mowed down spear-carrying warriors by the hundreds with "bullets that came like hail in a storm" (Wellington, 1967:245). In many areas, magical as well as empirical defenses were developed by tribal peoples to counteract such weapons. In New Guinea, natives invented a special salve that was supposed to deflect bullets (Reed, 1943:134), while on the American plains, the "ghost dance" shirt was intended to turn bullets to water, and in the Amazon Campa shamans attempted to blow at the bullets as protection. Guerrilla tactics generally proved more effective, however, and better still was the acquisition of firearms.

Although these campaigns were often short, one-sided affairs, tribal peoples were not infrequently capable of stubborn resistance and sometimes struck back major blows against their enemies. In Burma, the British spent more than ten years suppressing rebellious tribesmen (La Raw, 1967:131), and the Naga were even more resistant, as will be shown. The odyssey of Chief Joseph and the Nez Perce in 1877 is well known, as well as the massacre of General Custer and 264 men of the Seventh Cavalry in 1876. Perhaps even more dramatic was the destruction of more than 800 of the British forces sent against the Zulu in 1879 at Isandhlwana and Rorke's Drift. The soldiers were attempting to teach the Zulu that they were "hopelessly inferior," but in this case spears prevailed against guns. That same year in nearby Basutoland, 300 rebellious Pluthi warriors, armed with a few guns, withstood a siege of their fortified hilltop refuge for eight months against 1,800 soldiers with artillery. The most stubborn cases of resistance often occurred when tribal people were able to obtain firearms from traders and learned to use them before major conflicts broke out. This availability of firearms prolonged the Maori Wars and was an important factor in many other incidents of tribal resistance as well.

The distinction between these wars and the wars that Europeans waged among themselves was not merely the usual one-sidedness of the fighting, but rather that their purpose was often the destruction of a way of life and the subjugation if not destruction of entire populations. Military defeat of tribal peoples by industrial states involves far more than a mere change in political structure. When the Pluthi were defeated, their cattle and land were immediately taken from them, and their women and children became involuntary laborers for white farmers. In effect, the Pluthi ceased to exist as a distinct tribal entity.

In order to illustrate more fully the varied nature of the military conflicts between modern states and tribal peoples, the following specific examples are examined in greater detail: the defeat of the Indians in southern South America between 1870 and 1885; the Maori Wars of 1860–1872; the resistance of the Naga in Assam; the German extermination campaign against the Herero of Southwest Africa in 1904; and the Japanese method of controlling the Formosan Aborigines from 1902 to 1909.

The Conquest of 15,000 Leagues

We have six thousand soldiers armed with the latest modern inventions of war to oppose two thousand Indians that have no other defense but dispersion, nor other arms than the primitive lance.

Avellandeda-Roca, 1878, cited Portas 1967:7, my translation

In 1820 most of central Chile and the Argentine pampas were occupied by thousands of autonomous Araucanian and Tehuelche Indians who had successfully held back the frontiers of European settlement during nearly 300 years of continuous fighting. The Indians fell back, however, when the effects of the industrial revolution began being felt in southern South America and European immigrants began to arrive in greater numbers, bringing new patterns of warfare. By 1883, after a series of major military operations, the Indians were finally defeated, and vast areas of rich agricultural land were opened for the benefit of white settlers. On the pampas most tribes were virtually annihilated by the military campaigns, while in Chile, after the successful conclusion of the War of the Pacific, seasoned troops turned on the Araucanians and reduced them to disorganized and isolated pockets. These Indian wars in southern South America were strikingly similar to those occurring in North America at the same time, yet their scope, and the kind of military force that was required to defeat the Indians, is not widely appreciated.

In Argentina by the early 1870s, a semistatic defense system had evolved to protect the expanding agricultural settlements from attacks by dispossessed Indians. The system consisted of a continuous line of ten major forts and nearly seventy smaller forts stretching 1,600 kilometers from the Andes to the Atlantic. The large forts were bastions, each garrisoned by hundreds of soldiers, whereas the smaller were fortifications of walls, moats, and watchtowers, armed with cannon and perhaps ten to twenty troopers. Included in the line were 370 kilometers of walls, and trenches three meters wide and two meters deep, which were intended to impede the passage of Indian horsemen. Each fort sent daily patrols to the right and left along the line to check for incursions by the Indians. When Indians were detected in the vicinity, cavalry troops were quickly dispatched to intercept them, and if the Indians could be caught, bloody one-sided battles ensued. In one such action in 1872, the battle of San Carlos, 1,665 cavalrymen clashed with 3,500 Indians. Four soldiers and 200 Indians died. Lances and bolas proved ineffective against repeating rifles and artillery; the Indians' only defense was surprise attacks and rapid flight. This inability to match their enemies' armament was dramatically apparent in an 1878 incident, when a lone trooper with a rifle killed six Indians and captured nine. Earlier the Indians had successfully held their territory against the advances of soldiers and settlers, but modern firearms rapidly changed the situation. As one Argentine military official described it:

> The remington came, and with the remington, the offensive, the Indians were finished and the desert was conquered.
>
> General Ignacio Fotheringham, cited Portas, 1967:19, my translation

The defense network described above was actually neither static nor defensive, because it was constantly being moved forward and new land was declared free of Indians. As the Indians surrendered, they were required to sign treaties acknowledging the sovereignty of Argentina and pledging themselves to fight against rebel Indians. Many national leaders were dissatisfied with the relatively slow pace of the advance and openly called for an aggressive war against the Indians. Finally, in 1878 the government approved the "final solution"—a lightning "conquest of fifteen thousand leagues" in which five columns of 6,000 soldiers advanced into Indian territory to carry out what President Nicolás Avellaneda called "a great work of civilization" and a "conquest for humanity" (Garra, 1969:433). Within six months the frontier had been advanced some 640 kilometers until it stood on the south bank of the Rio Negro. More than 5,000 Indians were either killed or captured, and the nation's agricultural territory almost doubled at a cost of thirteen soldiers killed (Portas, 1967:7, 76). The campaign continued beyond the officially authorized frontier until 1885, when the general in charge of the forces south of the Rio Negro proudly reported the end of the humiliating frontier with the "savages":

> Today not any tribe remains in the field that is not voluntarily or forcibly reduced; and if any number of Indians still exist, they are isolated wanderers, without forming groups worthy of consideration.
>
> General Lorenzo Wintter, cited Garra, 1969:522, my translation

Indian settlements were indiscriminately destroyed and looted in the campaign, and it appears that many who were not killed were taken captive and removed to uncertain fates, while their women "voluntarily" became wives for the soldiers and settlers. This kind of culture contact had decisive effects. By 1913–1914 little more than a hundred Tehuelche still survived, and by 1925 the Puelche were nearly exterminated (Cooper, 1946:131, 138). The Argentine Araucanians apparently survived in greater numbers, but their total military defeat left them thoroughly demoralized and willing to accept the authority of the government.

Forcing the Maori into Civilization

> And the word of the Maori is, we'll fight for ever, for ever and ever.
>
> Maori answer to the call for their surrender at Oarakau, 1863, cited Harrop, 1937:190

In 1840 perhaps a thousand settlers, traders, and missionaries shared New Zealand with at least 100,000 Maori who were willing to tolerate the foreigners and even aid them in order to receive new manufactured goods such as muskets. By 1858, due to the usual frontier disturbances, the Maori population had dwindled to about 56,000, and thanks to rapidly increasing immigration the white population had risen to nearly 40,000. As the balance swung in its favor, the government felt strong enough to pursue a vigorous policy of Maori land alienation for sale to settlers and land speculators in spite of widespread Maori resistance. As usual in such situations, the colonists demanded the best land for farming and grazing; they rationalized their greed by pointing out that Maori possession of the land was an interference with the industrial and commercial progress of the colony. After all, the land was "the greatest curse the natives have" and taking it from them was "the greatest boon you could confer on them" (cited Sinclair, 1961:4–5). As early as 1854 the 12,000 colonists in Auckland Province in the North Island had already acquired some 324,000 hectares from the Maori, of which only 3.5 percent was actually being cultivated; and in Wellington Province, 6,000 colonists "purchased" 3.6 million hectares from the Maori and were cultivating less than one-tenth of a percent.

These proceedings caused considerable resentment among the Maori, who realized they were being rapidly dispossessed. Calling upon their traditions of warfare and chiefdom-level political organization, and borrowing from the British model, they began uniting to resist further land alienation. In 1858 they elected their own "king," designed flags, and organized troops. Declining Maori customs, such as tattooing, were revived, and there were moves to sever economic ties with the colonists and to demand that they be completely expelled from New Zealand. Soon a general feeling arose on both sides that war was inevitable. In 1860, when the Taranaki Maori passively resisted the work of a survey team preparing to subdivide a large block of their land, the governor of New Zealand declared martial law and called on the military to enforce the government's will. The colonists were eager to teach the Maori a lesson and were confident that the fighting would be short, decisive, and profitable.

In fact, the Maori proved to be formidable opponents, even though their total fighting force could hardly have numbered over 8,000 men. They managed to fight for twelve years against a force that in 1864 amounted to some 22,000 soldiers, including nearly 10,000 British regulars. The war cost the colony 1,500 casualties, including 500 killed, and a bill of approximately 1.3 million pounds from the Crown to pay for the military operations. The Maori suffered an estimated 4,000 casualties in killed and wounded, and in the end were forced to surrender their autonomy because of the greater fire power and overwhelming numbers of the government military forces (Cowan, 1922; Harrop, 1937:196, 312).

Although Maori resistance did not succeed, it was far stronger than the colonists expected, partly because the Maori were well armed and knew how to use their muskets. They were also skillful at fortifying positions and built numerous redoubts, with trenches, rifle pits, walls with loopholes, parapets, and towers, that rivaled those designed by the best-trained military engineers. Maori courage and fighting ability won frequent praise and admiration from their enemies. In the first major campaign in Taranaki in 1860–1861, a force of 1,500 Maori besieged the town of New Plymouth and prevented 3,000 troops from gaining any significant victories. The common British stereotype of colonial wars, involving a handful of red-coated infantry coolly fighting off hoards of natives, was often curiously reversed in the Maori Wars. In 1864 at Oarakau, 300 Maori men, women, and children entrenched themselves on a hilltop, where they were surrounded by 1,800 soldiers. The Maori, outnumbered six to one, were short of food, water, and ammunition, and were poorly armed, but they refused to surrender. For three days they withstood shellfire and grenades and repulsed four bayonet assaults before thirst forced them to retreat. In the final hours they were so short of ammunition that they were forced to improvise wooden bullets and fearlessly defused grenades thrown at them in order to use the powder. They withdrew in good order, advancing silently and deliberately into the fire of the troops surrounding them, but only a few escaped. In all, over half of their number were killed, and half of the survivors were wounded (Cowan, 1922:365–407). General Cameron, who led the British troops, spoke in tribute of their courage, and soldiers of the Sixty-fifth Regiment erected a tablet in a local church as a memorial to the Maori who fell at Oarakau (Harrop 1937:192).

Naga Resistance in Assam

The Naga hill tribesmen in Assam frustrated British attempts to extend administrative control over them and to end their headhunting and raiding for more than fifty years. In the nearly twenty years between 1832 and 1851, ten military expeditions were sent against them, inflicting incredible losses, but many of the Naga still refused to surrender their political autonomy.

The first British expedition to enter Naga territory in 1832 consisted of 700 well-armed soldiers, but the Naga resisted their advance with every weapon at their disposal and seemed to ignore the devastating effects of gunfire. They yelled and threw spears at the soldiers, rolled rocks on them from the ridgetops, burned grass in their paths, planted punji sticks, poisoned enemy wells, built stockades, and attacked continuously. In the face of such opposition the British managed only to temporarily occupy and destroy one village before withdrawing (Elwin, 1969:114). In 1850 another military expedition of 500 men and four artillery pieces besieged a Naga fortification for sixteen hours before capturing it. The 1851 expedition burned a village that refused to give it provisions and was thrown a fierce challenge by the Naga, who had nothing but scorn for its guns and muskets:

> We will fight with spear and shield and see who are the best men.
>
> Elwin, 1969:142

The British commander eagerly accepted the challenge and promptly attacked the Naga village of 2,000 warriors with 150 soldiers armed with muskets, 2 three-pounder artillery pieces, a mortar, and 800 native allies. The Naga were panic-stricken by the musketry and artillery, and lost 100 killed and another 200 wounded, whereas the soldiers escaped without a single casualty and proceeded to burn the village.

The fighting was not all one-sided, however, because the Naga continued to raid and constantly harassed the soldiers. In 1879 they killed an administrator and 35 troops, and 6,000 warriors besieged the administrative center for twelve days. In 1879–1880 expeditions sent to punish the Naga suffered over 100 soldiers killed (Elwin, 1969).

It gradually became apparent that regardless of how many villages were burned and how many Naga were killed, they remained unhumbled, and it became ridiculously costly to continue punishing them when their territory offered relatively little of economic value. Numerous suggestions began to be made that the Naga be left alone and that all attempts to extend British sovereignty and civilization over them be suspended. In 1854 all British troops were withdrawn, but by 1886 attempts at administrative control were renewed, and efforts were under way to build roads and establish economic contacts between the tribesmen and the lowlanders. These less militant efforts were moderately successful, but the Naga continued to resist penetration of their areas by lowlanders and still strongly resented any undue interference in their affairs. After India gained independence in 1947, the Naga openly rebelled again; this time they demanded to be recognized as an independent state. By 1956 they had organized a guerrilla force of 15,000 men armed with Japanese weapons hidden during World War II. The Indian Army attempted to end the rebellion, but the government was finally forced to make Nagaland a state within the Indian Union in 1963. However, the Naga have continued to fight for independence (Burling, 1967). Naga resistance was followed by the militarization of their territory. The Indian Army still occupies Nagaland and has been accused of many indiscriminate attacks on villagers and other human rights abuses. The army has also built roads and contributed directly to opening Nagaland to outside exploitation. Oil is now being extracted by at least two oil companies, Indians are invading in greater numbers, and deforestation is becoming a serious problem (IWGIA, 1986).

Extermination of the Herero

We tried to exterminate a native race, whom our lack of wisdom had goaded into rebellion.

German Professor Boon, in lecture to the Royal Colonial
Institute of London, 1914, cited Wellington, 1967:204

The Germans founded their protectorate of Southwest Africa in 1884 on the principle that native peoples must step aside and allow Europeans to use both their persons and their land as the Europeans desired. However, in this case they did not bother with any pretense of humanitarian concern for the advancement of what one governor had labeled "the most useless of natives" (cited Cornevin, 1969:387). The 300,000 tribal inhabitants of this arid desert region consisted primarily of nomadic cattle herders such as the Khoikhoi and the Bantu Herero, who numbered perhaps 100,000 (Cornevin, 1969:386; Murdock, 1959:370). Unfortunately, their interests in the land were incompatible with German plans. The German administration prepared to use military force against the tribes as soon as settlers began to arrive in 1892, seeking the few areas of valuable grazing and farmland that, of course, were already occupied by the tribal people. In 1893 an official policy of forced dispossession was initiated when 250 German soldiers and two artillery batteries surrounded a sleeping

FIGURE 3.1

A Herero woman of Botswana wearing traditional headpiece. The Germans attempted to
exterminate this tribe in 1904 and drove them
into the Kalahari Desert. (R. Lee, Anthro-
Photo.)

Hottentot village and massacred sixty men and ninety women and children. In
turn the Herero were attacked in 1896 and threatened with a "war of extermination" if they refused to surrender their best lands to the settlers and withdraw to
the waterless reserves designated for them (Wellington, 1967: 180–188).

The moral justification for this policy was a simple argument in favor of
social darwinism and economic efficiency, which was explained in 1907 by Paul
Rohrbach, leader of the territory's Settlement Commission:

*The native tribes must withdraw from the lands on which they have pastured their
cattle and so let the White man pasture his cattle on these self-same lands. If the
moral right of this standpoint is questioned, the answer is that for people of the culture
standard of the South African Natives, the loss of their free national barbarism and
the development of a class of workers in the service of and dependent on the Whites is*

primarily a law of existence in the highest degree. For a people, as for an individual, an existence appears to be justified in the degree that it is useful in the progress of general development. By no argument in the world can it be shown that the preservation of any degree of national independence, national prosperity and political organization by the races of South West Africa would be of greater or even of equal advantage for the development of mankind in general or the German people in particular than that these races should be made serviceable in the enjoyment of their former territories by the White races.

cited Wellington, 1967:196

The Herero soon were without grazing land and virtually cattle-less because an epidemic in 1897 carried off two-thirds of their cattle. By 1903 more than half of the remaining cattle had been appropriated by unscrupulous traders. They could tolerate their situation no longer. In 1904 some 8,000 Herero warriors rose against the colonists, and within a few days 150 Germans were killed. Two months after the outbreak of fighting, a Herero chief explained the causes of the war in a letter to the military governor. Speaking bitterly of German abuses, he stated that the war had been started by the whites, and he vowed to fight to the death.

The Germans were well prepared to make good on their earlier threats of a war of extermination. General Von Trotha was quickly dispatched from Germany and in 1904 surrounded 5,000 Herero with an army of 1,500 riflemen, thirty field guns, and twelve machine guns. Many Herero escaped in the fighting and were driven into the Kalahari Desert to die of thirst. Von Trotha refused to negotiate and proclaimed that anyone who remained in the country would be shot:

The Herero people must now leave the country, if they do not I will compel them with the big tube [artillery]. Within the German frontier every Herero, with or without a rifle, will be shot. I will not take any more women and children [prisoners], but I will drive them back to their people or have them fired on.

cited Wellington, 1967:208

The soldiers ruthlessly carried out these orders for months (even to the extent of deliberately poisoning waterholes), and thousands of Herero died. By 1906 their population had been reduced to 20,000 landless fugitives. The Khoikhoi also joined in the fighting, but by 1907 the war was officially declared over. It had been a disastrous campaign for the Germans as well. They lost over 1,600 men and had fielded a force of up to 19,000 men at an estimated cost of some 23 million pounds. The total native loss in life was estimated at some 100,000, or approximately two-thirds of the labor force as the Germans viewed it. In the end, even Rohrbach, whose policies of land confiscation had directly contributed to the fighting, was willing to admit his "blunder," because "the actual extermination of a race could be politically and economically disastrous" (Cana, 1946; Cornevin, 1969; Wellington, 1967:213).

Advancing the Guard-Line in Formosa

When the Japanese took over Formosa in 1895, some 3 million "civilized" people occupied less than half of the island while the remainder was occupied by 120,000 tribal people. Pressure on the tribal areas was understandable in view of their relatively light population and because of the resources in timber, camphor, gold, and agricultural land contained within them. As soon as the Japanese administration had succeeded in putting down the Formosan rebels in 1902, they turned their attention toward controlling the Aborigines and helping them progress toward civilization. The Aborigines were particularly bothersome because they frequently attacked and took the heads of outsiders who approached their frontiers too closely. This made it difficult for the Japanese to extract timber and camphor from aboriginal territory and virtually excluded the utilization of their agricultural land in the interests of the total economy. According to an official report published by the Formosan Bureau of Aboriginal Affairs (1911), the Japanese developed two methods for dealing with the problem. The first method was called "gradual development" and involved winning aboriginal cooperation through slow, peaceful penetration, but this did not always work quickly enough; the second, and more direct, "suppression" method was often resorted to.

Suppression of "savages" Japanese-style was similar to the Argentine approach, except that the Japanese were able to make use of much more sophisticated weaponry. The approach was to encircle virtually the entire aboriginal area with a military cordon and then gradually advance toward the center. The cordon itself, called a guard-line, consisted of a line of small guardhouse redoubts situated on ridgetops and paralleled by a road and a wide swath of cleared forest serving as a fire zone. Important innovations included the use of telephone communication, barbed-wire entanglements, electric fences, and land mines, which "have great effect in giving alarm of the invading savages" (Government of Formosa, 1911:16). The Japanese used grenades regularly in fighting and placed field guns in strategic locations where, according to the official report, "one gun is sufficient to withstand the attack of several tribes" (1911:16). In 1909 the guard-line was 493 kilometers long and throughout its length, approximately every 500 meters, guardhouses garrisoned with two to four armed guards were located, while every kilometer and a half there was a special superintendent station.

Like the Argentine line of forts, the Formosan guard-line was never intended to be a permanent frontier between state and tribal areas, but it was to be constantly advanced. The guards regularly conducted patrols and ambushes inside the line and moved the line forward at every opportunity, with or without the consent of the Aborigines. Between 1903 and 1909, seventy-five advances were made, eighteen under "hostile" conditions. Certainly the report was accurate in describing the advance as both "an aggression and progression into the savage territory" (1911:20).

"Punitive expeditions" were frequently sent across the guard-line to punish

FIGURE 3.2

A Taiwan hill tribesman, defeated by the
Japanese Army, 1902–1910. (Courtesy of
Government of Formosa, Bureau of Aboriginal
Affairs.)

the Aborigines for their attacks on outsiders. In 1897 one particularly "savage"
tribe killed a policeman and a year later killed two more officers at a pacification
station. In response, according to the report:

> *A punitive expedition, consisting of about 5 companies of infantry, was dispatched
> against this tribe. The Troops destroyed all the dwellings of the tribe. As a result, they
> surrendered to the Government.*

1911:35

The guards arranged a more elaborate punishment for another tribe that
had managed to kill thirty camphor workers and a policeman within their territory in 1906. A special eleven-kilometer guard-line was placed around the
area, and the tribe's villages were assaulted from the line while two cruisers
bombarded them from off the coast. In this action, six villages and their gardens
were destroyed and forty tribal people were killed.

In a typical advancement of the guard-line under hostile conditions—a campaign of 107 days, using 886 fighting men and 1,000 support forces for labor and transport—a tribal area of 222 square kilometers, "containing many camphor and other valuable trees" as well as tribal hunting grounds, was captured. The Aborigines constructed defenses and fought tenaciously but were finally overcome by rifles and grenades at close quarters. Territory captured in such a manner was immediately made available for outside exploitation, as the Formosan government's report carefully explained:

> *The territory thus included within the guard-line becomes a peaceful district, where various settlers may engage in the agricultural, timber and camphor industries with greater safety. . . . This act necessarily excites a dislike among the savages, but it intends, by no means, the plundering and destruction of the district occupied by them. It is simply intended to utilize the vast undeveloped territory now held by the Aborigines in the island.*

1911:20

Some measure of the intensity of the resistance in Formosa can be obtained by comparing the figure of 4,341 Japanese and Formosans killed by the Aborigines between 1896 and 1909, with the 500 Europeans killed by the Maori in New Zealand between 1860 and 1872.

Although these case studies of military force against tribals have been historical, many dating from the nineteenth century, the militarization of tribal areas is unfortunately still occurring. Since 1980 military force has supported the invasion of tribal areas by colonists in Bangladesh (cited in Chapter 1) and in Indonesian-controlled West Papua, where 14,000 native peoples were reportedly killed during a six-month military operation in 1981–1982 and as many as 150,000 may have been killed between 1963 and 1983 (Korwa, 1983; Nietschmann, 1985). Since 1980 government-sponsored (or condoned) terrorism has been used to suppress indigenous groups in India, the Philippines, Peru, Brazil, Guatemala, and Colombia. In many cases, indigenous groups have organized their own guerrilla forces in self-defense, as in the Sudan, West Papua, and the Philippines, or they have been caught between other military forces who have used their territory as a battleground as, for example, in Southeast Asia, Ethiopia, southern Africa, and Nicaragua. The arms race has also turned the lands of indigenous peoples into strategic military resources and resulted in their forced expulsion and exposure to nuclear radiation, as in the case of the Bikini islanders in Micronesia. Tribal groups have also been recruited to fight other peoples' battles, as was the case when the U.S. Central Intelligence Agency used Laotian hill tribes against communist forces and when the South African army used ethnic battalions, some drawn from the Bushmen, in their recent war against SWAPO (South West Africa Peoples Organization), the Namibian independence movement. The war was ended in 1989 by the UN-backed, but precarious, implementation of Namibian independence.

· 4 ·

The Extension of
Government Control

*The government of any race consists rather in implanting in them ideas
of right, of law and order, and making them obey such ideas.*

Bronislaw Malinowski, 1929

MILITARY FORCE BROUGHT GOVERNMENT control, which ended the lawless frontier process and initiated the formal, orderly process of native administration.
Such administration was designed to continue exploitation of natives through
legal means. It was a simple matter to assume political control over decimated
and defeated native populations that faced no alternative but submission. But
while governments did not hesitate to use armed force to crush native resistance,
in some areas humanitarian concerns prompted the use of peaceful pacification
techniques to subdue still hostile or potentially uncooperative native groups.

By whatever means necessary, agreements were made and treaties signed
with the natives that surrendered full and final authority for their lives to the
government and made them submissive wards of the state—whether or not they
understood what this meant. When large native populations survived and when
it was in the interest of the state to maintain them with minimal disturbance,
various systems of indirect rule were devised to ease the impact of government
control. Successful rule ultimately depended on census data, elaborate records,
and administrative bureaucracy, but it also required the accurate data on native customs that were provided by anthropologists working under direct government supervision or with the support of national and international research
institutions.

AIMS AND PHILOSOPHY OF ADMINISTRATION

Official statements frequently justify the extension of government control over tribal populations as an effort to bring them peace, health, happiness, and other benefits of civilization and minimize economic factors. But, undoubtedly, the extension of government control was directly related to protecting the economic interests of nonindigenous peoples moving into formerly exclusive tribal areas. Considering the incompatibilities between the economic and social systems of tribal and industrial cultures, it is clear that tribal cultures would have to give way and be transformed if the resources of their territories were to be efficiently exploited for the benefit of the world-market economy.

Governments could not allow the frontier process to continue indefinitely, even though it may have been extremely profitable for some individuals, because it was often destructive of native labor and other resources, and, as we have seen, it often led to expensive military campaigns. The maintenance of law and order became a critical concern. If settlers were to successfully acquire land and utilize native labor, the government had to provide security, because native unrest and uprisings could quickly sweep away the settlers' economic gains. Economic development of the tribal population itself also became important in many areas, but this will be treated in a separate chapter.

TRIBAL PEOPLES AND NATIONAL UNITY

Many newly independent nations have followed an active policy of exerting control over tribal areas in the professed interests of national unity. Economic considerations aside, government authorities see the existence of autonomous tribal populations within the boundaries of the state as a challenge to their authority and a possible invitation to aggression by foreign powers. This has been particularly true where, as is often the case in South Asia, tribal populations occupy remote border areas. Perhaps one of the principal reasons for the efforts of the Indian government to extend its control over the North East Frontier Agency (NEFA) was its proximity to her potential foe, the People's Republic of China, and the rising nationalism of the Naga. Prime Minister Nehru warned India of the dangers of leaving a political vacuum along the frontier and strongly emphasized the need for full integration of India's tribal populations.

Cunnision (1967) has noted the irritation of governments over the presence of tribal nomads in Asia and Africa, where they are regarded as a stigma, an affront to national pride. The main complaint is that the life style of the nomad is incompatible with the aims of the state. Nomads do not go to school, cannot easily be reached by state medical services, and are "lawless," but worst of all they may regard tribal loyalties above national loyalties.

It has become fashionable for governments to describe tribal peoples as na-

FIGURE 4.1

A Tswana tribal assembly in Botswana is addressed by government officials. Throughout the world, tribal populations have been forced to surrender their full political autonomy. (Irven DeVore, Anthro-Photo.)

tional minorities and, as such, even to speak of them as obstacles to national unity and sources of instability. Newly independent nations have been eager to politically incorporate zones that former colonial governments had left relatively undisturbed, on the theory that such zones had been deliberately perpetuated in order to create division within the country.

In many respects, use of the term *national minorities* or *ethnic minorities* undermines the legitimate claims of indigenous peoples to local autonomy. Calling a tribal group a "minority" requires an external reference point and needlessly implies inferiority and dependency. Many indigenous political activists, and some modern writers, such as geographer Bernard Nietschmann (1985), prefer to refer to tribal or indigenous peoples as "nations," emphasizing the original meaning of the term referring to common language, culture, and territory with an internal political organization. Nietschmann points out that most so-called nation-states are actually composed of many such "nations" that have been arbitrarily forced under the same government administration, often as a heritage of colonialism. Many conflicts around the world are related to efforts of these "ethnic" nations to reassert their independence. Furthermore, as large, composite national governments become increasingly unwieldy, both the desirability and the likelihood of their breaking down into more manageable constituent units increase (Kohr, 1978).

THE TRANSFER OF SOVEREIGNTY

Most nations throughout the modern period, and, indeed, many authorities on international law since the beginning of colonial expansion in the sixteenth century, have acknowledged tribal societies to be small independent sovereignties and have recognized that in order to legally govern them, tribal sovereignty would need to be transferred to the state either by conquest or by treaty. Many early Spanish publicists and theologians, such as Franciscus Victoria, Dominic Soto, Bartolomé de Las Casas, and Baltasar Ayala, stressed that non-Christian peoples constituted sovereign "nations." These writers challenged both the *validity* of European claims to sovereignty based solely on "discovery" and the *justice* of rights based on conquest. They generally agreed that non-Christian lands were not empty and, therefore, that they were not open to acquisition by Europeans.

Even after the industrial revolution had begun and the modern period of colonial expansion was under way, the prevalent opinion among legal authorities continued to recognize the sovereign rights of all peoples living in organized societies, regardless of their level of "civilization." In the nineteenth century, this opinion was supported by the French publicists M. P. Pradier-Fodéré, Charles Salomon, Henry Bonfils, and Gaston Jèze; the Italian Pasquale Fiore; and the German August Hefter.

As colonial expansion began to reach a peak in the late nineteenth century, however, important modifications of this position were begun. By an act of Congress in 1871 the United States declared, contrary to some 350 years of international legal opinion, that it would no longer make treaties with Indian tribes as if they constituted sovereign nations. The French annulled by decree all sovereign rights of traditional rulers in French Equatorial and French West Africa in 1899 and 1904, respectively. Legal authorities quickly fell in line. In 1876 the American lawyer Dudley Field (who helped found the International Law Association in 1873) argued that tribal lands could be acquired by direct occupation. In 1914 the British lawyer John Westlake opinioned that territorial claims could only be recognized in states that were organized strongly enough to protect the interests of white settlers. In the 1920s other authorities on international law, such as L. Oppenheim and T. J. Lawrence, asserted that tribal societies were not developed sufficiently to be considered sovereign entities and that these territories were therefore outside the family of nations where they could be legally claimed by any foreign power. In 1889 an Australian legal decision declared Australia to have been *territorium nullius*—unoccupied, waste territory, legally free for the taking—when it was annexed by Britain in 1788. This approach eliminates the costly inconvenience of paying land claims to dispossessed Aborigines and has also been the implicit policy of many Latin American nations expanding into Indian territory.

While the Institute of International Law, meeting in Lausanne, France, in 1888, rejected the notion that the rights of independent tribes could legally be ignored, and while it condemned wars of extermination against tribal peoples, useless severities, and tortures, it declared that the legal transfer of sovereignty could be carried out by simply extending government control over a region (Snow, 1921:173–201). There is certainly no question here of the morality of the procedure as a whole, aside from the details of how it is conducted, and this declaration suited perfectly the needs of colonial administrators.

TREATY-MAKING

Treaties with aboriginal tribes . . . are made for the purpose of arranging the terms of the guardianship to be exercised over the tribe.

Snow, 1921:207–208

Treaty-making as the first step in extending government control was carried out widely in North America and Africa as the frontiers of settlement were extended. Representatives of the governments involved merely located individuals who were assumed to be tribal leaders and obtained their marks on official documents transferring tribal sovereignty to the state and at times extinguishing their claims to the land. An example of the sweeping powers that governments assumed over tribal populations on the basis of such agreements is represented by the following treaty of 1884 between various Bechuanaland (now Botswana) chiefs and the British:

I give the queen to rule my country over white men and black men; I give her to publish laws and to change them . . . to appoint judges . . . and police . . . to arrest criminals . . . to hold them as prisoners . . . to collect money (taxes) . . . to impose fines.

cited Lindley, 1926:36

In the terms of the treaty of Waitangi in New Zealand in 1840, an assembly of chiefs ceded "absolutely, and without reservation, all the rights and powers of sovereignty . . . over their respective territories" to the British Crown. German treaties were, if anything, more inclusive: They could involve the transfer of a tribal people's rights to "have their own laws and administration, the right to levy customs and taxes, the right to maintain an armed force," and "all the rights" that Europeans recognize in a sovereign prince (Lindley, 1926:38–39). In several areas, the right to make such treaties was delegated by the government to special chartered companies. In Rhodesia, the British South Africa Company, under Cecil Rhodes, obtained an open-ended Royal Charter from Britain in 1888 that, like sixteenth-century Spanish charters, allowed the company

to acquire by any concession agreement grants or treaty all of any rights interests authorities jurisdictions and powers of any kind or nature whatever, including powers necessary for the purposes of Government and the preservation of public order.

cited Wellington, 1967:241–242

Treaty-making often concluded military campaigns as part of a formal surrender ceremony, but even under peaceful conditions, the threat of force was always in the background. It was also not unusual for lavish gifts to be presented to the signing tribal dignitaries, often accompanied by promises of new authority and special privileges to be accorded by the government. It appears that in signing these agreements many tribal leaders either acted largely in their own immediate self-interest or did not really understand the terms and full implications of the treaty and felt themselves under duress. Sometimes tribal leaders recognized the threat to their political independence that such treaties constituted but were unable to resist them. When the Germans approached a Hottentot chief in Southwest Africa in the 1880s, with a request that he accept German protection, the chief demanded to know what protection was and from what they were to be protected. He was promised continued jurisdiction over his people if he accepted protection, but he quickly recognized the inconsistency and pointed out that "everyone under protection is a subject of the one who protects him" (Wellington, 1967:177).

Bringing Government to the Tribes

As indicated above, treaty-signing was just a first step in establishing government authority, often intended merely to legitimatize sovereign claims to much larger areas. However, regardless of the dominion established over them on paper, tribal peoples remained autonomous until the government physically established contact with them and initiated their political integration into the national polity by

Appointing political authorities over them

Imposing the state's legal-judicial system, including police and imprisonment

Levying and collecting taxes

Instituting military recruitment

Collecting census data

Extending the national educational system and health services

The methods followed by states to initially break down tribal resistance in order to bring these national institutions to the tribes varied considerably in different parts of the world. But, in general, they were well-organized, large-scale programs based on the assumption that loyalties were to be developed and tribal hostilities were to be overcome by peaceful means. These efforts thus differed sharply from earlier attempts to overcome resistance by the use of overwhelming military force in raids and wars and could be correctly characterized as peaceful pacification. The emphasis was on the material benefits that the tribes could gain from cooperation with the government, and gift-giving was often a prominent part of the procedure of extending government control. (While the stress here is intentionally on the role of governments in reducing tribal political independence, it should be noted that tribal peoples themselves have sometimes taken the initiative in establishing peace when they saw it as beneficial to them.) The presence of government agents may be used to end intertribal feuding (for example, see several cases from Melanesia in Rodman & Cooper, 1979). Perhaps we can best visualize the pacification process by examining several specific examples from various parts of the world.

The Base-Camp System in New Guinea

Soon all villages in Australian New Guinea will have been formally brought under control of the Administration; most of them, in their turn, unwillingly, and resisting what must be, no matter how it is glossed over, an act of conquest.

Rowley, 1966:63

When the civil administration was established in Australia's Mandated Territory of New Guinea in 1921, a vigorous program for exploration and the peaceful extension of government control was immediately initiated. Material inducements were especially prominent in this procedure, and an important factor in the urgency of the program was the need for supplying the growing demand for laborers on the European copra plantations on the coast. At this time the territory was divided into areas according to the degree of government influence to help determine which areas had received least attention and to map progress as it was achieved. These categories are summarized in the following manner by Townsend (1933:424). They reflect the various degrees of influence and illustrate effectively how control was measured.

1. *Complete government control:* An area in which an unarmed native policeman could make an arrest and count on the assistance of local villagers.
2. *Partial government control:* Where arrests could be made, but where the local villagers would not necessarily assist.
3. *Government influence:* Where arrests would not be actively resisted and where European lives and property would be safe.
4. *Area penetrated by patrols:* Without opposition, but where "proper contact" still had not been established.
5. *Unknown area*

At the discretion of the government, various areas were declared "uncontrolled areas," and the entry of unauthorized individuals was strictly forbidden in order to prevent the usual frontier difficulties from disturbing the orderly process of peaceful penetration.

To extend control into the latter two categories, the government developed the base-camp system. In this system an armed patrol, well stocked with trade goods and headed by a European patrol officer with perhaps a dozen native police, established a base camp in an area already under government influence. The patrol carefully selected the camp site in order not to indicate any special alliance with any particular village, which might have been interpreted as an indication of hostility by neighboring villagers. While the patrol remained in this base camp, various highly prized trade goods such as steel tools, salt, and cloth were offered in exchange for food, thus establishing contact with many of the villagers in the surrounding area. At this point the patrol moved out to visit these villages for the first time and requested that the villagers build a rest house to make a longer visit possible for the patrol. Townsend indicates that the villagers were not always eager to fulfill this request because they "loathe interference in domestic affairs," but they were usually convinced through the services of an interpreter. When the rest house was completed, the patrol visited for perhaps several days and planted fruit trees for the use of future patrols.

The presence of a government camp distributing valuables in the partially controlled area would eventually attract visitors from the "unknown" areas, who might have arrived fully armed to receive their gifts and then quickly depart. They would return again, however, and would finally invite the patrol officer to visit their own village to distribute gifts to them directly. The officer would agree to do so on condition that they build a road for him. When the new village was visited, gifts were indeed distributed to the natives and the government's objectives were explained through interpreters, while the material rewards of "belonging to the government" were stressed. A few months later a feast would be conducted for all of the tribes in the area at government expense as further proof of good will. Peace agreements were negotiated between hostile native groups, and carefully selected native police were brought in to live at strategic points throughout the new area to help enforce the peace and to act as unobtrusive teachers. As soon as possible, *luluais*, or village chiefs, were appointed to serve as intermediaries between the government and the village. Each chief was presented with a red-banded, blue-peaked cap as a badge of honor and a village book that eventually would be filled with census data. Often the chief was assisted by an interpreter-assistant known as a *tultul*, who would be taken to the coast and given several months of training and who might also have served as a medical orderly in the village.

An average base-camp patrol operation lasted about three months and was normally a peaceful, successful procedure. Patrols were under orders not to use firearms except in self-defense, but occasionally trouble broke out and sometimes officers were killed while attempting to arrest participants in intertribal fighting. After friendly contact was established and luluais and tultuls were installed, a patrol officer made annual inspection tours. However, the real measure of successful penetration occurred when the labor recruiters were allowed to operate freely. As Townsend (1933:428) explains:

> It is not long before European recruiters of labour work through, and in the next few years each village has members who have worked for white men, and are strong advocates of the white man's Government.

FIGURE 4.2

A New Guinea *luluai*, government-appointed
chief, in official hat and clothes supplied by
the government. His cheek bulges with betel
nut. (Littlewood.)

Patrols experienced difficulties in New Guinea when pacifying the headhunting Sepik River district during the 1920s. In 1924 four European officers, a
detachment of thirty police, and a twelve-ton patrol boat established themselves
near the halfway point along the 800-kilometer river and began sending out
heavily armed patrols. The first patrol to be attacked responded with rifle fire,
and thereafter the tribal population resorted to passive resistance. Villagers informed the officers that they had no intentions of following their orders and
often simply deserted their villages when the patrol boat was sighted. To cope
with this problem the officers kidnapped the old men left behind in the deserted
villages and housed them in pacified enemy villages near headquarters until they
agreed to arrange for communication with the resisters. Within eighteen months,
400 kilometers of river inhabited by some 10,000 people was declared safe to
travel, but "ingrained hostility" still existed. Two years after the establishment
of district headquarters the district officer called a meeting of 200 men to gain
their approval for the government's acquisition of a plot of tribal land to be

leased to a mission station. The brief meeting ended when one man made the following statement and everyone filed out:

> *Several days' journey up the river there is a white man, the District Officer. Several days' journey downstream there is a white man, the missionary. That makes two. Two too many.*

Townsend, 1933:431

The last reported headhunting raid in the Sepik River district occurred in 1927, but the government arrested those involved, hung seven, and imprisoned the rest.

The Mokolkol people in New Britain probably were the most difficult case of resistance to pacification efforts anywhere in New Guinea. According to Fenbury's (1968) account, the Mokolkol were a small group of forest nomads who refused trade or any form of peaceful contact with outsiders and occasionally raided their neighbors to obtain steel tools. They occupied a small tract of mountain forest within just eighty air kilometers of Rabaul, the district capital, and were a constant source of embarrassment to the administration. In 1931 a patrol officer approached a Mokolkol village with his police, distributed his "gifts," and sat down to wait for the villagers to receive them. The Mokolkol ran out, grabbed the gifts, and disappeared—only to return four days later to attack the patiently waiting patrol. With this reception, the defeated patrol returned to the coast with two dead and four wounded. Two years later another officer was sent in, but this time with rolls of barbed wire and orders to construct a compound and lock up any "wild men" that he could capture. The Mokolkol played hide-and-seek with the patrol, which was able to capture only four children and three elderly men and women. These captives were taken to Rabaul, but the adults failed to adjust to their new surrounding and soon died. Finally, in 1950 a patrol of fifty-four men stealthily surrounded a village of twenty-seven people that had been located by aerial reconnaissance and rushed in, handcuffing captives. This time two men, one woman, and four children were arrested and taken to Rabaul, where they were successfully indoctrinated in the advantages of cooperation with the government of the Territory of New Guinea.

Throughout Australian New Guinea the process of peaceful penetration continued relentlessly from the 1920s into the 1970s, except for an unavoidable pause during World War II. By 1950 some 168,350 square kilometers of territory was not yet fully controlled, but by 1970 only 1,735 square kilometers remained in that category (Grosart, 1972:266–269).

Peaceful Pacification in Brazil

The techniques of government penetration used so effectively in New Guinea were first developed in Brazil by Candido Mariano da Silva Rondon, founder of the Indian Protection Service. Officials of the Indian Service worked under the strict motto "Die if necessary but never kill," and during given pacification efforts, perhaps lasting months or even years, they were not allowed to shoot Indians even in self-defense. The usual procedure called for a small team to enter hostile Indian territory and build a house and compound at a strategic location, placing gifts in conspicuous places in hopes of establishing a silent barter system with the natives. In many cases the Indians promptly attacked the team's base, but the house was well shielded with sheet metal, and the Indians' arrows usually had little effect. If the Indians approached too closely, the team was permitted to shoot over their heads to scare them away. Eventually the Indians would decide that the team intended no harm, and direct contact would take place. Pacification was usually followed by resettlement, schooling, and perhaps other forms of supervision by Indian Service officials at Indian "posts."

In 1967 the Indian Service was reorganized as the National Foundation for the Indian (FUNAI) after disclosure that many of its officials had been involved with wealthy investors in efforts to exterminate tribes that were impeding the development of tribal lands by outsiders. FUNAI continued the pacification techniques developed by the Indian Protection Service and applied them to relocate numerous groups that were in the pathway of highway construction, agricultural efforts, and mineral development in the Brazilian rain forest throughout the 1970s and 1980s. FUNAI's use of steel axes and knives as gifts to attract and "pacify" the Urueu-Wau-Wau in Rôndonia (a federal territory on the border with Bolivia) is one of the most recently described examples (McIntyre, 1988).

Unfortunately, in spite of the obvious humanitarian concerns of many of the former Indian Service officials and the present FUNAI workers, pacification has often had a disastrous impact on tribes who proved unable to adjust to their changed cultural environments.

In other areas of South America, such as Peru and Ecuador, the Summer Institute of Linguistics, a well-organized and equipped group of missionary-linguists, has established initial contacts with many isolated and potentially hostile groups in basically the same manner, except that they have been able to make widespread use of airplanes.

Soviet Reconstruction: Red Tents and Red Boats

The tribal peoples of Russia's Far East in Siberia were left virtually undisturbed by the government, and many groups, such as the Chukchi, had no idea that they were part of Russia until rivalry with Americans in nearby Alaska began developing around 1900 and focused special attention on the area. However, an effective policy toward the political incorporation of these peoples did not begin until after the Russian Revolution in 1917, when the new government discovered that the tribal peoples were living outside the Soviet Constitution and were in need of "extreme measures for their salvation" and of "rapid inclusion within the sphere of Soviet authority" (Levin & Potapov, 1964:490). In 1924 a special agency called the Committee for Assistance to the Peoples of the Northern Regions (the "Committee of the North") was assigned the task of bringing the tribal peoples into the Soviet system.

The scattered nature of the tribal population and their nomadic habits constantly frustrated efforts at political reorganization. Mobile red tents carried by reindeer or by boats ("red boats") attempted to follow the nomads and offer them political indoctrination, cultural programs, medicine, and education. By special decrees, the tribal populations were exempted from particularly bothersome duties of citizenship, such as payment of taxes, military recruitment, and work levies. "Capitalist" traders were thrown out, and the government became the sole supplier of desirable trade goods. An offensive was launched against traditional tribal leaders who resisted the new program, and they were ousted to be replaced by clan assemblies. The ultimate aim was the elimination of nomadism and the concentration of the tribal population in settlements for easier administration. Resettlement programs were developed to expedite this end, and thousands of nonnative immigrants were brought in concurrently. Stationary "cultural bases" equipped with hospital and veterinary facilities, boarding schools, radios and movie projectors, and model workshops were established in the most remote areas as inducements to facilitate the resettlement plan.

Tribal "Action Programs" in Southeast Asia

For thousands of years tribal peoples have occupied the interior hilly uplands of Southeast Asia, where they apparently maintained a balance with their environment and a successful symbiosis with the various civilizations on the lowland plains. Although trade and cultural diffusion occurred between the tribal populations and the civilizations surrounding them, the tribes retained their basic autonomy. This tribal independence was possible because the lowland civilizations were ecologically adapted to their own environment and were interested in maintaining the hill tribes as effective buffer zones separating them from neighboring states. World political considerations, beginning in the 1960s, suddenly made the "loyalty" of the hill peoples a matter of major concern for the governments claiming ultimate sovereignty over them, and a variety of programs were devised to win their support peacefully. An example of the recency of these efforts is the fact that Thailand's hill tribes, who may number some 200,000 people, were not even counted in the nation's 1960 census, and then there was no clear government policy on whether they were even to be considered citizens (Kunstadter, 1967:20, 375).

With the rise of antigovernment guerrilla activities, however, Thailand became very interested in the tribal peoples, and by 1967 numerous government agencies were showing a sudden new interest and often developing special programs for them. These organizations included the Provincial Police, the Border Patrol Police, and Ministry of Education, the Ministry of Health, the Ministry of Defense, the Department of Forestry, and the Hill Tribes Division of the Department of Public Health with its Hill Tribes Research Center and other programs. Considerable *international* involvement also began in direct support of these national efforts. This included the United States Information Service, the United States Operations Mission, the United States Department of Defense, the Southeast Asia Treaty Organization, UNESCO, the World Health Organization, the Asia Foundation, and at least eleven Protestant missionary organizations and several Roman Catholic orders.

The general intent and organization of these various programs parallels closely Soviet policy toward Siberian peoples described above, where the emphasis was on political indoctrination supported by the rapid provision of bountiful material rewards. Specifically, Thailand's Border Patrol Police Program and the Defense Ministry's Mobile Development Program offer striking parallels to Soviet Red Tent and Culture Base programs. The usual procedure for the border patrol police in carrying out their mission of befriending the hill tribes was to send patrols into the hills in order to persuade the tribal people to build airstrips in exchange for gifts of food, tools, and medical aid. The airstrips were then used to fly in other medical aid and technical assistance. During these visits the people were told "informally" about the national government, and photographs of Thailand's king and queen and the "emerald buddha," a symbol of the national religion, were distributed. In 1964 the border patrol police removed approximately a hundred young tribal leaders from some forty villages to a district town for technical training and political indoctrination. They were then sent back to their villages as instructors.

The Mobile Development Program also distributed thousands of photographs of the king and queen and the emerald buddha, but went a major step further with the establishment of model villages in the remote areas of Thailand.

Model villages were equipped with schools, TV sets, playgrounds, street lights, running water, toilets, and medical facilities, and were perhaps even more elaborate than the Soviet culture bases. Critics who suggested that such a life style was inappropriate within the hill tribe context, and that promoting such standards of material consumption might in the long run have a disastrous impact on the people, their culture, and their environments, are answered by Huff as follows:

> We must also be careful not to underestimate the villager's capacity to change his way of life. Arguments that he does not need, does not want, and cannot get TV, electric power, machinery, and other luxuries may turn out to be shortsighted, in which case the MDUs' [mobile development units] instinct in establishing and supporting the model village concept will look somewhat better in retrospect.
>
> Huff, 1967:463

THE POLITICAL INTEGRATION PROCESS

The extension of government control marks a highly significant event in the history of any tribal society, for it means that at this point they cease being politically autonomous "little sovereignties"; they cease being "tribes" as the term is being used here. Upon their official incorporation into the state, tribal peoples must conform to and become integrated with the social and political institutions characteristic of state organization. The tribe is no longer fully responsible for settling disputes and maintaining internal order and has limitations placed upon its political decision-making processes. At the same time, a new set of problems is created by the need to formally define the relationship between the tribal population and the state government, and with nontribal individuals who now have special interests in the tribal area and its resources.

There has been wide variation in different independent countries and colonial administrations in the extent to which political and legal powers have been delegated to or withheld from tribal peoples. At one extreme is the so-called direct rule system, in which *all* authority is held by outsiders, whereas at the other extreme is the creation of a political bureaucracy incorporating tribal individuals and extending down to the village level. Many variations on the theme of indirect rule lie between these two extremes, but regardless of which political integration strategy is followed, the result is always profound transformation of traditional tribal organization.

French Direct Rule

According to French colonial theory, control was to be imposed as rapidly as possible over native populations, with virtually no allowances made for incompatibilities between native sociopolitical organization and the French model. Native officials or canton chiefs were, of course, utilized, because it would have been impossible in many areas to have placed French administrators in every local village (in Africa in the 1920s, 12,500 Europeans controlled over 15 million natives), but these native officials were considered to be government employees, not representatives of traditional cultures.

René Maunier, a member of the French Academy of Colonial Sciences, argued that in the interests of utility, convenience, prosperity, and justice, it was necessary for the French to abolish the rights of traditional leaders and tribal councils and to replace them eventually with French administrators and French courts, presided over by Frenchmen. In many cases French authorities denied the legal existence of any tribal social unit above the family. It was felt that in this way the tribe could be remade, "to accommodate it to new needs" (Maunier, 1949:568–569). Direct rule seems to have been a deliberate and well-planned policy, reflecting a fundamental belief in French superiority.

Chiefs appointed by the French in tropical Africa were responsible for the collection of taxes, the requisition of forced corvée labor, forced crop cultivation, military recruitment, the provision of support for visiting dignitaries, and the maintenance of an armed police force. They themselves were subject to imprisonment and corporal punishment for failure to carry out these duties, and to complicate their situation, often their authority was not recognized by the villagers. Needless to say, this placed these puppet chiefs in extremely uncomfortable positions and led to many abuses.

Under direct rule in French tropical Africa, two legal systems operated side by side. French law and the French court applied to all cases involving natives and Europeans. The *indigénat* system, or indigenous justice, applied to all cases involving only natives. In this system at the village level, the canton chief was for a time allowed to judge minor cases and impose fines of up to five days in prison. But in 1912 the chief could no longer impose any fines and could only *mediate* disputes, and by 1924 full authority was entrusted to Europeans. French administrators operated with full discretionary powers to investigate, arrest, judge, and execute the sentence, and there was no practical appeal from their decisions. Infractions were defined by the administrator's interpretation of customary law and by decree and included such crimes as: "Any disrespectful act or offensive proposal vis-à-vis a representative or agent of authority" or songs, rumors, or speeches "intended to weaken respect for French authority" (Suret-Canale, 1971:331–336).

French-style direct rule was widely condemned by other colonial authorities, who claimed that it was too harsh on native custom, involved too much government, was too inconsistent and unstable, and, more specifically, that it deliberately refused to work through native political organization (Roberts, 1969:149–151).

Indirect Rule

By the 1920s and 1930s *indirect rule* came to be widely accepted as the only valid approach to native administration, although as an administrative structure it was often difficult to distinguish from *direct rule* on more than theoretical grounds. The method was pioneered and developed as both a practical working system and a philosophy by Lord Frederick Lugard during his service as high commissioner among the Islamic rulers of northern Nigeria between 1900 and 1907, and it was propagated through his book *The Dual Mandate in British Tropical Africa*, first published in 1922. Indirect rule involved maintaining and strengthening traditional native leaders and creating them where they did not exist. Tribes, tribal councils, clans, and villages were generally recognized as legal entities; native courts presided over by natives were encouraged, but with specific limits on their authority. In Lugard's view (1965:214–218), one of the primary purposes of indirect rule was the necessity to prevent the total breakdown of native society and the collapse of all social order, which was being initiated by the arrival of Europeans and would certainly be accelerated by the abuses unavoidably associated with arbitrary direct rule. The demands for recognition of native rights being made by anti-imperialists and humanitarian organizations, such as the Aboriginal Protection Society and the Congo Reform Movement, combined with the obvious failures of French direct rule, were all probably influential in fostering the acceptance of indirect rule, but practical considerations were undoubtedly paramount.

"Growth from within" was one of the key philosophical concepts behind indirect rule. It was assumed that tribal peoples would thereby be allowed to develop along their own lines, but precisely what this meant was never defined.

However, more cynical observers have called indirect rule, "direct rule by indirect means," and Pitt-Rivers (1927:276–277) argued that the only difference between the two forms of rule was that direct rule achieved the goal more rapidly and that in the long run detribalization and deculturation occurred either way. Indeed, there is considerable evidence to suggest that indirect rule was designed to preserve native political institutions only to the extent necessary to maintain order and to assure the availability of native labor. In areas where tribal populations were numerically insignificant, indirect rule was usually dispensed with in favor of more efficient or rapid methods. Indirect rule was clearly intended to involve the adaptation of the traditional political system to the political and economic requirements of the state, but this transformation was to be carefully directed.

The system of native administration in preindependence Kenya, as described by Dilley (1966:26–30), may be briefly examined as a typical example of indirect rule in operation.

In Kenya Colony, according to the guidelines of the Native Authority Ordinance of 1912, authority over the native population at the local level was vested in *headmen* or *councils of elders* who were selected by the local people subject to the recommendations of the white district commissioner and the final approval of the governor. Headmen were salaried and were given wide powers to maintain order and see that governmental regulations were carried out in the local area. In addition to the headmen, native councils existed in each district (sometimes paralleling European-run district councils), comprised of natives appointed and presided over by the district commissioner, but with considerable authority to pass resolutions and levy taxes. In addition, native tribunals or courts existed, which in 1932 under the supervision of the administration handled about 25,000 civil cases and 7,000 criminal cases. There were also tribal police at the province level.

Systems similar to this were applied by the British throughout Africa. In India the tribal peoples of the North East Frontier Agency were allowed to form tribal councils that also served as courts with broad powers. Australian New Guinea operated with the headmen, or *luluais*, until 1950 when local government councils were established.

In many areas indirect rule was eventually ended by "independence" in which a native elite, educated by the former colonial rulers, took over the state bureaucratic structure and local appointed headmen were abolished or became elected positions and dual (native-white) forms of local government were abolished in favor of a single administrative hierarchy.

The Protective Legislation Approach

In the case of tribal peoples who were greatly outnumbered by invading populations and were not themselves useful as sources of labor (such as in lowland South America, North America, and Australia), native administration tended to take the form of a welfare operation. After their traditional cultural autonomy had been destroyed by conquest or in some cases by treaty, these peoples were treated as incompetent and impoverished citizens to be sheltered in special institutions and managed by special legislation. Canada, for example, provided for the gradual development of some degree of self-government for reservation Indians in its Indian Act of 1869, but the United States did not allow any significant political activity among its Indian population until the Indian Reorganization Act of 1934, which permitted tribal councils. In lowland South America, isolated Indian populations are sometimes technically subject to special protective legislation, and there may be official state organizations, such as Colombia's commissions for Indian protection and welfare, Brazil's National Foundation for the Indian, and Venezuela's National Indigenist Commission—all in principle designed to look after Indian welfare—but there is little deliberate effort to preserve any semblance of traditional sociopolitical structure. Despite all of these organizations for their protection and regardless of special laws, Amazonian Indians continue to be exploited by outsiders taking advantage of their lack of sophistication because little effort is made to implement protectionist policies.

In British India there was a long tradition of protective legislation for tribal peoples in combination with a form of indirect rule. As early as 1855 the Santal Parganas District was declared a *nonregulation area*, making the general laws of the country inapplicable to it, and it was administered directly by special commissioners with full judicial authority. This approach was extended to other Indian tribal areas by the Scheduled Districts Act of 1874 and the *backward tract* provisions of the Government of India Act of 1919. *Scheduled tribes* and *tribal areas* were designated in the 1950 constitution of independent India, and tribal advisory councils were established under the supervision of the local governors, who could suspend any state laws at their discretion (Elwin, 1969; Ghurye, 1963).

Suspension of normal state laws or the creation of extraordinary political arrangements are everywhere viewed as only temporary measures to allow tribal peoples time to gain familiarity and competence with the normal political-legal structures of the state. In many countries few, if any, boundaries are maintained between the dominant society and the tribal population. In these cases tribal populations may participate in normal state political processes at least theoretically on an equal basis with any other citizen, and there is relatively little in the way of special protective legislation or distinctive administrative structures. This seems to be the approach of many independent African, Asian, and Pacific nations.

An exception to this general pattern is represented by the Soviet Union, which in 1926 began forming national *rayons*, or territorial political units ostensibly representing national minorities. At the lower levels the rayons were composed of clan assemblies and councils patterned after rural soviets and including clan federations and rayon native executive councils and congresses. This policy of recognizing nationalities or ethnic groups was merely an efficient way of following the larger national policy of helping tribal peoples "develop and consolidate Soviet state structure among themselves in the forms corresponding to the national ways of life of the peoples" and was to be "a gradual transition to the normal territorial system of soviets" (Levin & Potapov, 1964:492). In the People's Republic of China there has been a similar effort to recognize the existence of national minorities by designating *autonomous regions* that were to be integral parts of the nation but could enjoy considerable self-government subject to the approval of the National People's Congress (Diao, 1967:171–173).

ANTHROPOLOGY AND NATIVE ADMINISTRATION

Representatives of government have seldom questioned the value of ethnological data for purposes of administration. In modern times practically every nation with expanding frontiers has supported inquiries into the customs of native peoples in areas of projected or accomplished occupation. . . . Colonization programs, if they have not been dedicated to the destruction of indigenous populations, have necessitated a knowledge of local customs.

Barnett, 1956:2

Throughout most of the nineteenth century and before indirect rule and other administrative refinements became widely institutionalized, governments felt little need to acquire specialized knowledge of the cultures that were being transformed and eradicated. Gradually, however, it became apparent that such knowledge could make the task of administration and transformation much more efficient and effective and that it might even prevent tribal uprisings. Missionaries and administrators lacked the necessary training, were too busy with other duties, and were too biased by their roles to obtain reliable scientific data on tribal culture. The assistance of anthropologists was needed.

The United States led the way in 1879 by organizing the Bureau of American Ethnology, which, as its first director, J. W. Powell (1881:xiv), explained in his first annual report, endeavored to produce results of "practical value in the administration of Indian affairs." From about 1890 on, British colonial administrators became increasingly interested in anthropological research. Many gained some anthropological training at the Universities of Oxford and Cambridge and went on to publish significant monographs. In 1926 the International African Institute was founded with the primary purpose of relating scientific research to the "practical tasks" that were facing Europeans who were working for the "good" of Africa (Lugard, 1928). Support for this institute came from virtually all of the major colonial powers, including Great Britain, France, Belgium, Italy, South Africa, Germany, and the United States, but a great deal of the research effort of the institute was conducted by British social anthropologists in British colonies. Since the 1920s numerous national and international institutes have arisen in support of anthropological research in relation to native administration. Examples of the latter include the South Pacific Commission founded in 1948 and the Inter-American Indian Institute founded in 1940, while innumerable national research institutes have been founded. Most independent former colonies have also actively supported administration-related anthropological research (Barnett, 1956; Brokensha, 1966; Forde, 1953).

In general, government administrators have received the most support from anthropologists in such areas as sociopolitical organization, law and judicial processes, land tenure, and the general problem of economic development. British anthropologists were ardent supporters of indirect rule, which, according to Malinowski, was considered by all competent anthropologists to be "infinitely preferable" to direct rule (1929:23). They also stressed the functional inter-relatedness of culture in their research so that administrators could best evaluate the impact of their policies (Manners, 1956). Prominent British functionalists such as Malinowski and Radcliffe-Brown helped establish anthropology departments and special training programs for colonial administrators in South Africa and Australia. During their association with colonial governments, anthropologists generally assumed a neutral position in their work and limited themselves to providing data while they avoided direct involvement in policy making. The political implications of applied anthropology in relation to tribal peoples will be discussed further in Chapter 10.

· 5 ·

Land Policies

The land, of course, must be transferred from the hands of the Natives to those of the Whites. . . . So the Natives must give way and either become servants of the Whites or withdraw to the reserves allotted to them.

Newspaper Article, German Southwest Africa, 1901, cited Wellington, 1967

PERHAPS THE MOST CRITICAL government policies to affect tribal peoples were those relating to their possession of the land: Any modification of the traditional man-land relationship would undoubtedly have a major impact on all aspects of tribal culture. As soon as government control was firmly established and the administrative structures were in operation, attention turned to the problem of defining tribal land rights in order to maximize economic productivity. Although considerable variation existed in different countries, the general effect of the land policies imposed by governments was reduction of the territory available to tribal populations and modification of their traditional systems of tenure in favor of state-controlled systems. In turn, these results made traditional economic systems and related social and ideological patterns difficult, if not impossible, to maintain. None of these changes were due to mere "contact" and simple diffusion, but rather to deliberate state policy. These policies will be examined in this chapter, but to better appreciate their effects it is necessary to first understand traditional tribal systems of land tenure and how they contrast with state systems.

THE TRIBAL MAN-LAND RELATIONSHIP

In traditional tribal cultures, access to land was generally controlled by a complex network of kinship relationships, the principles of which were often incomprehensible to outsiders. It is common to encounter examples of complete misunderstanding of tribal land-tenure systems in the writings of government administrators and colonial experts who felt that native land rights were always obscure and confused. Tribal land rights *were* often complex, but certain facts do stand out. First, group boundaries were well defined and defended against encroachment from neighboring groups. Ownership was vested in the kin group or community, or figuratively in the chief, and it was inconceivable that anyone would have the right to permanently alienate land from the group. The concept of *ownership* at other than the group or tribal level was quite irrelevant, because land was to be *used* by individuals and not owned in the usual sense. Access to and use of land was virtually guaranteed to all tribal members. Even though specific rights were often overlapping and subject to numerous conditions, land allocation remained both well regulated and flexible. It was highly adaptive to have a variety of cultural mechanisms of land allocation to ensure an equitable balance between land resources and population. Aside from its obvious economic significance, the land itself often held important symbolic and emotional meaning for the native people as the repository for ancestral remains, clan origin points, and other sacred features in tribal mythology.

It is important to note that tribal land-use patterns make the concept of waste or unoccupied land as irrelevant as the concept of private ownership. Pastoralists, shifting agriculturalists, and hunter-gatherers often exploit their territory in long-term cycles and leave large areas undisturbed to recuperate before returning to them. Furthermore, not all portions of tribal land are necessarily exploited in exactly the same manner, because some zones might be reserved for specialized uses. These details are, of course, unlikely to be of much consequence to policy makers concerned primarily with increasing the cash value of the land. Governments have usually been quick to claim what they interpreted to be wasteland, and in the process have often destroyed the larger man-land equilibrium systems evolved by tribal cultures.

LAND POLICY VARIABLES

It is generally recognized in international law that the aboriginal inhabitants of a region possess rights in their lands that cannot legally be ignored (Bennett, 1978; Buffalo Law Review, 1978, 27[4]). This is acknowledged explicitly in Article Eleven of the International Labour Office's Convention 107, which provides that *the right of ownership, collective or individual, of the members of the populations concerned over the lands which these populations traditionally occupy shall be recognized.*

In fact, these rights have not always been recognized, or they have been legally circumvented through a variety of means, as will be shown.

Land laws are often complex, and in any discussion of land policies concerning tribal peoples several variables must be kept in mind. There may be no recognition of any native rights in the land, as was the case in Australia until the Land Rights (Northern Territory) Act of 1976, but more often *some* rights are recognized in *some* categories of tribal land. These rights and categories must be carefully distinguished because different effects on tribal culture may result. In terms of categories of tribal lands, the state may acknowledge tribal rights to any or none of the following:

Land traditionally exploited by the tribe

Land considered necessary to meet the future needs of an expanding or a recovering population

Land occupied or actively exploited at a given time

Land with registered title

In addition to these land categories are the critical questions of whether customary communal tenure will be allowed and how to deal with the problem of land transfers and alienation to outsiders. In theory, any tribal land could be considered inalienable and, therefore, the permanent possession of the tribe with no provisions for any acquisition by outsiders or the state. But most often governments have assumed responsibility for determining what tribal land can be alienated and for what purposes. It has also been common practice for governments to assume eminent domain over tribal lands in regard to certain categories of natural resources such as minerals, forests, and sometimes game, and to regulate tribal use of these resources accordingly.

The following sections examine general trends in government land policies as they relate to tribal peoples in different parts of the world. The policies of the United States concerning the Indians and Alaska natives are presented in detail as a basis for comparison with the situation in other countries, but in most areas only a brief survey is given. Despite the many divergent details, outstanding parallels throughout the world reside in the fact that governments have restricted the access of tribal peoples to their lands and have actively attempted to destroy customary patterns of land tenure.

The American Reservation System

The right of North American Indians to their lands was recognized in principle since the colonial period. For example, the British Royal Proclamation of 1763 stated that any lands that were not purchased or ceded to the crown would be reserved as Indian hunting grounds. This principle was reaffirmed by the new American government after the Revolution in the 1787 Ordinance for the Government of the Northwest Territory, which declared:

> *The utmost good faith shall always be observed towards the Indians; their lands and property shall never be taken from them without their consent; and in their property rights and liberty, they never shall be invaded or disturbed, unless in just and lawful wars authorized by congress.*
>
> Fey & McNickle, 1970:56

Such declarations were probably made in good faith and were apparently taken seriously—at least while the Indians were numerically strong enough to constitute a threat and when there was some danger that they might seek support from foreign governments. As soon as these dangers were no longer a problem and when settlers and speculators began clamoring for new lands, the government forgot these noble promises. There followed a steady reduction of the Indian land base through wars, removals, outright confiscations, and treaties that confined Indians on small reservations against their will.

The first major rejection of the policy of "utmost good faith" occurred with President Andrew Jackson's Indian Removal Act of 1830, which called for the removal of all eastern tribes to "permanent" Indian country in the Great American Desert west of the Mississippi, where it was thought that white men would never be able to settle. Some 90,000 Indians were removed, but not all tribes left their traditional homelands peacefully. The Florida Seminoles fought a war from 1836 to 1842 that cost the United States the lives of 1,500 soldiers and 20 million dollars to remove 4,000 Seminoles. The Cherokees of Georgia also presented a difficult case. They fought removal through the courts and obtained a favorable Supreme Court decision, but President Jackson refused to enforce it and the Cherokees had to surrender 2.8 million hectares to be distributed by lottery to Georgia's white population. Fourteen thousand men, women, and children were then herded into concentration camps and forced by federal troops to march to Oklahoma; 4,000 died en route. Unfortunately, not even their newly assigned land in Oklahoma was secure from further dispossession: They had to surrender much of it in a short time as punishment after they sided with the South during the Civil War.

By 1840 a "permanent" frontier had been established by a line on the map and a string of forts running west of the Mississippi from Texas to Canada. Within this Indian country, which extended to the crest of the Rockies and served as a vast buffer zone between the United States and disputed territories in the Far West, the Indians were to be allowed freedom to enjoy their lands. For a short time it appeared that the government intended to deal in the "utmost good faith." Regulations were passed prohibiting the entry of outsiders into Indian country without special permits and outlawing the sale of alcohol to the tribesmen. A few schools and training centers were to be established inside Indian country under the direction of the Bureau of Indian Affairs created in

1832, and troops were to be used to prevent intertribal conflicts. For the most part, however, the quarter of a million Indians in the area were to be left largely to their own devices. This scheme constituted what must have been the largest tribal "reserve" ever envisioned, and it even held some promise of success. But it was a regrettably short-lived experiment.

When Texas, the Oregon country, and the Southwest passed to American control in 1845, 1846, and 1848, respectively, the Indian country of the plains suddenly seemed to stand in the way of progress, and settlers began to stream across it in great numbers on their way farther west. The government quickly negotiated new land agreements with the tribes, including rights of passage. At the government's invitation in 1851, a general council with thousands of Indians representing many plains tribes was convened at Fort Laramie. In exchange for promises of abundant gifts in the future, the tribes agreed to grant rights-of-way for the Oregon Trail and accepted specific tribal boundaries. This was only the beginning of what was already a familiar process to the eastern tribes. Shortly thereafter, states and territories were carved out of what had been designated permanent Indian country, and all of the tribes were continually relocated on smaller and smaller reservations.

Land agreements were conducted in a similar manner to the transfers of political sovereignty described in an earlier chapter. While some writers will perhaps still defend the legality of the transactions and the good intentions of the government, there can be little doubt that coercion—if not outright deception—was often involved and that the Indians lost millions of acres of their best lands against their will. In his account of the plains wars, Andrist (1969:8) acknowledges that, strictly speaking, most Indian land was alienated with Indian consent, but he summarized the conditions under which "consent" was granted as follows:

> It was given by tribes which had just been broken in wars, it was given by peoples who had been threatened or cajoled into signing, or misled about what they were agreeing to. It was often consent granted by a minority of the tribe's leaders who had been subverted or liquored up; the Commissioners were never squeamish about hailing the voice of a few as the voice of all if that was the best that could be had. So, when the Indians gave up their land by their own consent, they were usually consenting with a knee in their groin.

Reservations grew smaller and smaller and in many cases became inadequate to support their Indian populations by traditional means. Furthermore, they were often outside traditional homelands. The tribesmen were forced to live on sporadic and insufficient government doles of unfamiliar food, and they had to accept the confinement and new regulations imposed on them. From 1789 to 1849 reservations were run by army officers, and even after agents of the Bureau of Indian Affairs took charge, army posts were located on most reservations. Reservations were not always happy places, and it is little wonder that the government often had to resort to force to keep the tribesmen on the land assigned to them.

Dull Knife's band of 320 Northern Cheyenne endured what they considered to be the intolerable conditions of their reservation in Oklahoma Indian Territory for a year and a half. Then, in 1878, they attempted to return to their homeland in Montana. After a flight of more than 600 miles they were recaptured and imprisoned, but they still refused to return to their designated reservation. After being deprived of food and warmth for five days in subzero weather, they attempted to escape again but were surrounded by soldiers and shot down (Andrist, 1969:320–330; Fey & McNickle, 1970:34–36).

In 1946 the government finally acknowledged that Indian grievances over past land deals were still of sufficient magnitude and presented such unique problems that special legal machinery in the form of the Indian Claims Commission was created to deal with them. Previously, between 1881 and 1950, 118 Indian land cases had been presented before the United States Court of Claims, but only 34 of these cases recovered damages (Lurie, 1957:57). The new Indian Claims Commission was more generous toward Indians in terms of the kinds of cases it would hear and the kinds of evidence that could be accepted. A specific category included "fraud, duress, unconscionable consideration, mutual or unilateral mistake" in the treaty signing, as a basis for claim, or simply the failure of the government to pay as promised (Lurie, 1957:62). Some 247 cases were tried by the commission between 1950 and 1967, and it awarded 250 million dollars in damages as at least partial restitution for past wrongs.

In spite of these belated efforts at compensation, the government had already embarked upon policies that were equally destructive of tribal land rights even before the last Indian wars ended. Indian administrators had long assumed that tribal forms of land ownership constituted an obstacle to progress, and as early as the 1830s an Indian commissioner had maintained that "common property and civilization cannot coexist" (Fey & McNickle, 1970:72). Finally these views found expression in the General Allotment Act of 1887, which called for the subdivision of reservations into small plots to be assigned to tribal individuals and held in trust for twenty-five years and then disposed of at the owners' discretion. "Surplus" land, remaining after the allotment, was purchased by the government and could also be disposed of at will. Indians often vigorously resisted allotment, but to no avail, and its effects were devastating. During the period of most active allotment between 1887 and 1932, more than 60 percent of the 56.7 million hectares then in Indian hands was lost, and the tribes were left with only 20 million hectares of often marginal land (Fey & McNickle, 1970:84).

The integrity of reservation lands was again threatened by implementation of House Concurrent Resolution 108 of 1953, which declared it was the "sense of Congress" that federal supervision of certain Indian reservations should be ended or, as it was more popularly understood, reservations should be *terminated* as soon as possible. In this process (which did not differ significantly from allotment except that it was more drastic), many reservations were legally disbanded and their land and other assets divided among their members. Termination proceedings touched off serious controversies on several reservations between those anxious for a quick cash settlement and those who wished to retain their land and tribal status. Unfortunately, as in the past, the government was willing to proceed with or without Indian cooperation or approval. In addition to outright termination, Indian lands have been allocated by the Bureau of Indian Affairs in long-term *leases* to large-scale development corporations for projects such as strip mining of coal and uranium mining.

The Alaska Natives Claims Settlement Act

All aboriginal titles, if any, and claims of aboriginal title in Alaska based on use and occupancy, including submerged land underneath all water areas, both inland and offshore, and including any aboriginal hunting or fishing rights that may exist, are hereby extinguished.

ANCSA P. L., 92-203 Sec. 4b

To clear the legal pathway for the construction of the Alaska pipeline following the discovery of oil at Prudhoe Bay in 1968, the United States Congress quickly put together formal legislation to permanently "extinguish" all aboriginal claims to the land. The act, passed in 1971 as the Alaska Natives Claims Settlement Act (ANCSA), provided for the payment of 962.5 million dollars in cash and royalties from oil revenues to native corporations set up by the act (Arnold, 1978). The natives were also to receive title to some 162,000 square kilometers of land to be held by regional and village native corporations. In comparison with the land settlements received by Indians in the lower 48 states, the Alaska claims settlement might seem like a generous arrangement. The natives, who in 1971 numbered approximately 78,500, or 25 percent of the Alaskan population, received roughly 17 percent of the total land area of Alaska, while the nonnative private sector of the state was left with less than 1 percent of the land. State and federal holdings accounted for the remaining 82 percent. There were a few catches, however. The Alaskan natives were to be turned instantly into corporate executives and stockholders and were required to use their cash payments and the natural resources of their land holdings to extract cash profits from their native corporations. Furthermore, by 1991 the stocks in native corporations can be sold to anyone and can, in effect, be bought up by outsiders.

ANCSA caused many difficulties for native peoples in Alaska and in the long run did not significantly increase their incomes or security. It undercut native control over subsistence resources, and it created new groups that were often at cross-purposes with each other. By 1983 dissatisfaction with ANCSA, and concern over what would happen in 1991, had reached such a point that an indigenous organization, the Inuit Circumpolar Conference, commissioned distinguished British Columbia Supreme Court Justice, and native rights advocate, Thomas R. Berger, to review the consequences of ANCSA and make recommendations for possible reforms before 1991. Berger spent nearly two years at his task, and interviewed 1,450 witnesses in sixty Alaskan villages, before issuing his report (Berger, 1985). He recommended the transfer of corporate lands to tribal governments and in effect called for native "retribalization." As he explains:

> *Alaska Natives regard the tribal government as the best means of keeping their lands in Native hands and the best means of defending their own subsistence activities and rights against further encroachments.*

Berger, 1985:158

Reservations and Dispossession in South America

Throughout the Amazon regions of South America up to the present, tribal Indians have been driven from their lands by settlers and military action, and the "reservations" established for them have either not been seriously protected by government authorities or they have been too small to allow continuation of traditional life styles. Thus, the situation closely resembles that in the United States. Like the Indian tribes of the American Great Plains, the Amazonian tribes utilize large areas of land, and, as hunters and shifting cultivators, in many cases they do not remain in a specific locality for more than two to three years. Their land rights have therefore been easily disregarded by governments. The national laws that frequently guarantee Indian land rights on paper are often in reality only lightly enforced, and the natives who most need them are usually unaware of the existence of these laws or else lack the means of seeking their enforcement. In the face of continual dispossession, for as long as possible Amazonian Indians merely abandoned their lands and withdrew into more remote areas.

In the 1850s Brazil's imperial government guaranteed the Indians' rights to the inalienable possession of lands needed for their survival. Under the republic, according to the constitutions of 1891, 1934, 1937, and 1946, this was modified to the extent that Indians were entitled to the possession of lands on which they were "permanently established" on the condition that they did not transfer this land to others. In some states, lands were reserved for Indians under the supervision of the Indian Protection Service, but often the boundaries were not considered inviolable by state governments. In Rio Grande do Sul, for example, tribal reserves that in 1913 had amounted to nearly 81,000 hectares had been reduced to only 32,000 hectares by 1967 (Moreira Neto, 1972:319), through a variety of legal and extralegal means.

The most ambitious Brazilian effort to "reserve" Indian land was begun in 1952, when some 85,000 square kilometers of unexplored territory in Mato Grosso were provisionally declared off-limits to white colonization. However, the local government of Mato Grosso proceeded to let out 75 percent of that area in concessions to land speculators. When the boundaries were finalized in 1961, only some 22,000 square kilometers remained as an Indian reserve designated as the Xingu National Park, but its area was later increased to 30,000 square kilometers. For many years the Xingu Park was left virtually undisturbed as an example of Brazil's ideal Indian policy, but it also became a sanctuary for Indians who were being displaced by the frontier in adjacent areas, and it was eventually invaded itself.

Previous legislative efforts to defend Brazilian Indian land rights were seriously undermined by the 1970 Federal Statute of the Indian. This law granted use rights to Indians, but ownership to the federal government, and legalized the physical removal of Indians from their traditional lands for almost any ill-defined reason ranging from national security and higher national interests to public health concerns or to prevent disturbances occurring when settlers invade Indian lands. In effect, Indian rights to their lands no longer needed to be respected at all. Even though Brazil's national Indian foundation (FUNAI) has designated millions of hectares as Indian parks and reserves on paper, since 1970 there has been little serious effort to prevent these areas from being invaded by powerful multinational development interests, highways, ranchers, and settlers (Davis, 1977; Presland, 1979). In 1980 the military took control of FUNAI and the most pro-Indian elements within the organization were removed, suggesting that the land situation would be even more desperate in the future (Davis, 1980). In fact, presidential decrees in 1983 and procedural changes initiated by FUNAI in 1986 modified the Federal Statute of the Indian to permit mining on Indian lands and favored land invaders and other special interest groups over Indians (Gray, 1987:19).

The situation of Indian lands in the Peruvian Amazon has not been much better. Official land regulations disregarded the jungle Indians, who were pushed aside by settlers until 1957, when Supreme Decree No. 3 called for the establishment of native reserves in traditionally occupied areas. The size of reserves was not to be determined with regard to traditional subsistence requirements but, rather, according to a formula that allowed up to ten hectares for each person over five years of age. The long-run policy objective was the introduction of private ownership to specific plots, because, according to the decree, the Indians *must* share in the benefits of progress and civilization. In 1974, Supreme Decree No. 3 was replaced by the "Law of Native Communities" and in 1975 by the "Forest and Wild Fauna Law," which called for the allotment of sufficient lands to native communities to meet their traditional subsistence needs (Chirif, 1975). However, implementation of these laws has been very slow, and it appears that in Peru, as in Brazil, Indian land rights are being overridden by corporate development interests (Cultural Survival Newsletter, 1980, 4[3]:9–10). The law was changed again in 1978 and 1980 and community titles to Indian lands were halted, while pressures to individualize land holdings and promote large-scale agricultural development and colonization of tribal lands have greatly increased.

Official Bolivian policy makes forest Indians the legal equals of any citizen; they are given no preferential treatment regarding land, even though their requirements are unique. They may legally claim title to lands they occupy, but they rarely do so, because the requirements of shifting cultivation do not encourage attachment to any small parcel of land. Consequently, they are subject to dispossession whenever an enterprising colonist applies for a title. The state makes no provision for protecting larger tracts of land for Indian hunting grounds or for long-term reuse of swidden plots (Kelm, 1972:165–167).

In Colombia an 1890 law provided for the establishment of Indian communal reserves (*resguardos*). However, this did not apply to uncivilized, non-Christian tribal groups, who were given no such rights and instead were placed under the legal guardianship of the Catholic missions delegated to civilize them. By 1961, however, Law 135 allowed reserves to be formed for uncivilized Indians, but unfortunately these have either not been established or they have been absurdly small; instead, tribal territories have been considered open for national expansion and colonization. For example, in the llanos in 1970, the Institute of Agrarian Reform reserved two hectares of arid savanna for each of 7,000 Guajibo (Guahibo) Indians, while 3,000 to 40,500 hectares were allotted to each of approximately sixty colonists for agricultural development (Arcand, 1972; Bonilla, 1972; Castillo-Cárdenas, 1972). Since then Indian groups in Colombia appear to have steadily lost ground, in spite of the creation in 1982 of a new government agency ostensibly to protect Indians: the National Development Program for Indigenous Populations (PRODEIN) (Gray, 1987:15).

In Venezuela the Agrarian Reform Act of 1960 recognized Indian rights "to hold the lands, woods and waterways which they occupy or which belong to them in those sites where they customarily dwell" (Coppens, 1972), but Jimenez (1972:38) reports that this law is ineffective because no rules for its implementation have been established. Even where community titles have been granted to Indians, they are not being effectively defended against invasion. According to Mosonyi (1972:48), Indian lands were steadily being appropriated by outsiders in the early 1970s:

> *This process is going on all over the country and no one seems seriously concerned to put an end to it. It is only in the last few years that some Indian leaders have decided to request title-deeds and legal delimitation of their respective possessions from the appropriate tribunals.*

Reports since 1985 indicate that invasions of Indian lands in Venezuela have continued (IWGIA Newsletter, 1985, 42:198–204; IWGIA Yearbook 1986:23, IWGIA Yearbook 1987:23).

Elsewhere in South America, reserves have been established in Chile and Argentina, but here, too, the allotment and individualization process has been applied. In 1940 only some 1,200 of 4.8 million hectares in Araucanian ownership remained under traditional tenure, and the tribal land base had been so reduced that most Araucanians found themselves facing a severe land shortage. Under the Allende government (1970–1973), generous communal reserves were established for the Mapuche, but these were undermined by the Pinochet government by a 1979 decree calling for "the division of the reserves and the liquidation of Indian communities" (cited Gray, 1987:17). The first Five-Year Plan in Argentina divided Indian lands into three categories (reservation, *reducción*, and *colonia*) that were actually stages leading to individual ownership on the same basis as that for other citizens (International Labour Office, 1953:308, 463). However, a 1984 law provides a basis for reestablishing communal reserves in Argentina (Gray, 1987:17).

While the Inini Statute was in effect from 1930 to 1968, the Indians of French Guiana enjoyed a favorable land rights situation. Under the provisions of the statute, the Indians were left in undisturbed possession of 90 percent of the country. The territory was administered directly by the governor, but effective control remained with the Indians. After 1965 there was a move to convert the Inini area into French communes (Hurault, 1972). In other areas in the Guianas, the situation of Indian lands is equally precarious. In Surinam, Indians occupy crown lands and have no special legal protection. In Guyana, some reservations have been set up and an Amerindian Land Commission recommended further entitlements of Indian lands in 1969. However, by 1975 plans were under way to inundate the traditional lands of 4,000 Akawaio Indians with the Mazaruni hydroelectric project (Bennett, Colson, & Wavell, 1978), and the Land Commission recommendations had not been acted upon. Fortunately for the Akawaio, as of 1989 an unresolved border dispute with Venezuela and funding problems were blocking the Mazaruni project.

Tribal Land in Colonial Africa

The pattern of government acquisition of tribal land for the economic benefit of outside interests was unfortunately as common in Africa as in the New World and sometimes even more blatant. The principal difference here was that very large tribal populations were involved, often far outnumbering the European colonists. However, except for a few outstanding exceptions such as in British-controlled West Africa, this did not hinder the alienation process.

In French-controlled West Africa the government declared that all lands for which the natives had no title belonged to the state. It then proceeded to dispose of such "unclaimed" lands by leasing them with full resource rights to European-owned concession companies for development purposes, whereas it offered dispossessed natives token "abandonment indemnities." In 1899, 70 percent of French Equatorial Africa was leased to only forty such companies, with one company receiving 140,000 square kilometers. Natives were, of course, free to apply for titles, but they rarely did so (by 1945 fewer than 2,000 out of 16 million had applied), because they either did not feel the need for them or did not want to risk the community conflicts that private ownership would introduce (Buell, 1928:1033; Suret-Canale, 1971:20, 255–261).

The Congo Free State followed a similar course from 1885 to 1908 with its *régime domanial*, which dictated that all "vacant" lands were claimed by the state. Vacant in this sense meant all land beyond the immediate vicinity of native villages and gardens. There were no provisions for tribal reserves or for any protection of native land rights beyond the islands of land occupied by villages at any given time, and natives were taxed for exploiting the state-owned resources in the forests surrounding their villages. The government strictly enforced this system, which consequently resulted in the incredible abuses described in an earlier chapter.

In areas of southern and eastern Africa considered particularly favorable for

TABLE 5.1

Amount of Land Reserved for
Indigenous Populations in Different Countries

	NATIVE POPULATION AS PERCENT OF TOTAL POPULATION	NATIVE LANDS AS PERCENT OF TOTAL AREA
Bechuanaland[a]	99+	38
Swaziland[a]	98	48
New Guinea[b]	98	97
So. Rhodesia[c]	95	33
S.W. Africa[a]	87	25
South Africa[d]	80	12
Canada[e]	3	0.2
Chile[f]	2	0.6
United States[g]	0.3	1

[a] Cole (1966:526). The British Protectorate of Bechuanaland became the independent republic of Botswana in 1966.
[b] Mair (1970:5, 146) population figures for 1960; "reserve" land here is actually nonalienated land as of 1967–1968.
[c] Barber (1967:1, 7) figures for 1960. Southern Rhodesia became independent Rhodesia in 1970 and Zimbabwe in 1980.
[d] Jabavu (1934:287).
[e] International Labour Office (1953:68, 332) population as of 1949, land figures 1951.
[f] International Labour Office (1953:40, 307) figures as of 1940.
[g] International Labour Office (1953:333, 69) population as of 1940, land figures 1949.

European settlement, colonial governments set up reserves to concentrate large tribal populations on small poor-quality tracts of land, which served as labor dormitories for the white farmers who cultivated vast holdings of the best land. This situation led to some incredible inequities, as the figures in Table 5.1 show. For example, although the natives of Southern Rhodesia constituted 95 percent of the total population, they were left with only a third of the land for their exclusive use.

The poor quality of African tribal reserves has frequently received comment. Writing of the Bantu reserves in southern Africa, Cole observed that they were generally poorer than the lands occupied by Europeans and indeed had not attracted European attention. These reserves were also overcrowded and the soil was highly susceptible to erosion, yet with wise management they were potentially productive (Cole, 1966:526–528). Wellington (1967) has noted how the reserves of Southwest Africa were purposefully located in the zones of lowest rainfall or, as a Herero chief complained in 1922, in deserts "where no human being ever lived before" (Wellington, 1967:279). In Kenya the reserves were structured to allow the Europeans, accounting for less than 1 percent of the population, to have full access to the agriculturally rich uplands that constituted

FIGURE 5.1

Maasai man with his herds in Kenya. In 1904
the Maasai were forced to surrender their
finest grazing lands. (Irven DeVore, Anthro-
Photo.)

20 percent of the country and became known as the *white highlands* (Manners,
1967:283). This policy of European priority in the best lands was established
early and was spelled out by the colony's first commissioner, Sir Charles Eliot
(1900–1904), in the following terms:

> *The interior of the protectorate is a white man's country, and it is mere hypocrisy not
> to admit that white interests must be paramount, and the main object of our policy
> and legislation should be to found a white colony.*

cited Lugard, 1965:324

Eliot rejected the notion of large reserves because he felt they would retard
civilization and perpetuate barbarism and customs that he disapproved of. Instead he favored a policy of interpenetration for Kenya, which would convert
native villages into islands within European estates that would serve as sources
of labor. The natives were to have full rights to lands they occupied, but here, as
elsewhere, the concept of unused land was interpreted to European advantage.

The cattle-herding tribes of Kenya fared particularly poorly under these
policies because of their nomadic habits, and like the North American Indians

they were forced to relocate frequently. The Maasai signed an agreement in 1904 in which they surrendered their finest lands to the whites in exchange for a reserve that would endure "so long as the Maasai as a race shall exist," but seven years later they were forced to move again (Soja, 1968:19). No reserves were secure, and any promises of permanence were shattered by the Crown Lands Ordinance of 1915, which "guaranteed" tribal land rights but allowed the governor to cancel any part of a reserve if he decided that the natives did not need it; any part could be excluded for railroads and highways or *any* public purpose. Kenya's tribal peoples in effect became tenants subject to dispossession at the whim of the government (Dilley, 1966:251–260).

Land Policies in Asia and the Pacific

In Asia and the Pacific region, almost the entire gamut of land policies are again represented. The harshest, most destructive policies occurred in Australia and areas under French, Japanese, and German control. Meanwhile in New Guinea, Fiji, and Micronesia (under American rule), substantial areas of land remained in native hands if not fully under native control. Where harsh colonial policies were followed in the Pacific, they mirrored the general trends noted elsewhere: An initial period of relatively uncontrolled dispossession is followed by the establishment of reserves or at least stricter controls on the alienation process, and finally, individual title registration schemes are imposed that undermine communal tenure systems and result in further alienation.

Australia in some respects represents a special case because the entire continent was occupied by hunter-gatherers and the government recognized neither the sovereignty nor the land ownership rights of these Aborigines. No land treaties or compensation payments were ever made to formalize their dispossession. Given the widespread practice in other areas of acknowledging native rights only in obviously occupied land, it is not surprising that the government declared all of Australia to be "unoccupied wasteland" and therefore state property. This was done in spite of the abundant testimony of early observers who were well aware of aboriginal land ownership and use practices. Anthropologists have even argued that every part of Australia was claimed by Aborigines and was exploited up to its maximum carrying capacity. According to Birdsell (1971:334), "There were no empty or unclaimed spaces." Australia had been occupied for perhaps 40–50,000 years before the arrival of Europeans, and this was plenty of time to develop effective land tenure systems. The European invaders realized that these traditional systems conflicted with the system they wished to impose and chose to ignore them. The aboriginal reserves that were eventually established in Australia were almost afterthoughts left largely to the discretion of the local state governments. Such reserves were usually in the least desirable locations, remained government property, and were never considered to be for the exclusive, undisturbed use of Aborigines. Until the Aboriginal Land Rights Act (Northern Territory) of 1976 (see pp. 169–172), the Australian government seemed convinced that ownership of land by Aborigines must be on

exactly the same basis as for any other "citizen" of Australia—that is, by individual title (see discussion by Rowley, 1971, and Pittock, 1972)—and it stubbornly refused to acknowledge the legitimacy of aboriginal claims. The official
position as of 1970 was clearly stated by the federal Minister for the Interior:

> *The Government believes that it is wholly wrong to encourage Aboriginals to think
> that because their ancestors have had a long association with a particular piece of land,
> Aboriginals of the present day have the right to demand ownership of it.*
>
> cited Pittock, 1972:17

The situation of aboriginal land rights began to change rapidly in 1972 with
the election of a new Australian government and the granting of some land holdings to Aborigines under the Land Rights Act. However, by 1980 the old
government was again in power and it was clear that corporate mineral development would have priority over aboriginal claims.

In New Caledonia the French dealt with the natives in their typically
straightforward manner. In 1855 the government assumed the exclusive right to
handle land transactions involving natives and nonnatives and claimed all land
that they considered to be unoccupied. In 1868 they introduced native reserves
as a temporary measure pending full native acceptance of individual titles. As
European planters became more interested in the island, the reserves proved to
be too generous, and in 1876 a ruling known as the *Confinement Decree* was
passed that, like the Indian Removal Act in the United States, called for the
removal of natives and their relocation on smaller, often already occupied reserves. The natives resisted the removal process, which had to be postponed until 1895, when it set off a rebellion that killed some 200 Europeans and 1,000
natives. When the rebellion was quelled, many of the defeated rebels were de-
ported to small islands, and others were forced to agree to voluntary renuncia-
tions of their lands in exchange for promises of annuities to be paid to the chiefs.
Some villages were moved as many as three times in a single year and were
sometimes even burned down by military authorities who were overly eager
that the land agreements be followed. By 1883 roughly 90 percent of the island
had been taken out of native hands (Saussol, 1971).

In New Zealand the Maori were guaranteed by the 1840 treaty of Waitangi
with the British:

> *the full, exclusive, and undisturbed possession of their lands and estates, forests, fish-
> eries, and other properties which they may collectively or individually possess.*
>
> cited Lindley, 1926:345

As in America, the British respected in principle Maori rights of land ownership, but pursued a steady policy of land "purchase" by government land agents
who were not always scrupulously fair in their dealings. The main difficulty
faced by the government agents was that of determining whether all individuals
with claims to a given piece of land were indeed willing to sell and that they

fully understood the transaction. It became obvious when fighting broke out in 1860 that the Maori felt that their land rights were not being properly respected. The familiar problem, as Sinclair (1961:44) noted in a careful understatement, was that "the chief aim of land policy was to benefit the Europeans."

After most of the fighting had stopped in 1865, the government established a Native Land Court to continue the registration and alienation process in a more orderly manner. By 1940 the Maori had surrendered some 94 percent of their 1840 holdings in spite of (or perhaps *because* of) government "protection." Furthermore, thanks to the individualization policy, much of the land remaining in Maori ownership quickly became so fragmented as to be almost useless. This reduction in land base was particularly serious because the Maori population had been increasing since 1896 and had nearly tripled by 1940. More recently, the alienation process had slowed (only 4,600 hectares were transferred to Europeans in 1958–1959), and the government attempted to consolidate fragmented individual Maori holdings, but little land remained under the traditional tribal system. The modern Maori have faced the unpleasant threat of an increasing population and a decreasing land base (International Labour Office, 1953:301–302, 555–556; New Zealand Official Yearbook, 1960:467–471). The Maori have continued a political struggle for control of their lands, but by 1987 they controlled less than 5 percent of their original holdings and their claims were still unrecognized. However, there are mechanisms in place, such as the Waitangi Tribunal, which suggest that the government is moving in a more favorable direction on the land question (IWGIA Yearbook 1987:42–43).

Australian land policy in New Guinea markedly contrasts with the government's policy toward the Aborigine in Australia. When the protectorate was declared over Papua New Guinea in 1884, the natives were assured that "evil-disposed men will not be able to occupy your country, to seize your lands or take you away from your homes" (cited Mair, 1970:135). The native title was recognized here and in the Mandated Territory from the beginning, as in New Zealand, and here too the government assumed exclusive control of the alienation process. This time, however, there seemed to be genuine concern that enough land be reserved for native use to protect their future interests (and to preserve the labor supply), and relatively little land was actually alienated. By 1967–1968, only about 3 percent of the total land area of Papua and New Guinea had been alienated, but, of course, this figure includes much of the most valuable land, and in some areas the natives were forced into overcrowded reserves. The government also embarked upon a policy of registering individual titles because, as usual, it was believed that communal tenure would not offer a satisfactory basis for economic development. In its 1964–1965 Report, the Papua New Guinea administration expressed its policy aims as follows:

The ultimate long-term objective is to introduce throughout the Territory a single system of landholding regulated by the Territorial Government . . . , and providing for secure individual registered titles after the pattern of the Australian system.

Australia, Department of Territories, Report for 1964–1965:43

Since 1975 independent Papua New Guinea has allowed local communities to retain traditional patterns of communal ownership, but this has not prevented environmental damage by large-scale multinational mining and lumbering activities on traditional lands (De'Ath & Michalenko, 1980; Hyndman, 1988) or the overriding of communal land rights by influential local political leaders (Grossman, 1983).

The Dutch were so protective of native land rights in their half of New Guinea and did so little to encourage colonization that by 1953 little more than 2,000 hectares had been alienated. This changed after the Indonesians took control in 1963 and, in typical colonial fashion, claimed all unoccupied land for the state and proceeded to introduce Javanese settlers into once exclusively tribal areas (Crocombe & Hide, 1971:314–315). Officially, this was part of Indonesia's transmigration program, which was designed to eradicate overpopulation and poverty in Java by moving people to the presumably underpopulated outer islands of Sumatra, Kalimantan, Sulawesi, East Timor, and West Irian (West Papua, the former Dutch New Guinea). By 1985 transmigration was considered to be the centerpiece of Indonesian development plans and called for the resettlement of at least 20 million Javanese (Otten, 1986:23). In the process, the land rights of the indigenous inhabitants have been largely ignored, and they are being displaced by incoming settlers. Military force has been used to overcome local resistance, especially in West Papua and East Timor.

In many of the smaller Pacific islands of Micronesia and Polynesia, where the land area is severely limited, colonization has usually been rigidly controlled. However, colonial governments have sometimes still sought to discourage communal tenure practices and replace them with individual tenure in hopes of facilitating cash-cropping activities and settling land disputes. Unfortunately, the result here, as elsewhere, has often been serious fragmentation of the land or its concentration in the hands of a few, even though alienation has not usually been a threat.

In both independent and colonial Asia there has been a general tendency not to create special reserves for tribal peoples. In India, Bangladesh, Thailand, and Malaysia, forest areas are claimed by the state, and in several cases forest reserves have been created in which tribal peoples are allowed to remain only by special permission and under special conditions. By 1987 shifting cultivators and foraging peoples in Malaysia, especially Sarawak, were being dispossessed by hydroelectric projects and lumbering operations (IWGIA Yearbook 1986:43, 1987:53).

The land regulations of 1947–1948 that were applied to the hill tribes of the North East Frontier Agency of India (NEFA) were unusually generous in that they allowed tribal communities full rights to the lands they normally cultivated in their shifting cycles and even recognized that villages might move within a general area without abandoning rights to the land (Elwin, 1959:65). In other areas of India, tribal peoples have lost large amounts of land due to their failure to register titles or when their temporarily abandoned plots were claimed by settlers in spite of the special provisions for tribal and scheduled areas. In

Bangladesh no lands are reserved for tribal peoples; instead, their use rights are "protected" and, as we have seen, are subject to government controls. The American administration in the Philippines specifically rejected the notion of tribal reserves, preferring instead to issue individual titles to tribal land. Later, the independent Philippine government created some small reserves that were to be allotted to individuals as they became sufficiently assimilated (International Labour Office, 1953:550; Keesing & Keesing, 1934:163–170). In Indochina, the French claimed all hill tribe areas as Crown lands and opened them for colonization. They specified that areas claimed by tribal peoples could not be *purchased* by outsiders, but these areas could be *leased* for ninety-nine years (Hickey, 1967:752). In Thailand, tribal peoples are presumably on equal terms in regard to land with other citizens. This "no special policy" policy is probably one of the simplest ways to accomplish the goal of replacing tribal peoples and their tenure systems with what the government considers to be more productive populations and ownership systems.

· 6 ·

Cultural Modification Policies

Cultural realities can be changed rapidly by governmental action if . . . massive, expensive, and highly organized coercive action is used.

R. Crocombe, 1971:380

UP TO THIS POINT we have seen how governments have destroyed the political autonomy of tribal populations and gained control of tribal lands. Although these actions are in themselves certain to bring about profound "acculturation," the almost total transformation of tribal cultures seems assured when these actions are combined with programs designed to eliminate all unique aspects of tribal culture and to bring about their full integration with civilization. Tribal peoples throughout the world have faced this situation, and it is a testimony to their courage and determination and the remarkable resilience of their cultures that so many groups have survived, as will be shown in Chapter 9.

From their positions of coercive power and authority, government administrators, their agents, and missionaries methodically set about to destroy tribal cultural patterns in the name of progress, to make the natives more amenable to the purposes of the industrial state. Every area of tribal life from language to marriage customs and religion came under attack by various crusading agencies and individuals anxious to reform and improve them. Any native custom that seemed immoral, offensive, or threatening was instantly abolished by decree, whereas other customs that were considered barriers to progress were either abolished outright or steps were taken to suppress them. Native offenders who

94

continued the then-illegal customs were fined, jailed, or subjected to various forms of corporal or capital punishment until they respected the new laws. However, despite all the forces brought against them, many customs proved difficult to eradicate and were often carried on covertly for years.

Forced cultural modification can be approached from many aspects, several of which have already been discussed or alluded to. This chapter describes the general attitude of governments and social scientists toward the subject and surveys the range and intensity of cultural modification practices in different countries with an emphasis on the colonial period, from approximately 1830 to 1950. (Economic development constitutes a special category of cultural modification and will be treated in a separate chapter.)

THESE ARE THE THINGS THAT OBSTRUCT PROGRESS

The political autonomy, economic habits, religious practices, and sexual customs of organized native groups, in so far as they threaten European control or offend Western notions of morality, must be abandoned.

Reed, 1943: xvii

Once the state embarks upon a policy of integrating a tribal people (and, as we have seen, this path is almost always taken), administrators must make policy decisions regarding how to deal with the many diverse elements of tribal culture that do not mesh easily with industrial civilization. The opening quote suggests that, given enough force, governments could completely destroy any tribal society's cultural diversity with massive cultural modification programs. However, such a rapid course has generally not been economically desirable, and governments have usually been more selective in their destruction of tribal culture.

More than a hundred years ago, Herman Merivale (1861:502–503), in his lectures on colonization, provided some guidelines for government administrators interested in the control of native customs. Objecting to what he considered to be the misguided philanthropy of some individuals who would leave tribal peoples alone except in matters directly involving Europeans, he discussed tribal customs in terms of three categories: (1) "violations of the eternal and universal laws of morality"; (2) "less horrible," but still "pernicious," customs; and (3) "absurd and impolitic" customs that were not directly injurious.

The first category included such practices as cannibalism, human sacrifice, and infanticide, all of which according to Merivale must be suppressed. As we shall see, most authorities have agreed that a category for "immoral" customs should be established, but there have been some different interpretations about which customs belonged in it. Merivale's second category was even less clearly defined. It included a variety of cultural traits that were considered to be "incompatible with civilization," many of which he felt should also be suppressed, although other authorities felt they would best be eliminated by gradual enlightenment rather than by outright force. Merivale's ethnocentric approach to the problem was apparent in his general conclusions:

> It will be necessary, in short, that the colonial authorities should act upon the assumption that they have the right in virtue of the relative position of civilized and Christian men to savages, to enforce abstinence from immoral and degrading practices, to compel outward conformity to the law of what we regard as better instructed reason.
>
> Merivale, 1861:502–503

This basic directive has been implicitly followed up to the present by government authorities throughout the world, although the "law" of "better instructed reason" has not always held the same meaning, and the question of which cultural traits should be modified is still being debated in some cases.

In general, states have suppressed headhunting and all forms of tribal feuding and warfare, along with cannibalism (including endocannibalism, the ritual eating of a people's own dead), infanticide, euthanasia, execution, and whatever was interpreted to be slavery. These traits all fall under the "inhuman or grossly immoral" category (Lindley, 1926:374), even though many, such as warfare and execution, are often institutionalized by states. It seems reasonable to assume that such traits are prohibited more because they represent challenges to state authority rather than because they are universally recognized as immoral. A good case could in fact be made in support of many of the above "immoral" traits on moral grounds. Euthanasia, for example, is now being openly advocated by some physicians. Also, the category of prohibited customs has been expanded to include almost every conceivable trait of tribal cultures. For example, in New Zealand by 1844, government authorities were likely to prevent anything done by the Maori that could be considered "inconsistent with good order and with the progress of civilization" (Snow, 1921:204). In practice, throughout the British Commonwealth tribal peoples were legally subjects of the crown and were expected to behave accordingly. They could retain their traditional cultures as long as they were compatible with "justice, humanity and *good government*" (Lindley, 1926:375, emphasis mine).

Many aspects of tribal kinship and social organization have been attacked as crimes against public order, shocking and injurious, cruel, or simply as obstacles to progress. A partial list of such traits that have been condemned at various times includes payment of bride price, infant betrothal, the levirate (a man marrying his brother's widow), polygamy, secret societies, kinship duties in general, and the extended family. The latter has been particularly criticized as an inappropriate "drag on economic development" and "a serious obstacle to economic progress" (Bauer & Yamey, 1957:64, 66), but it is doubtful that direct efforts have ever been made to abolish it.

The Indian government attempted to soften its policy of assimilation by taking care not to disturb traditional tribal customs, as long as they were considered to be proper (Iyer & Ratnam, 1961:227). In the North East Frontier

Agency, where greater liberality toward tribal cultures was followed than in India proper, it was standard practice for government administrators to prohibit the usual traits that offended against "law and order or the universal conscience of mankind," but here this came to include anything that was clearly "impoverishing" the population as well as "cruel" forms of animal sacrifice (Elwin, 1959:224, 250–251).

French policy toward cultural modification was summarized by the French authority on colonial science, René Maunier (1949), who explained that anything incompatible with French economic interests must be abolished:

> *Let us say that the French must—or think they must—abrogate the customary law of the colonies when it threatens to interfere with* security *or* prosperity.
>
> Maunier, 1949:501–502

This approach was combined with an assimilation theory that attempted to replace everything native with things French and gained for the French the title of "cultural imperialists," for "the wholesale attempt to impose an outside culture upon another people" (Buell, 1928:77). This was, of course, no different in fact from the native policies of every other major nation, but at that time the French were very blatant and at least seemed to be less sympathetic toward native cultures than, for example, were the British.

In the American dependencies, government directives regarding native culture were as ambiguous and open-ended as in other areas. A circular issued in 1932 by the Philippine Bureau of Non-Christian Tribes urged government officials to respect cultural practices that were "not contrary to law, morals, and good customs" but reaffirmed that tribesmen were still to be assimilated as rapidly as possible (Keesing & Keesing 1934:33).

According to Schapera (1934:x–xii), by the 1930s South Africa was following the *adaptationist* policy as the most reasonable and economical means of "facilitating the transition to assimilation." This policy assumed that where necessary, tribal culture might be allowed to persist, but administrators and missionaries did not always agree on this point. Native customs were recognized by the courts if they were not "repugnant to elementary ideas of justice and humanity" or "*illegal!*" (Schapera, 1934:x–xii, emphasis mine). Here as elsewhere, this policy gave local officials considerable room for independent action, and attitudes toward tribal culture varied widely even among the country's scholars. In his discussion of the "native problem," the South African economist W. H. Hutt (1934:195–237) called for sympathetic understanding of native culture but stressed that assumptions regarding the necessity or permanence of any traits should be avoided. His conclusion on the matter was that probably the entire native culture would have to "go":

> *Fortunately there is now almost universal agreement that the "cattle cult," animal sacrifices, the doctoring of land [magic], and many other obviously effete primitive customs and taboos must go. What is not so readily admitted is that with them must*

also go the native mode of life and probably the language which was adapted to that life.

Hutt, 1934:209–210

In New Guinea the Germans prohibited whatever they considered to be antisocial, whereas the Australian mandate government declared on the *positive* side that its policy would be to *improve* the moral and physical environment of village life and to introduce "healthy forms of amusement." Reed observed that this policy resulted in the natives' being forced to abandon everything threatening or offensive to Europeans; it extended to the extreme that in the 1930s a native who used "obscene" language could end up in court (Reed, 1943:xvii, 138–139, 176–177). By the late 1960s the Australian administration in Papua New Guinea was still prohibiting certain religious practices thought to be "repugnant to the general principles of humanity," illegal, or "not in the best interest of a child." There were also official complaints that cultural diversity presented "obstacles to orderly social change" and that "adherence to custom can hinder progress" (Australia, Department of Territories, Report for 1967–1968:3, 8, 10–11, 19).

The cultural modification policies of the independent, modernizing nations have sometimes been more sweeping in their destruction of tribal culture than were the earlier colonial authorities, particularly where they have followed the ruthless prescriptions of development experts such as Heilbroner, who recommended the following measures to help transform "tradition-bound" societies into "modern" societies:

Nothing short of a pervasive social transformation will suffice: a wholesale metamorphosis of habits, a wrenching reorientation of values concerning time, status, money, work; and an unweaving and reweaving of the fabric of daily existence itself.

Heilbroner, 1963:53

It seems that anything remotely considered to be an obstacle to progress might be slated for elimination by the new leaders of developing nations acting on the advice of development specialists. One such expert who has written widely on the development problems of Africa and Asia lists a number of "nonadaptable" African tribal institutions, such as tribal organization, matrilyny, and shifting cultivation, which he feels are unsuitable in a modernizing society and presumably should be abandoned (Hunter, 1967:72). In a similar manner Goulet (1971:326) lumps chattel marriages along with infanticide as incompatible with human rights and positively harmful impediments to development, and he therefore considers them to be expendable cultural traits. Almost in the same breath he observes that the African value system based on cattle might also be "doomed to disappear." Paradoxically, Goulet earlier complained that in such matters social engineers lacked "clear universal directives" and faced "perplexing questions" over "which cultural peculiarities are to be allowed and which eliminated" (Goulet, 1971:268–270). Such problems are unavoidable when individuals attempt to program a way of life for people in alien cultures.

Social Engineering: How to Do It

When a change that is to be applied to the common man, usually a village peasant, has been agreed upon by a member of the ruling elite and the overseas specialist, the problem is how to convince this common man to accept the new ideas without using force.
                                                        Arensberg & Niehoff, 1964:68

It is no easy task for an outsider to get people to change their pattern of doing things.
                                                        Arensberg & Niehoff, 1964:87

Designating what aspects of a tribal culture to eliminate and selecting suitable replacements are relatively simple problems compared with the difficulties of executing such decisions. During the early period of colonial expansion, governments allowed most of their cultural modification work to be carried out by "natural" frontier processes, or they resorted to direct military or police force to suppress "illegal" customs, while the remaining unsuitable customs were attended to by missionaries. Naked force has been widely applied against tribal cultures and continues to be used even at the present time because of the speed and apparent efficiency of its results. In the late 1960s the Uganda government, for example, abolished a bothersome hunting-and-gathering culture virtually overnight when they loaded the entire population of Ik into trucks and drove them out of their homeland (Turnbull, 1972). More commonly, direct coercion has been used to suppress specific aspects of a traditional culture that have been declared illegal. Maunier (1949:504) explained the French approach to this kind of legal abolition or "civilization by legislation" as follows: "Such and such an act may be absolutely, totally, unreservedly, forbidden." Later in this chapter, numerous examples of such use of direct force in culture change are presented, but indirect force, or "social engineering," will be discussed first because since the 1960s it has become far more common and deserves special treatment.

In the post–World War II decolonization period, with its emphasis on self-determination of peoples, the use of force in culture change has generally been frowned upon by international agencies and social scientists concerned with human rights. Although the 1948 United Nations Declaration of Human Rights does not specifically mention forced culture change programs, it does state in Article 22 that everyone is entitled to the realization of the "cultural rights indispensable for his dignity and the free development of his personality," and forced change could certainly threaten such rights. This interpretation was affirmed, enlarged upon, and made directly applicable to tribal peoples by the International Covenant of Human Rights, adopted by the UN General Assembly in 1966, which states unequivocally in its convention on civil and political rights that

> *in those states in which ethnic, religious or linguistic minorities exist, persons belonging to such minorities shall not be denied the right, in community with the other members of their group, to enjoy their own culture, to profess and practice their own religion or to use their own language.*

Any program of directed culture change imposed upon a "target" population against their will would almost unavoidably violate these rights, and in principle at least such programs are usually rejected by social engineers. In 1968 the Permanent Council of the International Congress of Anthropological and Ethnological Sciences acknowledged that force was still being widely used and unanimously passed a resolution on forced acculturation that called upon governments to respect the Declaration of Human Rights.

Applied anthropologists have in general rejected the use of any change techniques that the target or recipient population might interpret as coercive, in part because as Goodenough (1963:16) explained, "We have scruples against attempting to impose blueprints on others," but perhaps more importantly because it was long realized that force did not always achieve permanent results. Even Maunier (1949:513) warned that force often generated resistance and caused undesirable cultural traits to go underground. Goodenough was concerned with the same problem and felt that from a strictly "practical" viewpoint, successful "reform" could not depend on external force, because "the truth is that to accomplish purposive change in another usually requires the other's cooperation." Cultural modification then becomes "helping others to reform themselves." Goodenough specifically rejected the notion that force might still be involved even when it may not be directly perceived by the target group, and he stated flatly that his book outlining how change agents can gain the "cooperation" of their targets was not a book on "how to get other people to do what you want and like it" (Goodenough, 1963:16–17). A closer look at the general techniques of social engineering as it developed in the early postwar period suggests otherwise.

Mead, in her discussion of culture change in Manus Island, New Guinea, was convinced that tribal peoples there were eager for change, and she too seemed unwilling to recognize how force could possibly be involved. As she stated:

> We do not conceive of people being forcibly changed by other human beings. We conceive of them as seeing a light and following it freely.
>
> Mead, 1961:19–20

Such firm conviction that if cooperation is gained, force is not involved is perhaps understandable in change agents who were convinced of the desirability of the changes sought. Indeed, to many change experts, the ends appeared to justify the means, regardless of the likelihood that outsiders might make ethnocentric judgments concerning "benefits" and in spite of the unpredictability of the long-term effects of change. This reckless attitude seems to be expressed in the formal code of ethics adopted by the Society for Applied Anthropology in 1963, which spoke of the need for respecting the "dignity and general well-being" of target peoples, but which was silent on the specific issue of the use of force and appeared to condone it under the proper circumstances. Action that might adversely affect the "lives, well-being, dignity and self-respect" of targets was considered unethical, *unless* efforts are made to *minimize* such adverse side effects and *unless* such action was thought to be beneficial (Anonymous, 1963–1964).

In other words, as long as your intentions were good, whatever techniques achieved the desired results most effectively were considered acceptable.

The indirect manipulation of tribal peoples is not an invention of applied anthropologists, but it probably has been employed as long as direct force. Maunier advised French colonial authorities that it was generally more advantageous to "conditionally" eliminate undesirable customs through such measures as taxation, licensing, or other forms of control. The secret was to make the change imperceptible:

> If reform is necessary, it ought to be carried out after preparation and with due consideration, leaving the subject people under the illusion that their old traditions will be maintained, even if they are in fact being gradually, unobtrusively, progressively, modified—as is necessary. That seems to be sound psychology.
>
> Maunier, 1949:513

Elsewhere Maunier observes that there are "thousands of ways" of achieving culture change against the real wishes of the natives. In addition to the general method of regulating without directly abolishing customs, Maunier described what could be called the *enlightenment* approach, in which "reform" was sought by convincing argument, example, and education—all aimed at showing how inferior native ways were and how advantageous it would be for the natives to abandon them in favor of superior French ways. The formal education approach will be examined more closely in another section, but here it can be pointed out that the creation of dissatisfactions as a stimulus for change has been widely recommended by modern change experts. Goulet suggests that traditional peoples must be shocked into the realization that they are living in abnormal, inhuman conditions as psychological preparation for modernization (Goulet, 1971:25–26). In Goodenough's view:

> The problem that faces development agents, then, is to find ways of stimulating in others a desire for change in such a way that the desire is theirs independent of further prompting from outside. Restated, the problem is one of creating in another a sufficient dissatisfaction with his present condition of self so that he wants to change it. This calls for some kind of experience that leads him to reappraise his self-image and reevaluate his self-esteem.
>
> Goodenough, 1963:219

Applied anthropologists have no secret weapons for achieving culture change: Their recommendations, as they evolved during the 1960s, were usually in the form of commonsense advice or sound psychology, based on an understanding of the culture to be modified and embodying proven methods of persuasion. For example, in addition to the obvious tactic of tampering with self-images, change agents were advised to:

1. Involve traditional leaders in their programs
2. Work through bilingual, acculturated individuals who have some knowledge of both the dominant and the *target* culture

3. Modify circumstances or deliberately tamper with the equilibrium of the traditional culture so that change will become imperative

4. Attempt to change underlying core values before attacking superficial customs

The change agent was furthermore advised to gain the respect and confidence of the native people; to manipulate traditional attitudes toward status and prestige to his advantage; to make certain that modifications sought are actually possible; and to time them carefully (Arensberg & Niehoff, 1964; Foster, 1969; Goodenough, 1963; Jones, 1965). The judicious employment of material rewards or "benefits" was perhaps one of the strongest change strategies because these may be offered to the target group "when it performs in a manner prescribed by the agent of change," not unlike pigeons being taught to peck at appropriately colored disks (Jones, 1965).

While anthropologists trained and advised change agents, they themselves could work directly in change programs where they could use their specialized knowledge of social structure, value systems, and the functional interrelatedness of culture to identify both the "barriers" to change and the "progressive forces" within a specific target culture (Foster, 1969:120).

Clearly, the change strategies just outlined did not rely on the *direct* use of force, but in terms of the larger context of most change programs, coercion was almost always implicit. Change *was* being deliberately initiated by outsiders. In the final analysis, blueprints *were* being handed down from above, by individuals and agencies in the dominant culture who were making the policy decisions for a submissive target culture that ultimately had no power to resist. The critical problems here are that not only are basic human cultural rights being threatened, but the changes themselves, though they may have been well intentioned, all too often were tragically destructive. What is really being questioned here is what Foster has called the "rationale" for *directed* culture change programs:

> that technical experts can and should evaluate the practices of other people and decide which ones should be modified.
>
> Foster, 1969:136

When "other people" are people with a radically different culture, and when they are ultimately powerless to resist such change programs, perhaps the rationale needs to be reconsidered. The views of seemingly well-informed anthropologists on the appropriateness and value of particular cultural practices have sometimes been dangerously wrong. For example, A. P. Elkin, for many years the principal authority on Australian Aborigines, understood the intricacies of aboriginal beliefs in totemic ancestors and sacred sites, but Elkin was also a Christian minister and felt that such beliefs were wrong. He argued that Christianity and science should replace aboriginal reverence for sacred sites. He thought that for their own benefit, Aborigines needed to be convinced that "their own spiritual life and the future of natural species is not bound up with the integrity of particular spots on the earth's surface" (Elkin, 1934:7). In fact, the Aborigines were right—their spirituality and the future of their natural resources were tied to the integrity of their sacred sites, but it was more than forty years before the Australian government acknowledged this point. Since the Land Rights Act of 1976 (see Chapter 9), sacred sites have been the foundation of the Aborigines' struggle to regain control of their lands.

The following sections present specific examples of cultural modification policies in action against tribal peoples in different parts of the world. Education policies in colonial settings and American Indian schools are briefly examined, and both direct and indirect change strategies are illustrated with cases involving government attempts to destroy shamanism and ceremonial activities, desert pastoral nomadism, the East African cattle complex, and swidden agriculture.

Education for Progress

People must learn to be scientific and progressive in outlook instead of living by ancestral laws and long-tried rules of thumb.

Jones, 1965

In many countries schooling has been the prime coercive instrument of cultural modification and has proven to be a highly effective means of destroying self-esteem, fostering new needs, creating dissatisfactions, and generally disrupting traditional cultures. As representatives of the prestige and power of the dominant culture, teachers assume positions of authority over students, overshadowing parents and traditional tribal leaders. But even more important, schooling conflicts with the education that children gain from participation in their own cultures. Tribal cultures generally require mastery of a specialized knowledge of the natural environment, as well as special training in folklore, religion, ritual, technology, and other skills. The years that children are required to spend studying the dominant culture's textbooks are in direct competition with the normal enculturation process. Furthermore, schooling deprives the traditional community of the important contribution that children often make to the subsistence economy. Cunnison (1966:40–41) reports that children of Sudanese tribal nomads who spent as little as two years in schools returned to their homes without the skills needed of cattle herders, and they also became physically too "soft" to readapt to the demands of traditional life. This example no doubt overstates the incompatibility between formal schooling and effective participation in subsistence pursuits, but this issue *is* too often overlooked.

Under colonial conditions, schooling was often a direct means of cultural modification. According to Buell (1928:55), in French colonial schools two basic subjects were taught. The first was *morale*, which aimed at instilling French ideals of "good habits, cleanliness, order, politeness, respect, and obedience." *French* was the second subject and the principal language of instruction, while in some colonies all use of native language in schools was forbidden by decree. Lessons included "simple ideas of France and the French people," and advanced students were instructed in the meanings of such terms as justice, respect, altruism, charity, pity, and compassion—all of which were presumed to be unfamiliar concepts. The most important lesson was "the need of loyalty to France" and the importance of cooperating with French interests. Schoolchildren were taught to despise their own traditions and cultures in a direct and ethnocentric manner, as illustrated by the following excerpt from a French reader designed in 1919 for use by French West African schoolchildren:

> It is . . . an advantage for a native to work for a white man, because the Whites are better educated, more advanced in civilization than the natives, and because, thanks to them, the natives will make more rapid progress . . . and become one day really useful men. . . . You who are intelligent and industrious, my children, always help the Whites in their task. This is a duty.

Moussa et Gi-gla, Histoire de deux Petits Noir, cited Buell, 1928:63

In the government schools of Italian East Africa, tribal children were taught discipline, respect, and obedience—to Italian authority. With amazing ethnocentrism, teachers also proceeded to teach tribal boys arts and crafts and how to farm, while girls were taught how to cook native food! Italian textbooks, described as "didactic aids adapted to the attitudes and capacities of the natives," contained such choice readings as:

> I am happy to be subject to the Italian government and I love Italy with the affection of a son.

or simply:

> Help me, oh God, to become a good Italian!

cited De Marco, 1943:36, 40

For many years in the United States the government delegated the formal education of Indian children to missionaries such as Stephen Riggs, whose attitude to Indian culture was summarized by his 1846 statement that "as tribes and nations the Indians must perish and live only as men!" (his emphasis, cited Berkhofer, 1965:7). Boarding schools were considered one of the best means of destroying Indian culture because here even very young children could be almost permanently separated from the influences of their parents. Mission teachers imposed haircuts, Western dress, new English names, and rigid schedules on their charges, and they emphasized religion and manual labor.

A similar approach to missionary boarding schools was recently applied in South America. For example, the Salesian boarding school of La Esmeralda, which was opened in 1972 in Venezuela for the Yanomamo and Makiritari Indians, was apparently being operated with little regard for the traditional culture. Children were kept within the school's walled-in compound, often against their wills. Their hair was cut, their clothing was changed, and they were given

Spanish names. Outside observers reported that the children complained of the restrictions, lack of food, homesickness, ridicule of their traditions, and being beaten. They also frequently attempted to run away (Lizot, 1976).

In the Peruvian Amazon in 1964 I found Seventh-Day Adventist missions promoting profound changes among the Ashaninka Campa Indians. The Adventists forbade polygyny, shamanism, drinking manioc beer, dancing, body ornaments, and the eating of a long list of fish and game considered "unclean." These prohibitions struck at the very core of Ashaninka culture, but the missions went further by discouraging use of the Ashaninka language in the schools.

Eliminating Shamanism

Leaders in traditional religion and specialized knowledge such as tribal curers and shamans have often been singled out for special attention by both missionaries and government authorities because they seem to represent direct challenges to Western medicine and Christianity and because they have sometimes come to symbolize the traditional culture in opposition to progress.

One of the strongest antishaman campaigns was carried out during the Stalin era, especially before World War II, by the Soviet Union in the Soviet Far East, where shamans were classified along with other tribal leaders (or ruling cliques) as wealthy "exploiters" and "parasitic groups" who "battled bitterly against the new regime and actively attempted to sabotage its projects" (Levin & Potapov, 1964:10, 497–498). According to Soviet officials, shamans played an extremely negative role among the tribal people, in part because they made "wasteful" animal sacrifices and were the principal exponents of an "outdated religious ideology," but also because they apparently did lead the resistance to Soviet schools, medical centers, "culture-bases," and collective farms. One shamanistic activity that must have been particularly frustrating for Soviet authorities was the continuing effort of the shamans to regulate the tribe's resource exploitation practices by enjoining hunting and fishing on certain days and even prohibiting the killing of certain animals. Clearly, in Soviet eyes, shamans were a "reactionary, counter-revolutionary force" (Kosokov, 1930:70, cited Kolarz, 1954:76).

An offensive was launched against the shamans in which they were arrested and exiled or forced to publicly renounce their activities. The local representatives of the "League of Militant Godless" were enlisted to gather information on shamans and to generally conduct antireligious propaganda among the tribes. As part of the campaign, efforts were also made to replace shamans with what Kolarz (1954:79–80) refers to as the "Lenin-Stalin Cult." The government circulated poems and folk tales among the tribal population in which Lenin and Stalin were represented as all-powerful solar deities capable of defeating all evils, in hopes of overshadowing the role of shaman. The extravagant nature of these tales is well represented by the following quote from *Sun of the People*, a story that refers to Stalin and was designed for the hunting and fishing Nanai:

Nobody can equal the strength of that hero [Stalin]. His eyes see everything that goes on on earth. His brain knows all that people think. His heart contains the happiness and the woe of all peoples. The depth of his thought is as deep as the ocean. His voice is heard by all that inhabit the earth. Such is the greatest of the very greatest in the whole world.

cited Kolarz, 1954:80

What shaman could compete with that kind of power and authority?

Shamans and the practice of tribal religions in general also came under similar attacks in other parts of the world. Speaking of Bantu shamans in South Africa, Schapera (1934:33–34) stated that their influence was unhealthy and that they constituted a "powerful obstacle to progress" because of their "almost fanatical" conservatism. He felt that the best way to eliminate their influence and their belief in witchcraft and magic would be through "the effective teaching of scientific principles."

In nearby Rhodesia (now Zambia and Zimbabwe), witchcraft and certain forms of divination were outlawed by the Witchcraft Regulations of 1895 and the Witchcraft Suppression Act of 1899. The latter act, which was vigorously enforced in the 1960s, provided punishments of up to seven years of imprisonment and/or thirty-six lashes for anyone proven to be "by habit and repute a witch doctor or witch finder" (Witchcraft Suppression Act, Articles 4 and 8) or for the use of charms to locate lost or stolen articles. The law also declared that anyone receiving money for any "exercise of so-called witchcraft or the use of charms," or who gives any instruction or advice on the subject, will be punished for fraud (Crawford, 1967).

In New Guinea, native curers were often regarded as illegal and were not infrequently prosecuted for practicing their art. Medical doctors sometimes attempted to shame and embarrass them by using modern drugs and even imposed medical attention on unwilling patients, who sometimes had to be literally dragged into operating rooms because of their fear of foreign practitioners (Ryan, 1969:41).

Every Ceremony Must Go

Conspicuous ceremonial activities or particularly unusual customs have very often been candidates for elimination, because even if they were not contrary to universal morality, they were certain to be considered obstacles to progress.

In the United States from 1884 to 1933, there were laws forbidding "pagan" Indian ceremonies that the Indian Bureau felt would inhibit the spread of Christianity. The sun-dance ceremony of the Plains Indians, which was their highest expression of tribal unity and identity, was specifically outlawed, presumably because it involved immoral physical ordeals. In 1926 the leaders of Taos Pueblo in New Mexico were jailed for participating in illegal religious ceremonies described as pagan, horrible, sadistic, and obscene. Efforts were even made to prevent Pueblo youth from being initiated in traditional tribal fashion (Collier, 1947:233–234, 256).

The French acted with characteristic thoroughness in areas under their jurisdiction. In the Marquesas in the 1850s, tattooing, singing, dancing, and performance of the traditional religion were abolished at one sweep (Maunier, 1949:500–501). The Dutch treated ceremonies more cautiously than did the French. In the Celebes, ceremonies "which could be vested with a Christian mantle" could remain, but this sometimes required some special engineering such as allowing certain ceremonies to take place at different dates, renaming them, and so on (Kruyt, 1929:7–8).

In New Guinea, missionaries took it upon themselves to speed culture change by destroying "pagan" ceremonial art and burning down spirit houses (Ryan, 1969:68). Missionaries in Assam forbade singing, dancing, and the wearing of all distinctive ornaments by their Naga converts, while government schools went even further by not allowing their pupils to wear flowers in their hair (Elwin, 1939:512; 1959:196, 220). In the Naga case, the missionary rationale for their action was simple, as Elwin explains:

> As religion plays a part in every Naga ceremony and as that religion is not Christianity, every ceremony must go.
>
> Elwin, 1959:220

Whereas missionary efforts to clothe natives are notorious, it is often forgotten that government efforts in the same direction have often been just as vigorous and even harder for tribal people to ignore. For example, a local government order in Burma in 1957 prohibited hill tribesmen from wearing their traditional red cane belts and specified how wide their loincloths were to be, as well as the length of women's skirts (Lehman, 1963:211). By Royal Decree in 1881, the Spanish attempted to force Philippine hill tribesmen in northern Luzon to wear breeches and coats in the presence of government officials (Keesing & Keesing, 1934:67–68). It has also been common practice for government edicts to require the distribution of clothing to native labor forces and to insist that it be worn.

Even the simple dignity of burial according to the forms prescribed by their traditional cultures has sometimes been denied tribal peoples. In 1918 and 1922 the American administration in the Philippines passed laws requiring the tribesmen to bury their dead in proper fashion in approved cemeteries. In order to eliminate lengthy processes of smoking and tending of the bodies, regulations specified that burial must take place within forty-eight hours (Keesing & Keesing, 1934:238–239). Practices involving platform burials or secondary burial have almost always been prohibited. Even the normally liberal-minded Dutch authorities refused to allow tribal peoples in the Celebes to clean the bones of their dead (Kruyt, 1929:6). Tribal peoples in New Guinea protested bitterly when medical researchers and government coroners desecrated their dead against their wishes, and as recently as 1968 riot police were called out to prevent native "interference" with official autopsies (Ryan, 1969:41).

It may seem incredible that any society would accept so much interference in their lives, but after government control has been firmly established over a tribal population there is little alternative but conformity, at least with conspicuous customs. However, *before* government authority is complete the situation is different. For example, in Assam a British survey party and escort totaling some eighty men was massacred by the Wancho in 1875 after the people had been ridiculed for their peculiar burial practices and when a chief's tomb was desecrated (Elwin, 1959:250). In New Guinea in 1904, ten missionaries were killed in a single incident when they attempted to outlaw polygyny (Ryan, 1969:65). It seems that formerly autonomous tribal peoples did not always welcome interference even *after* control was established and that they managed to keep many aspects of their cultures alive covertly in the face of constant government efforts at suppression.

Settling Nomads

In the corridors of international agencies and the desert capitals, the cry goes up, "How do we settle the nomads?"

Cunnison, 1967:10

The pastoral nomads of North Africa, the Middle East, and Southwest Asia have evolved a successful ecological adaptation to extremely arid conditions and for thousands of years have maintained a stable symbiotic relationship with their sedentary "civilized" village neighbors (Spooner, 1973). Few tribal groups in other parts of the world have made such a satisfactory adjustment to both civilization and their natural environment. However, in recent years this adaptation has been increasingly threatened because governments have set about to solve what they consider to be the nomad problem by abolishing the nomadic way of life. The "problem" of the nomads is that their mobility makes it difficult for governments to impose controls over them and that they seem to place tribal loyalties above national loyalties. Furthermore, there are sometimes misleading official complaints that nomadism is wasteful and that nomads infringe on the rights of settled farmers. Perhaps closer to the truth, some writers have explained that nomadism constitutes a "challenge to the orderly mind" of the government administrator eager to do something to improve the "wretched" living conditions of nomads (Brémaud & Pagot, 1962:320). Cunnison (1967:9) boils all the charges against nomads into one: "incompatibility with the aims of a modern state and the modern world." This means, of course, that most states refuse to compromise and will not recognize either the special contribution that nomads make to the national economy or their special needs. Actually, nomads efficiently exploit vast arid lands in the only way that the peculiar ecological conditions of many of these areas will probably ever allow, and in the process nomads are often better fed and wealthier than village agriculturalists.

Governments have generally followed the "solution" to the nomad "problem," which calls for converting all nomads into sedentary villagers. In some countries this had been expressed as clear government policy, such as in Syria, where the 1950 Constitution declared "the government shall endeavor to sedentarize all nomads" (Article 158). A certain degree of continuous sedentarization has probably always been a necessary part of the nomadic adaptation and has even included some nomadization of the sedentary population, but in the last few decades the process has been drastically accelerated by deliberate government action. Certainly the pacification of the desert, which ended intertribal feuding and raids, has served to weaken tribal political organization, but would not in itself destroy the nomadic way of life. More significant have been government settlement schemes involving outright propaganda programs on the virtues of settled life and the drilling of wells, land allotments, and schooling. These direct measures have been facilitated by the roads and trucks that have replaced camel caravans and by the oil companies that have made extensive use of nomad labor. Governments are fighting powerful ecological and cultural forces, however, and it is possible to assume that they will not be entirely successful without the use of even greater coercion. In 1960 nearly 7 million people in the Sahara, Arabia, and Southwest Asia were estimated to still be following the nomadic life (Awad, 1962; Barth, 1962; Capot-Rey, 1962). In 1987, IWGIA (Yearbook 1987) estimated that there were 21 million nomads or pastoral peoples in North and East Africa and Southwest Asia.

Nomadism in general (and the Arab Bedouin form in particular) has been highly romanticized in the Western world, but fortunately this has not prevented all anthropologists from defending the nomadic way of life. Some social scientists, however, have supported the prevailing government policies of assimilation. For example, Awad, who in 1960 participated as chairman of UNESCO's executive board in the UN-sponsored international symposium on "The Problem of the Arid Zone," in no way questioned the need to settle nomads and reported optimistically that converting them to a sedentary life was not impossible, although he cautioned that the process would be slow and that "no initiative can be expected from the nomads themselves." He felt that the initiative must come from the governments concerned, and he recommended that the end should be achieved as rapidly as possible whether the motives were humanitarian, political, economic, strategic, or administrative (Awad, 1962:336). Interestingly, other participants in the symposium, such as Capot-Rey and Barth, felt that total elimination of the nomadic way of life was undesirable and would result in the impoverishment of the people involved. Along with Cunnison (1967), they made the radical suggestion that governments might attempt to cooperate with the nomads.

Combating the Cattle Complex

Closely paralleling the drive to settle the desert nomads are the efforts of East African governments to end the seminomadism of their tribal cattle herders and to convert them into settled village farmers or isolated ranchers with "improved" herds. These cultures are characterized by a so-called cattle complex because subsistence, kinship organization, politics, religion, folklore, and personal identity and worth all center on cattle (Netting, 1977). This great value placed on cattle extends to the point that the loss of a native's favorite cow might be cause for his suicide. Much to the frustration of administrators, African cattle herders are almost totally self-sufficient and find that very little from the outside world is of any use to them. This, of course, makes it difficult to replace their cattle values with equally compelling money values and in general makes their overall life style difficult to modify. While administrators complain of the poor quality of tribal cattle, anthropological research has repeatedly emphasized that African pastoralists are interested in cattle for *subsistence* purposes, not for marketability. Their herds are designed to support as many people as possible, and the system is not an inefficient, irrational, and wasteful use of natural resources as many development experts and government planners ethnocentrically suppose. It is simply a specialized economic system based on principles in complete opposition to those underlying cattle raising in an industrial society (Dyson-Hudson & Dyson-Hudson, 1969). Any highly successful economic system is bound to be persistent.

The Karimojong of northeastern Uganda represent a specific case of one such East African cattle-herding society that has been subjected to intensive government-directed pressure to abandon their nomadic life style and modify their cattle complex. According to Dyson-Hudson (1962), pressure for change began for the Karimojong in 1921, when the British established a civil administration after several years of military patroling during which "chiefs" had been appointed. In rapid succession, missionaries, a poll tax, and controls on population movement were introduced, and administrative boundaries were drawn in disregard for traditional cultural groupings. Perhaps most seriously, the tribe was prohibited from using its normal dry-season grazing areas without special permission from the district commissioner, and anyone making unauthorized moves was subject to a fine of four head of cattle or imprisonment. Movements between settlements, which had helped distribute the population, were prohibited, and the administration itself freely moved communities about to suit its own purposes. The Karimojong often openly defied the new orders in spite of the punishments that were meted out, and in 1923 they even speared to death one of the government-appointed chiefs who had attempted to prevent their annual cattle movements. Restrictions on cattle and population movements were followed by measures to reduce the number of cattle and "improve" their quality to suit them for the market. The administration urged the Karimojong to sell their cattle and raise cash crops instead. As a further inducement, entire regions traditionally used as pasturage were closed to the Karimojong and opened to use by the neighboring tribes, cattle markets were organized, and inoculation programs for cattle were initiated. These actions only caused further resentment, and the Karimojong responded by hiding their herds and refusing to sell. They were particularly disturbed when some of their inoculated cattle died and correctly assumed that their way of life was being attacked by a government that "eats our cattle."

On the basis of his study of the Karimojong, Dyson-Hudson concluded (along with numerous other observers) that pastoral societies are "generally slow and difficult to change." By 1958, after facing nearly forty years of deliberate cultural modification policies, the 60,000 Karimojong had managed to maintain their basic value system intact, even to the extent that they still engaged in cattle raiding against neighboring groups.

In nearby Kenya the government-sponsored Konza Scheme was designed in 1947 as a pilot program to convert the nomadic Maasai into settled ranchers, but it failed to overcome traditional pastoral values. Ten families were settled on individually fenced plots that were provided with wells, dams, and dipping tanks, but they refused to sell their cattle, retained their social ties with their nomadic kin, and within ten years had completely undermined the scheme (Allan, 1965: 322–324).

More direct action was taken by Tanzania, an independent country with an avowed goal of blending socialism and African culture. Perhaps recognizing the difficulties of changing pastoralists when the cattle complex remained intact, they attempted to force the Barabaig to stop herding cattle and to settle down as gardeners. The government program included a ban on traditional dress and forced "reeducation" of tribal youth, and was pushed so vigorously that George Klima, who conducted anthropological research in the area, concluded that:

All of these changes and more will eventually destroy the traditional life-ways the Barabaig have created over the centuries. Another island of cultural diversity will have disappeared into oblivion.

Klima, 1970:112

Unfortunately, the result of such modification policies has meant far more than merely the loss of cultural diversity, but as will be shown in Chapter 8, it also brings social, economic, and environmental disaster. Forced modification of the subsistence practices of cattle-herding peoples has been carried out in the name of environmental protection, but evidence that tribals are degrading the environment seems questionable and other facts may well be at work (Homewood & Rodgers, 1984; also see Chapter 8). Cattle herders such as the Maasai have recently been excluded from certain areas that they have traditionally used, because conservationists feel that cattle herding is incompatible with the maintenance of wildlife. Such incompatibility seems unlikely, however; the value of maintaining "pure wilderness" for tourism is probably the real objective for government planners (Arhem, 1985).

Weaning from the Axe

Shifting, or swidden agriculture, has come under government attack almost as frequently as pastoral nomadism. Swidden agriculture involves cutting and burning a small opening in the forest, cultivating it for two years or so, and then allowing the forest to regrow. Within fifteen to twenty-five years the same plot may be recleared and planted again. To administrators it appears to be a wasteful process, but in most tropical forest environments under aboriginal

FIGURE 6.1

A young Batangan man of Mindoro planting his swidden plot. Under traditional conditions, shifting cultivation may often be the only ecologically sound form of agriculture in many areas, but this practice has been almost universally condemned by government officials. (Pennoyer.)

conditions it has proven to be a sound and stable form of adaptation where shallow soils and heavy rainfall place severe limitations on agricultural activities. Like nomads, shifting agriculturalists tend to be independent, self-sufficient peoples, characterized by frequent population movements, and their entire cultures are often neatly integrated with their agricultural cycles. None of these features fits neatly with the interests of government planners.

The Baiga of India, who have been described by Elwin (1939), exemplify the kinds of pressures that governments have used in many countries to destroy the swidden life style. In 1868, in the interests of both civilizing the Baiga and opening their forests for commercial exploitation, the government declared that the Baiga had no occupancy rights in their forests and completely forbade shifting cultivation in certain zones. To enforce the new laws, crops were destroyed, and since hunting and fishing were also important components of the Baiga subsistence system, they too were declared illegal by the Game Act, which prohibited even the killing of hares. The bows and arrows that the Baiga were not allowed to carry were confiscated and burned by officials, whereas outsiders who could purchase licenses were, of course, allowed to hunt within Baiga territory. In Elwin's estimation, forbidding shifting cultivation was equivalent to taking food from Baiga mouths and thus constituted a direct assault on their entire culture. Under some administrators the policy was softened to a gradual "weaning" from the axe because, as an official report complained in 1893, the Baiga insisted on clinging "like a spoilt child to their axe and fire" (cited Elwin, 1939:119). Axes were taxed and the Baiga were permitted to continue their traditional farming practices only in carefully selected reserve zones considered to be useless for any other purposes. Even within these reserves, the government attempted to make the Baiga take up sedentary plow agriculture on individually allotted plots, and outsiders were brought in to farm reserve land as examples for the Baiga. These efforts were supplemented by attempts to remove Baiga tribesmen and integrate them with sedentary villagers, where they could be supplied with plows, seed, land, and bullocks. Some successes were claimed, but many Baiga chose to flee rather than give up their traditional culture. Weaning from the axe also caused the population to plummet from some 1,500 individuals in 1891 to a low of 600 in 1939, and those who survived faced poverty and destitution.

· 7 ·

Economic Development

In other words, it is now held that economic development can be induced or even imposed, the goals being determined by governments who become responsible for the coordination and planning deemed necessary to attain them.

Mountjoy, 1967:28

GIVEN THE FUNDAMENTAL IMPORTANCE of economic patterns in all cultures, and considering the extreme contrasts between tribal and industrial economies, the economic incorporation of tribal cultures into the world-market economy is a critically important phenomenon. A tribal culture may surrender its political autonomy but can still continue to be an essentially tribal culture if it is allowed to retain its self-sufficient, subsistence economy and if it remains unexploited by outsiders. The degree of a tribal group's participation in the cash economy must be determined by the people themselves and on their own terms. Only in this way can economic self-sufficiency and cultural autonomy be safeguarded and the "price of progress" be minimized.

Development experts widely assume that the economic development of tribal peoples is *development* in the usual meaning of the word, that is, "a process of *natural* evolution or growth." But, in fact, outside coercion and deliberate manipulation have usually been necessary both to destroy the tribal economy and to carefully channel its conversion into a market-oriented economy. *Development* is an ethnocentric term, based on assumptions of progress and inevitability, but it might better be replaced by a more accurate and less ethnocentric term such as *transformation*.

114

In many areas of the world the initial breakdown of tribal economies began under the coercive pressure of the policies of colonial governments designed to develop native labor resources or to promote cash cropping for the benefit of the colonists. These efforts were successful in initiating widespread migratory wage-labor and many forms of marginal production for the market economy, but most tribal cultures still managed to retain many of their traditional features, including partial self-sufficiency and low levels of consumption. Following World War II, government pressures on tribal economies greatly intensified as a result of a new worldwide campaign for rapid economic growth. Under the technical and financial assistance of the leading industrial countries, nations everywhere attempted to raise their GNPs and initiate self-perpetuating economic growth. Professional development experts including economists, anthropologists, sociologists, geographers, agriculturalists, and other specialists from various countries and the United Nations all turned their attention to tribal peoples, who, because of their "backward" cultures, were considered to be major obstacles to national and international economic goals. These experts devised elaborate programs to bring unwilling tribal peoples fully into national economies, to further raise their agricultural productivity and per capita cash incomes, and to promote whatever socioeconomic transformations they deemed necessary to achieve these goals.

In this chapter the primary concern is to examine the attitudes of governments and development writers toward this kind of economic development directed at self-sufficient tribal peoples. Emphasis is given to the strategies employed and the obstacles encountered. The purpose is to demonstrate that tribal peoples have not always been enthusiastic recipients of industrial economic values and techniques, but rather that their participation in the world-market economy has often been brought about by government-supported compulsion, persuasion, and deliberately altered circumstances. The consequences of this economic transformation will be examined in the following chapter.

FORCED LABOR: HARNESSING THE HEATHENS

The natives must be induced to work.
> Report to the League of Nations for 1923, Australian Trust
> Territory of New Guinea, cited Reed, 1943:179

Throughout Africa, Asia, and the Pacific the economic pursuits of European colonists depended almost entirely upon native labor, but as these new areas were opened, government administrators and colonists soon realized to their dismay that tribal peoples were neither willing nor eager to labor for the white man. Undisturbed tribal cultures *really are* well-integrated, self-contained, satisfying systems, and their members cannot be expected to suddenly begin working for the material rewards of an alien culture without some form of compulsion.

Many governments openly indulged in direct compulsion in the form of *corvée*, or forced, labor. In British colonies it was common practice to demand an annual period of labor from tribal villagers, sometimes for up to a month of road construction work. In the Dutch Celebes nearly two months of labor per year were required of tribal peoples. This was considered to be a tax and was justified in terms of its effectiveness for dealing with *cashless* tribal economies.

The force involved in the recruitment of labor by the "blackbirders" has already been described, but by the 1880s, when New Guinea was being opened for settlement after the Queensland labor trade had subsided, both German and Australian government officers engaged in their own kidnapping of labor recruits. Reed assures us that this was done primarily in cases of undisturbed villages that refused to supply recruits and where kidnapping seemed to be the only way of "breaking the ice." We are told that *trickery* was used more often than force and that the procedure would only resemble slavery if done too often. In some instances small groups of highland Papuans were flown by the government to work in coastal plantations, but this operation was not very successful because the tribesmen soon wanted to return home and suffered high mortality rates in the strange environment. In its 1923 Report to the League of Nations, the Australian mandate government of New Guinea defended such labor policies with the novel argument that if they were not forced to work, the natives were likely to die out from lack of exercise!

The French made liberal use of forced tribal labor in both Africa and Indochina. The Fifteen-Year Plan for the economic development of French West Africa received a major boost by a decree in 1926 creating a conscript labor force that allowed three years of labor per man toward the construction of highways, railroads, irrigation works, and other development projects. Such measures became necessary when the native population proved unwilling to volunteer for year-round labor at incredibly low wages, sometimes thousands of miles from home, and in the face of high mortality rates. The extent of this corvée labor force was staggering. For example, in 1923 nearly 5 million man-days of free labor were reportedly employed in Senegal. Conditions were so poor in some areas that annual death rates in the labor forces sometimes ran as high as 60 percent (Buell, 1928:937–1044). Elsewhere in Africa, forced labor was used extensively by the Congo Free State, where a 1903 decree called for forty hours of labor a month from each native in exchange for a token wage.

At best, corvée labor was a traumatic introduction for tribal peoples to the benefits of labor in the market economy; at worst it was an inhuman and destructive form of slavery. However, clear evidence for the apparent necessity of the procedure can be seen in the fact that the world community did not officially outlaw corvée labor until 1957—long after it had served its purpose. In that year the International Labour Office formally abolished corvée labor in member nations, regardless of whether it was justified as a means of education, labor discipline, or economic development.

LEARNING THE DIGNITY OF LABOR: TAXES AND DISCIPLINE

Under all circumstances the progress of natives toward civilization is only secured when they shall be convinced of the necessity and dignity of labour; and therefore I think that everything we reasonably do to encourage the natives to work is highly desirable.

Joseph Chamberlain, 1926 speech to the House
of Commons, cited Wellington, 1967:250

Even where direct corvée labor was not practiced, tribal people were still co-erced into the labor force by other means and were often subjected to rigid discipline so that they would not fail to learn the dignity of labor. The most popular and effective form of indirect compulsion was taxation. There were head taxes, poll taxes, even dog taxes, all payable only in cash, which in turn was obtainable only through labor or cash cropping. In many cases the primary purpose was not to obtain revenue for the state directly. Rather, it was to create an artificial need for money and to thereby force reluctant tribesmen to either seek labor in the mines, on the farms and plantations of the colonists, or in the towns, or else to take up cash cropping. This is clearly indicated by official gov-ernment statements and by contemporary observations but is also confirmed by the manner in which these taxes were applied. For example, in Australian New Guinea the head tax did not apply to anyone who had already signed up as an indentured laborer. South African scholars had no doubts about the pur-poses of the various taxes that their government directed at the Bantu. As Hutt (1934:212–213) observed in 1934:

The poll tax and hut tax to which natives are subjected have been used as a means of forcing them into the European economic system.

He felt that the more backward a given tribe proved to be, the greater the pres-sure must be in order to overcome their reluctance to join the labor force. The poll tax itself was initiated around 1900 and demanded the equivalent of up to two months of annual labor for all male tribe members over age eighteen. A jail sentence awaited those who failed to pay up. Significantly, this tax applied only to natives and recognized their adulthood three years earlier than that of Euro-peans, but it was defended as a relatively mild and effective device:

As the natives were often reluctant to leave their homes, a little gentle pressure was brought to bear upon them by the introduction of a poll tax. This measure quite effec-tively stimulated their desire for earning the white man's money.

Eiselen, 1934:71

Merely forcing tribesmen to obtain a cash income was not sufficient to con-vert them into permanent full-time employees, because they frequently re-sponded to these pressures by becoming unenthusiastic "target workers" who

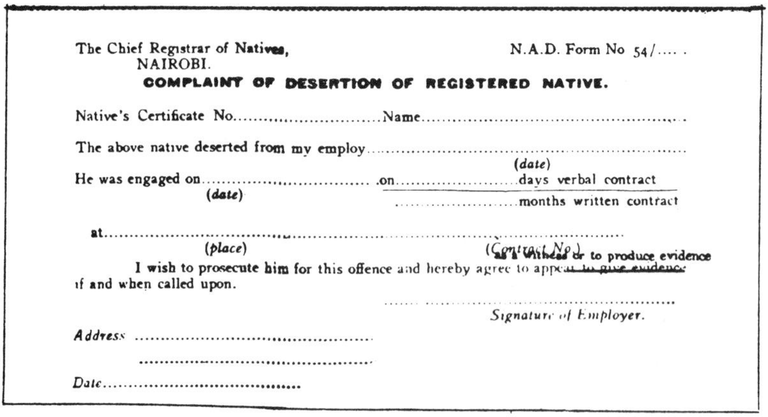

The Chief Registrar of Natives,
NAIROBI.   N.A.D. Form No 54/..... .
COMPLAINT OF DESERTION OF REGISTERED NATIVE.

Native's Certificate No...........................Name..

The above native deserted from my employ..
                                                         (date)
He was engaged on.............................. .on......................days verbal contract
             (date)   ....months written contract

at...............................
          (place)   (......Withheld or to produce evidence
     I wish to prosecute him for this offence and hereby agree to appear to give evidence
if and when called upon.

                                       ....
                                          Signature of Employer.

Address ....

          ....

Date..............................

FIGURE 7.1

While learning "the dignity of labor," in Kenya in 1922 it was a crime for a
tribal person to quit work without authorization. (W. McGregor Ross, 1927,
Kenya From Within. London: George Allen & Unwin Ltd.)

returned to their villages when they had earned enough to pay their taxes or to
purchase a few specific items. Further "instruction" was needed in the dignities
of labor, and sympathetic governments readily provided concerned European
planters and miners with laws allowing various forms of corporal punishment to
correct the "negligence" and "ignorance" of their native employees. In German
Southwest Africa, the Imperial Ordinance of 1896 prescribed imprisonment in
irons and other forms of corporal punishment for natives if their employers
found them guilty of "continued neglect of duty and idleness" or "unwarranted
desertion" from their places of work. Deaths resulting from such "fatherly correction" were not considered to be murder by German law, but it was recognized
that the natives might not understand such subtle distinctions (Wellington,
1967:230–231). In German New Guinea, European plantation owners could
obtain a special disciplinary license permitting them to administer floggings to
their native employees "for sufficient cause." Under the Australians, punishments for labor offenses were strictly a government prerogative and officially
took place only after trial in the district courts, which seemed particularly dedicated to this problem. Reed reports that in 1937–1938 nearly half of all district
court cases involved handing out two-week jail sentences to natives accused of
deserting or neglecting their duties (Reed, 1943:143, 177).

All of these measures have been stoutly defended by apologists for the colonial system as fulfilling the necessary responsibilities of a civilized guardian
over his childlike ward. The American legal authority Alpheus Snow (1921:163)
pointed out that natives simply lack the acquisitive drive characteristic of civilized man, and doing virtually anything that will correct this mental deficiency
is permissible and even a moral duty of the state.

CREATING PROGRESSIVE CONSUMERS

The Australian Government's expenditure on general administration, social services and education helps to raise consumption levels and thus assists the growth of local commercial enterprises.

Australia, Department of Territories, Report for 1967–1968:24

One of the most significant obstacles blocking native economic "progress" was the ability of the natives to find satisfaction at relatively low and stable consumption levels and the fact that their cultures were self-sufficient. Independent tribal peoples with viable economies often expressed little desire to obtain any foreign manufactured goods except those of immediate practical utility such as metal axes, knives, and mirrors. Demand for these simple, utilitarian articles often initiated certain changes in tribal life but did not mean a rejection of traditional culture. Therefore, this demand was often not powerful enough to ensure full "progress." Outsiders quickly realized that if tribal peoples could somehow be made to reject the material satisfactions provided by their own cultures and if they could be successfully urged to desire more and more industrial goods, they would become more willing participants in the cash economy.

Raising tribal consumption levels was not as simple as it might seem. As pointed out previously, acquisitiveness is not a universal trait, and tribal cultures have developed numerous means of limiting the overaccumulation of material goods. Special pressures were necessary to overcome these built-in defenses against alien material goods and standards of value. The first and most obvious pressures for increased consumption of foreign goods were brought about by disturbances in tribal socioeconomic organization that accompanied the uncontrolled frontier and the end of tribal political autonomy. Forced labor, depopulation, reduced land base, loss of traditional food sources, and taxation all helped create a dependency on external goods. When these factors were combined with the ready availability of such goods—whether given out by missionaries and government welfare posts or offered by traders—increasing demand was almost certain to follow. Certainly, government development projects that have pushed new communication networks into formerly isolated tribal areas and have encouraged or even subsidized the work of commercial agents have contributed to increased demand for manufactured goods. It seems doubtful, however, that the mere *availability* of these goods, in the absence of the disturbances accompanying this availability, would be sufficient to create significant demand for them. Many proponents of the demonstration effects theory would argue just the opposite—attributing the disturbance and demise of tribal cultures largely to their demands for the superior goods of industrial civilization. But it would seem equally valid and certainly less ethnocentric to assume that these new demands are more *symptomatic* of tribal disruptions that were already in progress, rather than their immediate causes.

Since the establishment of administrative control, governments have been able to manipulate conditions to unobtrusively stimulate new needs within tribal cultures almost at will through such means as community development programs and formal schooling. Schools have served the double function of creating new needs and preparing individuals for their roles as consumers. Illich (1970) has argued that this double function is one of the primary purposes of schools, even in highly industrialized societies.

PROMOTING TECHNOLOGICAL CHANGE

Governments around the world have been engaged in a massive effort to replace traditional tribal crops, livestock, and productive techniques with what development experts consider to be superior crops, livestock, and techniques. What makes this phenomenon so different from "natural" diffusion is that the recipients, or target peoples, are not generally allowed to pick and choose what suits them. Choices are made by distant officials who are primarily concerned with increasing the production of a certain region. The task of implementing those decisions is delegated to local administrators, extension agents, and applied anthropologists who must present tangible results within specified program timetables. Not only are the choices made by outsiders who have their own goals in mind, but the technologies themselves are usually the products of foreign environments and cultures and in many cases must still be considered experimental even in their countries of origin.

Accepting novel technologies in most cases must mean abandonment of traditional economic self-sufficiency, which is not always easy to promote. Many of the innovations are, in fact, tailored specifically to the needs of the world market. Accepting them often means also accepting a variety of related innovations and an ever-increasing dependence on the world economy. Growing a miracle hybrid grain may require expensive applications of purchased chemical fertilizers and pesticides, and the grain seed itself may need to be purchased again each year. Cash crops may also undermine self-reliance in other, less obvious ways. In many areas under the influence of government-directed agricultural development programs, all of the productive land in entire regions may be transformed from subsistence farming to production of a nonfood cash crop. Such a transformation means, of course, that people who were formerly feeding themselves directly must now purchase their food from external sources by selling their crops. In less extreme cases, some subsistence farming may be carried on, but substantial amounts of imported food still must be purchased. An unforeseen hazard in cash cropping is that it is often difficult to return to full self-sufficiency if crops fail or if world-market prices fall—and tropical mono-crops are particularly vulnerable to both of these problems.

Traditional peoples' frequent resistance to technological change can thus be readily appreciated. The uncertain benefits of new crops and techniques must be carefully weighed against the certain loss of both economic independence and reliable subsistence pursuits, as well as against the *unknown* hazards involved in any experiment with complex cultural and natural systems. Unfortunately, governments have pushed innovations with little appreciation of the problems involved. In many areas, they have imposed new crops by direct force. New Guinea, for example, resorted to a Compulsory Planting Ordinance in 1919, requiring villagers to plant a specified number of coconut palms under penalty of fines or jail sentences. Coffee planting was forced by both the Spanish in the Philippines and the Dutch in the East Indies, and forced planting was common practice in many other colonial countries. Since the postwar emphasis on increasing agricultural production, under way since the 1950s, reluctant tribal peoples have been cajoled and harassed by eager agricultural extension agents and have been plied with free seeds and special subsidies, in order to overcome their justified caution.

In the following sections, three specific case studies illustrate the argument presented in the preceding sections. The first case involves the initial efforts of Dutch colonial administrators to force a self-sufficient, autonomous tribal population into the world-market economy. In the second case, the Zande Scheme, a colonial government is shown using a massive and coercive development scheme designed to introduce a new cash crop after the establishment of administrative control and initial involvement with a cash economy. The final example is an extended treatment of the noncoercive methods employed by the American administration of Micronesia to introduce American standards of consumption to a subsistence-oriented population where local resources will not support such developments. Although these three examples by no means represent the full range of development strategies, they do illustrate several major trends.

Dutch Colonial Development in the Celebes

A brief case study of how Dutch colonial administrators prepared the way for the "healthy" development of the Toradjas, tribal peoples of the Poso district in central Celebes (now Sulawesi), is an example of classic colonial development techniques designed to force an unwilling population into the world economy. According to Kruyt (1929:1–9), when mission efforts began in 1892 the Dutch government deemed the Toradjas completely incapable of progress without outside intervention. Kruyt found and described several of the basic stabilizing features of tribal societies in full operation among the Toradjas. He concluded that because of these features, "development and progress were impossible"—the Toradjas were "bound to remain at the same level." Toradja society was cashless and there was neither desire to earn money nor unfulfilled needs for which it might be required. Wealth-leveling mechanisms, such as reciprocal kinship obligations, religious sacrifices and feasting, and special values on generosity, helped maintain the balance.

Mission work in this relatively undisturbed setting proved a dismal failure. The Toradjas were entirely self-satisfied and quite uninterested in converting to any new religion, in sending their children to the mission schools, or in planting coconuts and coffee as cash crops. Obviously, drastic measures were required to break through their "wall of conservatism." In 1905 the Netherlands Indies government brought the Poso region under administrative control, using armed force to crush all attempts at resistance. In rapid succession, headhunting was stopped, a head tax was imposed, roads were built with conscript labor, and the entire Toradja population was forcibly removed from their traditional hilltop homes where they had grown dry rice and was relocated along the new roads in the lowlands where tribe members were persuaded to grow wet rice for their own good.

The Toradjas were understandably resentful and bewildered by these actions, especially when their mortality rates suddenly soared and they found themselves being punished continually by the administration for offenses that they did not understand. They turned to the missionaries for help, became "converted," and began sending their children to school. Eventually they were cultivating their own coconut and coffee plantations and began to acquire the appropriate new *needs* for such goods as oil lamps, sewing machines, and "better" clothing. Within twenty years the self-sufficient tribal economy had been replaced by deliberate government action. However, in spite of the enormous changes to which they have been subjected, the Toradjas have retained their strong ethnic identity and cultural distinctiveness.

The Zande Development Scheme

The Zande Development Scheme, which has been described in detail by Reining (1966), represents a massive economic development effort aimed at raising the cash income and agricultural productivity of a subsistence-oriented native population after the usual colonial development techniques proved too slow and ineffective. The scheme deserves special attention as a pioneer effort at the *directed* economic transformation of tribal society and as an illustration of how even well-intentioned development plans may often be executed with coercion and little regard for the real wishes of their "targets."

Prior to extensive European intervention the Azande were a large population of shifting cultivators and hunters living in the isolated southwest corner of the Sudan in self-sufficient, dispersed homesteads and recognizing the political authority of local chiefs. The termination of Azande political autonomy in 1905 and the initial administrative assaults on their subsistence economy followed the familiar pattern. To establish "law and order," the British disbanded warrior groups, collected firearms, outlawed the manufacture or possession of shields, and, according to the Azande, banned the smelting of iron. The traditional authority of chiefs was limited, and they were converted into government agents under indirect rule.

After civil administration began in 1911 the entire Azande population was relocated along roads constructed by conscript native labor. Ostensibly, the move was designed to prevent people from living in tsetse fly zones, but it was also intended to facilitate administration. This first major disturbance of the traditional ecological balances was quickly followed by other "improvements." In the interest of conservation, the Azande were forbidden to locate their swiddens in the most favored locations in the gallery forests along the streams, and traditional hunting techniques were seriously restricted or forbidden. Participation in the cash economy was stimulated by a head tax introduced in the 1920s. At that point deliberate efforts at economic development were pushed no further, although the importation of manufactured goods by licensed traders and missionary education were encouraged. Further development seemed frustrated by the region's extreme isolation and lack of significant natural resources for the world market. In spite of the disturbances already introduced, the Azande remained largely self-sufficient subsistence farmers. They had developed a taste for a limited range of consumer goods offered by the traders, but they were content to obtain these by selling wild honey, beeswax, and wild peppers. They remained uninterested in augmenting this meager cash income by migratory wage labor because, it was said, they were too fond of their own country and did not want to leave it. When prices on their limited salable resources fell or when the price of the foreign goods rose too high, they readily returned to their traditional goods. According to Reining, the Azande had not yet passed the point of no return in their economic involvement with the industrial economy and could easily have reverted to full self-sufficiency. Unfortunately, administration planners had other ideas.

In the late 1930s the government began to favor expanded economic development—regardless of cultural and environmental "barriers"—and experiments were begun with cotton as a possible cash crop for the Azande. In 1938 J. D. Tothill, an agricultural development specialist, was appointed to conduct research and make policy recommendations. Within five years he presented his views to the administration in the form of a memorandum entitled "An Experiment in the Social Emergence of Indigenous Races." He called for the conversion of the Azande into "happy, prosperous, literate communities . . . participating in the benefits of civilization" through the cultivation of cotton and the establishment of factories to produce exportable products on the spot (cited Reining, 1966:143). His plans found support in the government although, of course, no one thought of consulting the Azande themselves, and in 1944 the civil secretary urged the governor-general's council to approve an intensive economic development policy for the entire southern Sudan. Blaming the region's "backwardness" on "tribal apathy and conservatism," he made an appeal to the wardship principle as a justification for renewed efforts and stated with familiar ethnocentrism:

We have a moral obligation to redeem its [the southern Sudan] inhabitants from ignorance, superstition, poverty, malnutrition, etc.

cited Beshir, 1968:55

By 1946 a modified scheme for the total economic transformation of the Azande was under way. A small industrial complex was built that included spinning, weaving, cotton oil, and soap mills, an electrical power station, a water system, and a dairy. All of these industrial plants were to be operated by 1,500 Azande workers, who would be trained and supervised by Europeans and northern Sudanese. Telephone lines, improved motor roads, and concrete bridges soon spread across the landscape.

The scheme was envisioned and entirely directed by British planners, and the Azande, who had not been consulted at any point, were called upon to furnish labor for the initial construction at the rate of approximately 1,000 men a month for nearly seven years. Every man in the district was required to work at least one month per year for pay of from $.85 to $1.30 a month! The administration decided that the cotton planting could be most efficiently regulated by introducing a carefully laid out, geometrically precise settlement pattern that would allow the Azande to live in an "accessible and rational manner, not as beasts in the wilderness." Consequently, over a five-year period 50,000 Azande families—nearly the entire district population of some 170,000 people—were removed from their roadside locations (where they had been placed thirty years earlier) and distributed along a grid of sixteen-hectare individual household plots covering thousands of square kilometers of dry scrub forest. Plots were arbitrarily assigned by a clerk escorted by police, with no regard for individual Azande desires to live near their kin, and restrictions were imposed against any future moves.

The key to the entire scheme was the growing of cotton, but this presented some difficulties because the Azande were not interested in growing cotton. Deliberate efforts were made to train Azande merchants and to supply them with consumer goods, because planners believed that what the Azande lacked was a "realization of what money can do for them." The planners felt that as soon as the Azande had learned to desire money they would become eager cash croppers. However, along with these deliberate attempts to increase consumerism, direct compulsion was felt to be necessary. This compulsion took the form of forcing anyone who refused to plant or properly cultivate cotton to do a month of public works labor on the roads as punishment. When yields declined as a result of low prices, and dissatisfaction occurred over food shortages that were caused by this new stress on normal subsistence activities, the number of cotton "defaulters" and the frequency of punishment increased accordingly.

In the face of this degree of direct compulsion, and with a social-engineering scheme of this magnitude, it seems incredible that the planners were motivated by the best intentions, but this seems to be the case. In 1948 the chairman of the project's board of directors reiterated in a memorandum that the underlying purpose of the Zande Scheme was "to bring progress, prosperity, and the reasonable decencies and amenities of human existence to the Azande" (cited Reining, 1966:156). Herein, of course, lay the difficulty. Outsiders applied their own ethnocentric judgments on what should constitute progress, prosperity, decency, and amenities, and then proceeded to impose this blueprint on a totally different culture, assuming that the noble ends justified the apparently drastic means. While the scheme was in progress, the administration operated under the incredible illusion that the traditional culture was being respected, whereas it was in fact being eliminated. According to the district commissioner's platitudes: "The object throughout has been to interfere as little as possible with the people's own way of life" (cited Reining, 1966: 108).

Overall, it appears that the Zande Scheme did succeed somewhat in raising production, income, and consumption levels. These successes were apparently illusory, however, because as soon as the independent Sudanese government was instituted, a new team of development experts was called in to submit further recommendations for the entire southern Sudan. Their report, submitted in 1954 to the Development Branch of the Ministry of Finance and Economics, concluded that *greater* agricultural output was needed to provide *steady improvement* in the standard of living. What was needed was new crops, improved techniques, mechanization, better marketing, and so on. By 1960 an all-new Ten-Year Development Plan was under way.

In 1965, some 20 years after the first development project was begun and halfway through the Ten-Year Plan, a Sudanese journalist, Mohammed Said (1965: 141), reported enthusiastically that the standard of living in Zandeland was higher; consumption of sugar had doubled in just nine years; there were no naked people left; Azande women were dressed in the fashionable northern Sudanese style; and everyone had bicycles and lived in clean houses equipped with beds and mattresses. And Said reported that, best of all, there were now swarms of children everywhere! A more cynical observer might well have wondered who would be setting the development goals for the burgeoning next generation and how long Zandeland's shallow lateritic soils and the Azande themselves could support their newly attained standard of affluence.

Purchasing Progress and Dependency in Micronesia

Micronesia represents another outstanding example of the close relationship between government policy and the transformation of a traditional subsistence economy. In contrast to the Zande Scheme, in which overt coercion was an integral part of development strategy, in Micronesia the transformation has been readily accomplished without coercion. Instead, it was accomplished by a lavish distribution of material rewards by a wealthy government and by massive spending on administration, education, and special development programs. By the late 1960s, many Micronesians who only a few years earlier were participants in presumably satisfying traditional cultures, and who were self-sufficient in food and material needs, were consuming costly imported goods in the American style. The Micronesian subsistence economy was undermined in favor of dependence on a cash system in a manner that is perhaps unique but that dramatically magnifies the general processes involved in the "development" of traditional economies around the world.

The Micronesian environment imposes several rigid limitations on economic activity, one of the most obvious being the severe limitation on land area, combined with vast distances and extreme isolation. There are approximately 2,000 islands with a total combined land surface of only 1,864 square kilometers, scattered over 7.7 million square kilometers of ocean—an area roughly the size of the United States. Many of these islands are low coral atolls, and agricultural potential on even the larger islands is limited. A further complication is the fact that the region is swept regularly by devastating typhoons. This seemingly unpromising environment has been populated by a rich variety of self-sufficient cultures for more than a thousand years and has been in contact with the "civilized" world for some 450 years. Spain, Germany, Japan, and the United States have successively claimed political control over the islands, but thanks to the area's isolation and because relatively few of Micronesia's limited resources have found a place on the world market, the traditional economies have been only slightly disturbed by foreign influences until recently. There were some efforts under the German administration, beginning in 1899, to promote copra plantations, but major efforts at economic development did not occur until the Japanese took control in 1914.

Under the Japanese, the typical colonial pressures were applied to bring the native Micronesians into the economy. All "unoccupied" land was claimed by the government, and the best areas were opened to Japanese colonists or developed as sugar plantations. "Vulgar" native dances and kava drinking were suppressed; over half of the native children were placed in schools to learn Japanese and "ethics"; all males over age sixteen were required to pay a head tax; and subsidies were offered for the planting of coconuts. In spite of these inducements, the natives still proved to be unwilling laborers. The economic development that did occur during this period was centered on the larger islands and was undertaken largely by the Japanese colonists, who outnumbered the native Micronesians by 1937. Except for a general increase in copra production, the outlying islands were relatively undisturbed (Clyde, 1935; Nishi, 1968).

World War II brought large-scale devastation to Micronesia because many of the islands had been fortified by the Japanese and bitter fighting was necessary to dislodge them. The United States Navy assumed administrative control in 1945, and the pattern for large-scale intervention in the lives of the people was soon reestablished. In 1946, within a few months after gaining control, the navy launched a major survey of Micronesia's economic potential in order to guide the military administration in the formulation of policy. The survey was undertaken by twenty-three specialists from the United States Commercial Company, a branch of the Foreign Economic Administration, and included anthropologists, geologists, nutritionists, geographers, economists, botanists, and agronomists. According to Douglas Oliver, who edited a summary of the final report, the astonishing objective of the survey was

> the sobering one of attempting to prescribe a way of life for people who have no effective voice in deciding their own destinies.

> Oliver, 1951:vi

The report clearly recognized that the administration was assuming ultimate power over the lives and welfare of the indigenous population and would, in effect, shape their cultures after whatever pattern the administrators chose. It contained a curious mixture of caution over the dangers involved in manipulating other cultures and of blatantly ethnocentric and even contradictory recommendations. According to the report the traditional cultures were still intact and they represented "more or less delicately balanced adaptations to specific sets of environmental and historical factors and could be badly unbalanced by unwise forced changes" (Oliver, 1951:8). It was stressed that the population should be helped to return to its prewar economic self-sufficiency and that the government should not attempt to attract natives to settle in administrative centers for government convenience, because this was contrary to their traditional ecological patterns and would threaten their self-reliance. The report also indicated that some of the more isolated areas might not even need permanent administrators.

It seems obvious in retrospect that at this point the administering authorities had an opportunity to permit a resumption of an essentially indigenous way of life, free even of the modifications introduced by the Japanese. The aboriginal cultures were familiar with the disruption and devastation of typhoons and were therefore equipped with traditional patterns for dealing with the kinds of problems presented by the war's destruction. Some segments of the population undoubtedly missed the foreign luxuries made possible by the massive Japanese colonization, but everywhere proven traditional patterns of subsistence and technology were being resumed. Even people who had become familiar with motor-driven boats were repairing and rebuilding their sailing canoes. Inspired by premature speeches and naval authorities promising "liberty," the people of Ponape returned enthusiastically to their traditional subsistence activities and feasting. According to Bascom (1965:15), who conducted anthropological research on Ponape, such speeches caused the natives to ignore their copra plantations and served only to "retard" economic development.

It soon became apparent that the policy makers were not considering a return to cultural autonomy: Rather, these cultures were to be remade and reformed, this time according to *American* ideals.

After just four months of field work, the team of experts of the United States Commercial Company Economic Survey proceeded to lay the groundwork for policy decisions that would completely transform cultures that possessed the accumulated knowledge of a thousand years of successful adaptation to a unique and complex environment. Micronesian culture was to be replaced by foreign cultural patterns that policy makers assumed would provide a more satisfying way of life. With colossal ethnocentrism, reinforced by ignorance of the complexities of Micronesian culture, these "experts" made judgments in the light of their own misplaced values and recklessly proceeded to prescribe a way of life for an entire people.

The basic assumptions of the survey team were apparent in the report, which spoke of economic reform and the need to establish an expanding economy and an expanding population (Oliver, 1951). The native people were described as impoverished because they were not enjoying the standards of consumption of luxury goods established by the Japanese, and it was repeatedly emphasized that these foreign goods were now necessities. A taste for such exotic foods as rice, flour, canned meat, and cheese had been cultivated among the conscript labor forces at military camps. Because some of these men were now anxious to continue eating these foods, *they were to be supplied*—regardless of their expense or inappropriateness. One member of the survey later advised that new *needs* should be deliberately promoted among the natives: "Acquaintance with new ideas should be encouraged and desires to try new articles or products should in general be facilitated" (Bascom, 1965:53). Apparently no one recognized the incompatibility between self-sufficiency and dependence on foreign foods and consumer goods.

According to the team's report, traditional Micronesian gardening practices were undeveloped by American standards and native food was monotonous, bland, and not well balanced, even though no signs of nutritional deficiency could be found. The report stated that the people were not eating enough fruit and that for their own benefit they should learn to grow vegetables, "in spite of the present native resistance to a vegetable diet" (Oliver, 1951:13–19). The team felt that agricultural advisers should be provided to teach the population "elementary practices of horticulture," even though it should have been obvious that perhaps the natives might have had more to teach the advisers about such basics as plant varieties and their special requirements, soil conditions, growing seasons, and so on. Along with dietary changes, new crops, and new gardening techniques, the experts recommended that, where possible, every family should be provided with a cow, two pigs, and as many chickens as they wanted. This was surprising in view of the fact that the traditional economy was already solidly based on ample *marine* protein sources. Pigs and chickens were not needed (and there was little to feed them), while cattle, having pasturage requirements, were absurdly out of place in an area as short of land as Micronesia.

The report piously affirmed, almost as a self-evident truth, that economic change in Micronesia was inevitable, implying that the natives were bringing it on themselves and that it could therefore not be prevented:

> *Micronesians will, for better or worse, continue to expand their participation in western systems. In the kind of world we live in, that is inevitable, and no one but a nostalgic antiquary would imagine otherwise.*
>
> Oliver, 1951:85–86

Curiously, however, the report ominously warned that the "inevitable" changes "must occur gradually and voluntarily" (Oliver, 1951:8). Administrators were advised not to use force; rather, the people were to be *directed*, not compelled, into proper economic patterns. As the report explained:

> *Much can be accomplished positively if natives are led rather than pushed into channels which are intended for their economic benefit.*
>
> Oliver, 1951:91

In spite of this strange double talk, Oliver explicitly noted in his conclusions that the Micronesians would probably not "be permitted the absolute freedom of choice to decide their own destinies." Obviously, the government was deciding what was to be inevitable and was deliberately setting about to create the conditions under which the inevitable new economic style would be chosen. In one remarkable passage in a report full of paradoxes, the team of experts recommended that Micronesians should be made to think they were choosing freely even though they really were not:

> *Attempts to bring about economic reform in conformance with western modes of living, before the natives are ready to make the changes, would undermine their faith in our avowed intentions. Natives should be given the opportunity of learning about and considering cultural alternatives, but the desire for change should come from within the society. No penalties in any form should be invoked for refusal to accept a proposed change over which they were told they had a free choice.*

Oliver, 1951:91

When the administration of Micronesia was transferred in 1951 to civilian authorities of the United States Department of the Interior (under the United Nations Trust Territory agreements), the newly appointed high commissioner proclaimed to the natives that "your existing customs, religious beliefs, and property rights will be respected," but this proved to be as misleading as the navy's promise of liberty (Proclamation No. 2, Annual Report on the Administration of the Territory of the Pacific Islands, 1953:79–80, hereafter abbreviated as TTR—Trust Territory Report). In the same proclamation, the high commissioner also promised an administration based on "applied science," and the tone of the annual administrative report for 1951–1952 leaves no doubt that *respect* was being pushed aside by the need for *advancement*. While there was talk of "gradual evolution," and it was claimed that "no pressure has been used to force the native Micronesians to discard their customs in favor of western institutions," there were complaints that the "divisive effect of ethnocentricity must be overcome" and that a more democratic form of government with a broader outlook was being carefully created through "well nurtured growth . . . education and civil guidance by administrative officials" (TTR, 1953:13–14). The "ethnocentrism" to be overcome was, of course, the native belief in the superiority of their own institutions, not the ethnocentrism of government officials who, after all, were dealing in applied science to further a natural evolutionary process.

In the economic field, subsistence activities were to be fostered, but it was felt that the "fullest possible development of land resources" was impeded by traditional land tenure practices. The official program for Micronesian economic advancement followed the lines recommended by the 1946 survey and overflowed with extravagant promises and American values. Everything was to be improved—more and better, better and greater. Production would be increased, new practices and superior crops would be introduced, and the environment would be dealt with *more effectively* (TTR, 1953:26–31). In effect, a thousand years of Micronesian cultural development was declared obsolete, and

FIGURE 7.2

Traditional houses in Yap, Micronesia (above). A tourist hotel on Yap (below) was made possible by an outpouring of American dollars for Micronesian development beginning in the 1960s. (Price.)

applied science was to miraculously replace it. In the eyes of the administration, the traditional culture was simply standing in the way of a better life.

Within two years the administration's development strategy was taking shape. The territory's natural isolation would be ended by the introduction of radio communication and a modern air and sea shipping network. The reluctance of Micronesians to abandon their traditional cultures would be overcome by large doses of administrative advice and education, while the natural limitations on economic growth imposed by the restricted resource base would be circumvented by the massive importation of American dollars in the form of wages for indigenous government employees. In 1953, 15 percent of the native population of 57,000 was enrolled in schools. This figure included 1,300 high school and college students who were preparing for government employment and acquiring first-hand experience in American standards of consumption at schools in Guam, Hawaii, and the United States mainland. By 1954 the success of the program was already becoming apparent in the fact that more than 1,200 Micronesians were on the administration's payroll, 200 cars were in native hands, and 1.3 million dollars worth of imports were now flowing into the islands. An annual government operating budget of nearly 6 million dollars was needed to support these activities, but only 1.6 million dollars could be obtained in revenue from local resources—the remainder was appropriated as a direct subsidy from the federal government (statistical tables TTR, 1954, 1955).

The motivation for this policy of creating native dependency on the government seems to have resulted largely from the government's desire to strengthen its dominance in the region in order to retain it as a strategic military resource, rather than from any real need for the area's other meager resources. The exploitation of Micronesia by the American military did not end with the war. In 1946 the navy removed the 170 Marshallese residents of Bikini Atoll and relocated them on other islands so that nuclear bombs could be exploded over and under the lagoon in Operation Crossroads (Kiste, 1974). By 1988 radioactive contamination still made reoccupation of Bikini impossible. Guam was used as a base for B-52 bombers during the Vietnam War, and Kwajalein Atoll in the Marshall Islands is still a target for test nuclear missiles fired from California.

By 1958 the American administration was even prouder of the success of its development strategy. Native houses were now more substantial, power boats were being purchased more widely, and some 500 private vehicles, 275 radios, and various other electric appliances could now be pointed to as evidence of an increased standard of living. However, some isolated pockets of cultural resistance still remained. *Improvement* in the remote islands was slower and less evident, necessitating more education and greater effort:

> *In such remote areas the basic problem is one of educating the local inhabitants to the need for or desirability of improvement and the development of local means to accomplish such improvements.*
>
> *Further improvement of living standards can be accomplished throughout the Territory. . . . The policy and programs of the Administration are planned and intended to develop an awareness and understanding of community needs and the desirability of improvement, and to develop local community resources and means to a maximum extent to achieve the improvement desired.*
>
> TTR, 1959:90–91

For ten years the pace of development input from the administration increased steadily but gradually, until the annual budget stood at approximately 7.4 million dollars. Micronesians were now consuming over sixty dollars worth of imported goods per capita annually, while exports of island resources remained at approximately their prior levels. It was obvious that the value of exports had reached an absolute ceiling even by the mid-1950s, but *apparent* economic growth continued as more and more natives were placed on the government payroll and more capital improvements were made. Clearly, dependency was growing and the native culture was being gradually overwhelmed in a tide of dollars and foreign consumer luxuries. (For example, see Peoples [1978] for a detailed examination of dependency on the island of Kosrae.) If at this point the world price of copra had fallen, and if the government payroll had been drastically reduced, several thousand impoverished Micronesians would have been left to fend for themselves, in which case, if enough of the traditional culture had survived in the outlying islands, it would have been possible for the natives to return to self-sufficiency. The government, however, had no intention of reducing its development efforts and actually had even greater things in store.

In 1962 the government more than doubled its spending in Micronesia to facilitate more rapid development and to "meet the needs of the Micronesian people." Official reports explained that this represented a major shift in the administration's commitment to Micronesia (TTR, 1973:41), but this was a careful understatement. A massive, all-new development machine was being cranked into motion, fueled by a seemingly endless stream of American dollars. By 1965 government spending had tripled the pre-1962 annual levels and was still climbing, until the projected 1973 budget reached an incredible 78.6 million dollars—more than eleven times the pre-1962 levels! Between 1962 and 1972 the administration spent some 397.4 million dollars, much of this directed toward what was called an accelerated *emergency* program to upgrade and speed development of essential public services, including schools, transportation, communication, and power plants. The results of some of this money could be seen immediately in the educational plant, where by 1972, 80 percent of the public elementary schools met American standards—approximately eighty square meters of working space and concrete and metal to replace coral floors and thatch.

In a dramatic rejection of earlier policy emphasizing self-reliance, the territory was opened to U.S. capital investment by presidential decree in 1962 to stimulate new economic activity for the "maximum economic and cultural benefit of all Micronesians" (TTR, 1964:49–50; 1973:54). Progress based on local resources and capabilities was no longer adequate:

> The government recognizes that outside capital and expertise, particularly for large-scale, sophisticated enterprises, are needed for maximum efficiency and profit.
>
> TTR, 1973:54

The subsistence economy was now out:

> The Administration continues to seek means to promote development of the economy of Micronesia so that it will become geared to a world money economy and thus, its subsistence aspects will become supplemental.

TTR, 1973:45

An enormous tide of exotic material wealth was beginning to engulf the islands, but the official administration position was that these changes would be good and they would be *voluntarily chosen*. According to the 1972 report to the United Nations, the "Administering Authority"

> encourages Micronesians to voluntarily integrate into their own culture useful features of other civilizations to enable them to lead more meaningful and rewarding lives in today's changing world.

TTR, 1973:93

Predictably, the "useful features" were all drawn from American civilization and represented the material trappings that Americans considered essential for a "more meaningful and rewarding" life. In a remarkable exercise in self-deception, the administration observed that it would permit only those foreign investments that would contribute to the territory's overall economic well-being "without adversely affecting the existing social and cultural values and ethnic conditions of the district" (TTR, 1973:54).

Evidence of progress suddenly began to appear throughout the territory in direct proportion to government spending and foreign investment. Jetports sprang up on Truk, Ponape, and Majuro, and by 1972 Continental Airlines was operating tourist hotels on three islands. Nearly 7,000 private motor vehicles were now spilling over 960 kilometers of roads, and 26 million dollars worth of imported food, clothing, gasoline, machinery, and other consumer goods were pouring in. There were 415 licensed commercial business outlets where there had been only 54 in 1958. Electrical power plants were in place or being installed that would have a total capacity of 30,000 kW; twenty-two movie houses were in operation, one television and eight radio stations were broadcasting, and an estimated 50,000 radios were in private homes and cars.

A multitude of special programs and new institutions were needed to channel native participation in these developments. A massive effort at the recruitment, training, and placement of future civil servants was soon under way to help swell the government payrolls even further. In 1972 there were already over 5,700 native employees in the government receiving some 18 million dollars in salaries, and more than 600 natives were enrolled in special training programs designed to increase incomes. These programs were sponsored by the United States federal government under Public Service Careers and Public Employment Programs; the United Nations; the South Pacific Commission; and the World Health Organization. Credit unions, the Small Business Administration loan program, and the Economic Development Loan Fund were all "making it easy to borrow money for useful purposes." Useful purposes included such diverse, but thoroughly American, enterprises as the establishment of cattle ranches, laundromats, jewelry and upholstery shops, car rentals, and the purchase of outboard motors and motorcycles. In 1972 the Economic Development Loan Fund alone had made over a million dollars worth of direct and guaranteed loans, while 3 million dollars worth of applications were pending.

To help overcome the last remnants of resistance in the remaining backward areas, in 1966 the Peace Corps was called in for community development work. In their peak year, 700 volunteers were on duty teaching English, organizing self-help programs, advising on business matters, promoting increased agricultural production, and spending money. As an underdeveloped, impoverished region, Micronesia also qualified for a number of federal War On Poverty programs, and soon there were federally funded Community Action programs, Head Start programs, Economic Opportunity Office programs, special scholarships, workshops, and a bewildering array of other "opportunities," plus a Neighborhood Youth Corps and a special Grant-in Aid program. As a final touch, the most isolated communities were visited every year by Santa Claus, the supreme cultural hero of American materialism, who air-dropped free consumer goods on needy children, courtesy of the U.S. Navy and Air Force based on Guam.

Beginning with the creation of the Commonwealth of the Northern Mariana Islands in 1976 as a U.S. territory, the United Nations Trust Territory administration of Micronesia has been replaced by other political arrangements. In 1978 the Marshall Islands became a constitutional republic and the Caroline Islands formed the Federated States of Micronesia. Local political autonomy has not yet overcome Micronesia's problems, and the United States continues to exert a powerful influence by taking advantage of Micronesian economic dependency. For example, between 1980 and 1983 the Palauan people voted four times to keep the self-governing Republic of Palau a nuclear-free zone, thus excluding U.S. ships that might be carrying nuclear weapons, but the United States refused to accept this decision (IWGIA Newsletter, 34:91–92). The Compact of Free Association between the United States and Palau, which the U.S. government wanted the Palauans to approve, would permit considerable U.S. military presence in Palau, including the storage of nuclear weapons and possibly the dumping of nuclear waste. As an incentive, the agreement offered 1 billion dollars in aid money to Palau. As of late 1988, the Free Association issue was still unresolved. In recognition of Palau's opposition to nuclear weapons, it was awarded an alternate Nobel Peace Prize in 1983 (IWGIA Newsletter, 35/36:161–165).

TRIBALS AND TOURISM

The economic, technical and cultural marginalisation of tourism exposes cultural minorities to discontinuity, disturbance, divergence, even disintegration, and usually to a dangerous dependency.

Rossel, 1988:13

The development of tourism cited in the previous Micronesian example involves a larger issue that has affected tribal populations throughout the world: the exploitation of tribal territory and culture as exotic tourist attractions and symbols of national identity. This topic has been examined in detail by anthropologists (Cultural Survival Quarterly, 1982, 6[3]; Graburn, 1976; Rossel, 1988; Smith, 1977), but in this section only a few major points will be raised. Tourism in the Third World is a product of global economic inequality and often disproportionately favors a few special-interest groups. Furthermore, it often leads to distorted national development and obscures the realities of exploitation.

Tourism involving tribal peoples can be attacked on several grounds, as in the quote from Rossel above. First, tribal peoples are "marginalized," or made to feel like inferior outsiders, by tourism when they must interact with wealthy outsiders who flaunt their economic, technological, and cultural superiority. They are also marginalized in that they often have no direct control over the tourist trade, cannot set prices, and enjoy only a small proportion of the profit from tourism. In extreme cases, such as with the Yagua Indians in the Peruvian and Colombian Amazon (Chaumeil, 1984; Seiler-Baldinger, 1988), tour organizers have set up artificial villages and relocated native groups for the convenience of tourists. Indians then are coerced into maintaining an ethnographically "primitive" image and must perform on cue to be observed and photographed. The Tasaday in the Philippines, who were "discovered" in 1971, appear to have been deliberately set up to be exhibited as primitive cave dwellers to make the Marcos administration appear as a benevolent protector of tribal groups. These sorts of "human zoos" can be readily identified as demeaning and exploitative, but in many cases the detrimental impact of tourism may be less obvious. For example, where large numbers of backpacking trekkers hike into "authentic" native areas, they may unwittingly degrade the environment, increase pressure on local resources, distort local value systems by the sudden injection of cash into the economy, and create internal inequalities and dependency because only a few native people are able to benefit from the trekkers' presence. More serious consequences of tourism have occurred when tribal groups, such as the Maasai in East Africa, have been removed from their traditional lands to allow tourists greater access to observe wildlife (see Chapter 6).

Tourism officials and tourist agencies sometimes defend cultural tourism as a form of cross-cultural education in which members of dominant, urban, industrial societies gain knowledge and respect for indigenous peoples. This may be true under certain conditions, but more often tourism creates and maintains illusions about exotic cultures. Tourists are escorted about and insulated from unpleasant truths, and often return home believing themselves to be "experts" on the peoples they visited, but knowing nothing about the larger realities of land rights, discrimination, and economic exploitation.

The cultural tourism industry is not entirely negative, however. Where indigenous peoples are able to control the conditions of interaction with tourists, set prices, and obtain a fair share of the profits, a modest income from tourism can help these groups maintain economic self-sufficiency. Where native groups have retained ownership over territory within national parks, such as in the

Kakadu in the Northern Territory of Australia, they may be able to combine cultural tourism and wildlife tourism in beneficial ways. Indigenous peoples can market their arts and crafts, while educating the public about contemporary tribal realities. The critical element is that indigenous peoples must be allowed to control their own cultural and territorial resources.

· 8 ·

The Price of Progress

In aiming at progress . . . you must let no one suffer by too drastic a measure, nor pay too high a price in upheaval and devastation, for your innovation.

Maunier, 1949:725

UNTIL RECENTLY, GOVERNMENT PLANNERS have always considered economic development and progress beneficial goals that all societies should want to strive toward. The social advantages of progress—as defined in terms of increased incomes, higher standards of living, greater security, and better health—are thought to be positive, *universal* goods, to be obtained at any price. Although one may argue that tribal peoples must sacrifice their traditional cultures to obtain these benefits, government planners generally feel that this is a small price to pay for such obvious advantages.

In earlier chapters, evidence was presented to demonstrate that autonomous tribal peoples have not *chosen* progress to enjoy its advantages, but that governments have *pushed* progress upon them to obtain tribal resources, not primarily to share with the tribal peoples the benefits of progress. It has also been shown that the price of forcing progress on unwilling recipients has involved the deaths of millions of tribal people, as well as their loss of land, political sovereignty, and the right to follow their own life style. This chapter does not attempt to further summarize that aspect of the cost of progress, but instead analyzes the specific effects of the participation of tribal peoples in the world-market economy. In direct opposition to the usual interpretation, it is argued here that the benefits of progress are often both illusory and detrimental to tribal peoples when they have not been allowed to control their own resources and define their relationship to the market economy.

PROGRESS AND THE QUALITY OF LIFE

One of the primary difficulties in assessing the benefits of progress and economic development for any culture is that of establishing a meaningful measure of both benefit and detriment. It is widely recognized that *standard of living*, which is the most frequently used measure of progress, is an intrinsically ethnocentric concept relying heavily upon indicators that lack universal cultural relevance. Such factors as GNP, per capita income, capital formation, employment rates, literacy, formal education, consumption of manufactured goods, number of doctors and hospital beds per thousand persons, and the amount of money spent on government welfare and health programs may be irrelevant measures of actual *quality* of life for autonomous or even semiautonomous tribal cultures. In its 1954 report, the Trust Territory government indicated that since the Micronesian population was still largely satisfying its own needs within a cashless subsistence economy, "Money income is not a significant measure of living standards, production, or well-being in this area" (TTR, 1953:44). Unfortunately, within a short time the government began to rely on an enumeration of certain imported consumer goods as indicators of a higher standard of living in the islands, even though many tradition-oriented islanders felt that these new goods symbolized a lowering of the quality of life.

A more useful measure of the benefits of progress might be based on a formula for evaluating cultures devised by Goldschmidt (1952:135). According to these less ethnocentric criteria, the important question to ask is: Does progress or economic development increase or decrease a given culture's ability to satisfy the physical and psychological needs of its population, or its stability? This question is a far more direct measure of quality of life than are the standard economic correlates of development, and it is universally relevant. Specific indication of this *standard* of living could be found for any society in the nutritional status and general physical and mental health of its population, the incidence of crime and delinquency, the demographic structure, family stability, and the society's relationship to its natural resource base. A society with high rates of malnutrition and crime, and one degrading its natural environment to the extent of threatening its continued existence, might be described as at a lower standard of living than is another society where these problems did not exist.

Careful examination of the data, which compare, on these specific points, the former condition of self-sufficient tribal peoples with their condition following their incorporation into the world-market economy, leads to the conclusion that their standard of living is *lowered*, not raised, by economic progress—and often to a dramatic degree. This is perhaps the most outstanding and inescap-

FIGURE 8.1

Trash litters a lagoon in Micronesia. Quality of life often suffers as economic development accelerates. (Price.)

able fact to emerge from the years of research that anthropologists have devoted to the study of culture change and modernization. Despite the best intentions of those who have promoted change and improvement, all too often the results have been poverty, longer working hours, and much greater physical exertion, poor health, social disorder, discontent, discrimination, overpopulation, and environmental deterioration—combined with the destruction of the traditional culture.

Diseases of Development

Perhaps it would be useful for public health specialists to start talking about a new category of diseases. . . . Such diseases could be called the "diseases of development" and would consist of those pathological conditions which are based on the usually unanticipated consequences of the implementation of developmental schemes.

Hughes & Hunter, 1972:93

Economic development increases the disease rate of affected peoples in at least three ways. First, to the extent that development is successful, it makes developed populations suddenly become vulnerable to all of the diseases suffered almost exclusively by "advanced" peoples. Among these are diabetes, obesity, hypertension, and a variety of circulatory problems. Second, development disturbs traditional environmental balances and may dramatically increase certain bacterial and parasite diseases. Finally, when development goals prove unattainable, an assortment of poverty diseases may appear in association with the crowded conditions of urban slums and the general breakdown in traditional socioeconomic systems.

Outstanding examples of the first situation can be seen in the Pacific, where some of the most successfully developed native peoples are found. In Micronesia, where development has progressed more rapidly than perhaps anywhere else, between 1958 and 1972 the population doubled, but the number of patients treated for heart disease in the local hospitals nearly tripled, mental disorder increased eightfold, and by 1972 hypertension and nutritional deficiencies began to make significant appearances for the first time (TTR, 1959, 1973, statistical tables).

Although some critics argue that the Micronesian figures simply represent better health monitoring due to economic progress, rigorously controlled data from Polynesia show a similar trend. The progressive acquisition of modern degenerative diseases was documented by an eight-member team of New Zealand medical specialists, anthropologists, and nutritionists, whose research was funded by the Medical Research Council of New Zealand and the World Health Organization. These researchers investigated the health status of a genetically related population at various points along a continuum of increasing cash income, modernizing diet, and urbanization. The extremes on this acculturation continuum were represented by the relatively traditional Pukapukans of the Cook Islands and the essentially Europeanized New Zealand Maori, while the busily developing Rarotongans, also of the Cook Islands, occupied the intermediate position. In 1971, after eight years of work, the team's preliminary findings were summarized by Dr. Ian Prior, cardiologist and leader of the research, as follows:

> We are beginning to observe that the more an islander takes on the ways of the West, the more prone he is to succumb to our degenerative diseases. In fact, it does not seem too much to say our evidence now shows that the farther the Pacific natives move from the quiet, carefree life of their ancestors, the closer they come to gout, diabetes, atherosclerosis, obesity, and hypertension.
>
> Prior, 1971:2

In Pukapuka, where progress was limited by the island's small size and its isolated location some 480 kilometers from the nearest port, the annual per capita income was only about thirty-six dollars and the economy remained essentially at a subsistence level. Resources were limited and the area was visited by trading ships only three or four times a year; thus, there was little opportunity for intensive economic development. Predictably, the population of Pukapuka was characterized by relatively low levels of imported sugar and salt intake, and a presumably related low level of heart disease, high blood pressure, and diabetes. In Rarotonga, where economic success was introducing town life, imported food, and motorcycles, sugar and salt intakes nearly tripled, high blood pressure increased approximately ninefold, diabetes two- to threefold, and heart disease doubled for men and more than quadrupled for women, while the number of grossly obese women increased more than tenfold. Among the New Zealand Maori, sugar intake was nearly eight times that of the Pukapukans, gout in men was nearly double its rate on Pukapuka, and diabetes in men was more than fivefold higher, while heart disease in women had increased more than sixfold. The Maori were, in fact, dying of "European" diseases at a greater rate than was the average New Zealand European.

Government development policies designed to bring about changes in local hydrology, vegetation, and settlement patterns and to increase population mobility, and even programs aimed at reducing certain diseases, have frequently led to dramatic increases in disease rates because of the unforeseen effects of disturbing the preexisting order. Hughes and Hunter (1972) published an excellent survey of cases in which development led directly to increased disease rates in Africa. They concluded that hasty development intervention in relatively balanced local cultures and environments resulted in "a drastic deterioration in the social and economic conditions of life."

Traditional populations in general have presumably learned to live with the endemic pathogens of their environments, and in some cases they have evolved genetic adaptations to specific diseases, such as the sickle-cell trait, which provided an immunity to malaria. Unfortunately, however, outside intervention has entirely changed this picture. In the late 1960s, sleeping sickness suddenly increased in many areas of Africa and even spread to areas where it did not formerly occur, due to the building of new roads and migratory labor, both of which caused increased population movement. Large-scale relocation schemes, such as the Zande Scheme, had disastrous results when natives were moved from their traditional disease-free refuges into infected areas. Dams and irrigation developments inadvertently created ideal conditions for the rapid proliferation of snails carrying schistosomiasis (a liver fluke disease), and major epidemics suddenly occurred in areas where this disease had never before been a problem. DDT spraying programs have been temporarily successful in controlling malaria, but there is often a rebound effect that increases the problem when spraying is discontinued, and the malarial mosquitoes are continually evolving resistant strains.

Urbanization is one of the prime measures of development, but it is a mixed blessing for most former tribal peoples. Urban health standards are abysmally poor and generally worse than in rural areas for the detribalized individuals who have crowded into the towns and cities throughout Africa, Asia, and Latin America seeking wage employment out of new economic necessity. Infectious diseases related to crowding and poor sanitation are rampant in urban centers, while greatly increased stress and poor nutrition aggravate a variety of other health problems. Malnutrition and other diet-related conditions are, in fact, one of the characteristic hazards of progress faced by tribal peoples and are discussed in the following sections.

The Hazards of Dietary Change

The traditional diets of tribal peoples are admirably adapted to their nutritional needs and available food resources. Even though these diets may seem bizarre, absurd, and unpalatable to outsiders, they are unlikely to be improved by drastic modifications. Given the delicate balances and complexities involved in any subsistence system, change always involves risks, but for tribal people the effects of dietary change have been catastrophic.

Under normal conditions, food habits are remarkably resistant to change, and indeed people are unlikely to abandon their traditional diets voluntarily in favor of dependence on difficult-to-obtain exotic imports. In some cases it is true that imported foods may be identified with powerful outsiders and are therefore sought as symbols of greater prestige. This may lead to such absurdities as Amazonian Indians choosing to consume imported canned tunafish when abundant high-quality fish is available in their own rivers. Another example of this situation occurs in tribes where mothers prefer to feed their infants expensive and nutritionally inadequate canned milk from unsanitary, but *high status*, baby bottles. The high status of these items is often promoted by clever traders and clever advertising campaigns.

Aside from these apparently voluntary changes, it appears that more often dietary changes are forced upon unwilling tribal peoples by circumstances beyond their control. In some areas, new food crops have been introduced by government decree, or as a consequence of forced relocation or other policies designed to end hunting, pastoralism, or shifting cultivation. Food habits have also been modified by massive disruption of the natural environment by outsiders—as when sheepherders transformed the Australian Aborigines' foraging territory or when European invaders destroyed the bison herds that were the primary element in the Plains Indians' subsistence patterns. Perhaps the most frequent cause of diet change occurs when formerly self-sufficient peoples find that wage labor, cash cropping, and other economic development activities that feed tribal resources into the world-market economy must inevitably divert time and energy away from the production of subsistence foods. Many developing peoples suddenly discover that, like it or not, they are unable to secure traditional foods and must spend their newly acquired cash on costly, and often nutritionally inferior, manufactured foods.

Overall, the available data seem to indicate that the dietary changes that are linked to involvement in the world-market economy have tended to *lower* rather than raise the nutritional levels of the affected tribal peoples. Specifically, the vitamin, mineral, and protein components of their diets are often drastically reduced and replaced by enormous increases in starch and carbohydrates, often in the form of white flour and refined sugar.

Any deterioration in the quality of a given population's diet is almost certain

FIGURE 8.2

A Batangan woman of Mindoro, Philippines,
with empty Pepsi-Cola bottle. Dietary change
is a critical aspect of culture change in general,
and for tribal peoples it often results in lowered
nutritional status and poor health. (Pennoyer.)

to be reflected in an increase in deficiency diseases and a general decline in
health status. Indeed, as tribal peoples have shifted to a diet based on imported
manufactured or processed foods, there has been a dramatic rise in malnutrition, a massive increase in dental problems, and a variety of other nutrition-
related disorders. Nutritional physiology is so complex that even well-meaning
dietary changes have had tragic consequences. In many areas of Southeast Asia,
government-sponsored protein supplementation programs supplying milk to
protein-deficient populations caused unexpected health problems and increased
mortality. Officials failed to anticipate that in cultures where adults do not normally drink milk, the enzymes needed to digest it are no longer produced and
milk *intolerance* results (Davis & Bolin, 1972). In Brazil, a similar milk distribution program caused an epidemic of permanent blindness by aggravating a
preexisting vitamin A deficiency (Bunce, 1972).

Teeth and Progress

There is nothing new in the observation that savages, or peoples living under primitive conditions, have, in general, excellent teeth. . . . Nor is it news that most civilized populations possess wretched teeth which begin to decay almost before they have erupted completely, and that dental caries is likely to be accompanied by peridontal disease with further reaching complications.

Hooton, 1945:xviii

Anthropologists have long recognized that undisturbed tribal peoples are often in excellent physical condition. And it has often been noted specifically that dental caries and the other dental abnormalities that plague industrialized societies are absent or rare among tribal peoples who have retained their traditional diets. The fact that tribal food habits may contribute to the development of sound teeth, whereas modernized diets may do just the opposite, was illustrated as long ago as 1894 in an article in the *Journal of the Royal Anthropological Institute* that described the results of a comparison between the teeth of ten Sioux Indians and a comparable group of Londoners (Smith, 1894:109–116). The Indians were examined when they came to London as members of Buffalo Bill's Wild West Show and were found to be completely free of caries and in possession of all their teeth, even though half of the group were over thirty-nine years of age. Londoners' teeth were conspicuous for both their caries and their steady reduction in number with advancing age. The difference was attributed primarily to the wear and polishing caused by the traditional Indian diet of coarse food and the fact that they chewed their food longer, encouraged by the absence of tableware.

One of the most remarkable studies of the dental conditions of tribal peoples and the impact of dietary change was conducted in the 1930s by Weston Price (1945), an American dentist who was interested in determining what caused normal, healthy teeth. Between 1931 and 1936, Price systematically explored tribal areas throughout the world to locate and examine the most isolated peoples who were still living on traditional foods. His fieldwork covered Alaska, the Canadian Yukon, Hudson Bay, Vancouver Island, Florida, the Andes, the Amazon, Samoa, Tahiti, New Zealand, Australia, New Caledonia, Fiji, the Torres Strait, East Africa, and the Nile. The study demonstrated both the superior quality of aboriginal dentition and the devastation that occurs as modern diets are adopted. In nearly every area where traditional foods were still being eaten, Price found perfect teeth with normal dental arches and virtually no decay, whereas caries and abnormalities increased steadily as new diets were adopted. In many cases the change was sudden and striking. Among Eskimo groups subsisting entirely on traditional food he found caries totally absent, whereas in groups eating a considerable quantity of store-bought food approximately 20 percent of their teeth were decayed. This figure rose to more than 30 percent with Eskimo groups subsisting almost exclusively on purchased or government-supplied food, and reached an incredible 48 percent among the Vancouver Island Indians. Unfortunately for many of these people, modern dental treatment did not accompany the new food, and their suffering was appalling. The loss of teeth was, of course, bad enough in itself, and it certainly undermined the population's resistance to many new diseases, including tuberculosis. But new foods were also accompanied by crowded, misplaced teeth, gum diseases, distortion of the face, and pinching of the nasal cavity. Abnormalities in the dental arch appeared in the new generation following the change in diet, while caries appeared almost immediately even in adults.

Price reported that in many areas the affected peoples were conscious of their own physical deterioration. At a mission school in Africa, the principal asked him to explain to the native schoolchildren why they were not physically as strong as children who had had no contact with schools. On an island in the Torres Strait the natives knew exactly what was causing their problems and resisted—almost to the point of bloodshed—government efforts to establish a store that would make imported food available. The government prevailed, however, and Price was able to establish a relationship between the length of time the government store had been established and the increasing incidence of caries among a population that showed an almost 100 percent immunity to them before the store had been opened.

In New Zealand, the Maori, who in their aboriginal state are often considered to have been among the healthiest, most perfectly developed of peoples, were found to have "advanced" the furthest. According to Price:

> *Their modernization was demonstrated not only by the high incidence of dental caries but also by the fact that 90 percent of the adults and 100 percent of the children had abnormalities of the dental arches.*

Price, 1945:206

Malnutrition

Malnutrition, particularly in the form of protein deficiency, has become a critical problem for tribal peoples who must adopt new economic patterns. Population pressures, cash cropping, and government programs all have tended to encourage the replacement of traditional crops and other food sources that were rich in protein with substitutes high in calories but low in protein. In Africa, for example, protein-rich staples such as millet and sorghum are being replaced systematically by high-yielding manioc and plantains, which have insignificant amounts of protein. The problem is increased for cash croppers and wage laborers whose earnings are too low and unpredictable to allow purchase of adequate amounts of protein. In some rural areas, agricultural laborers have been forced systematically to deprive nonproductive members (principally children) of their households of their minimal nutritional requirements to satisfy the need of the productive members. This process has been documented in northeastern Brazil following the introduction of large-scale sisal plantations (Gross & Underwood, 1971). In urban centers the difficulties of obtaining nutritionally adequate diets are even more serious for tribal immigrants, because costs are higher and poor quality foods are more tempting.

One of the most tragic, and largely overlooked, aspects of chronic malnutrition is that it can lead to abnormally undersized brain development and apparently irreversible brain damage; it has been associated with various forms of mental impairment or retardation. Malnutrition has been linked clinically with mental retardation in both Africa and Latin America (see, for example, Mönckeberg, 1968), and this appears to be a worldwide phenomenon with serious implications (Montagu, 1972).

Optimistic supporters of progress will surely say that all of these new health problems are being overstressed and that the introduction of hospitals, clinics, and the other modern health institutions will overcome or at least compensate for all of these difficulties. However, it appears that uncontrolled population growth and economic impoverishment probably will keep most of these benefits out of reach for many tribal peoples, and the intervention of modern medicine has at least partly contributed to the problem in the first place.

The generalization that civilization frequently has a broad negative impact on tribal health has found broad empirical support (see especially Kroeger & Barbira-Freedman [1982] on Amazonia; Reinhard [1976] on the Arctic; and Wirsing [1985] globally), but these conclusions have not gone unchallenged. Some critics argue that tribal health was often poor before modernization, and they point specifically to tribals' low life expectancy and high infant mortality rates. Demographic statistics on tribal populations are often problematic because precise data are scarce, but they do show a less favorable profile than that enjoyed by many industrial societies. However, it should be remembered that our present life expectancy is a recent phenomenon that has been very costly in terms of medical research and technological advances. Furthermore, the benefits of our health system are not enjoyed equally by all members of our society. High infant mortality could be viewed as a relatively inexpensive and egalitarian tribal public health program that offered the reasonable expectation of a healthy and productive life for those surviving to age fifteen.

Some critics also suggest that certain tribal populations, such as the New Guinea highlanders, were "stunted" by nutritional deficiencies created by tribal culture and are "improved" by "acculturation" and cash cropping (Dennett & Connell, 1988). Although this argument does suggest that the health question requires careful evaluation, it does not invalidate the empirical generalizations already established. Nutritional deficiencies undoubtedly occurred in densely populated zones in the central New Guinea highlands. However, the specific case cited above may not be widely representative of other tribal groups even in New Guinea, and it does not address the facts of outside intrusion or the inequities inherent in the contemporary development process.

ECOCIDE

"How is it," asked a herdsman . . . "how is it that these hills can no longer give pasture to my cattle? In my father's day they were green and cattle thrived there; today there is no grass and my cattle starve." As one looked one saw that what had once been a green hill had become a raw red rock.

Jones, 1934

Progress not only brings new threats to the health of tribal peoples, but it also imposes new strains on the ecosystems upon which they must depend for their ultimate survival. The introduction of new technology, increased consumption, lowered mortality, and the eradication of all traditional controls have combined to replace what for most tribal peoples was a relatively stable balance between population and natural resources, with a new system that is imbalanced. Economic development is forcing *ecocide* on peoples who were once careful stewards of their resources. There is already a trend toward widespread environmental deterioration in tribal areas, involving resource depletion, erosion, plant and animal extinction, and a disturbing series of other previously unforeseen changes.

After the initial depopulation suffered by most tribal peoples during their engulfment by frontiers of national expansion, most tribal populations began to experience rapid growth. Authorities generally attribute this growth to the introduction of modern medicine and new health measures and the termination of intertribal warfare, which lowered mortality rates, as well as to new technology, which increased food production. Certainly all of these factors played a part, but merely lowering mortality rates would not have produced the rapid population growth that most tribal areas have experienced if traditional birth-spacing mechanisms had not been eliminated at the same time. Regardless of which factors were most important, it is clear that all of the natural and cultural checks on population growth have suddenly been pushed aside by culture change, while tribal lands have been steadily reduced and consumption levels have risen. In many tribal areas, environmental deterioration due to overuse of resources has set in, and in other areas such deterioration is imminent as resources continue to dwindle relative to the expanding population and increased use. Of course, population expansion by tribal peoples may have positive political consequences, because where tribals can retain or regain their status as local majorities they may be in a more favorable position to defend their resources against intruders.

Swidden systems and pastoralism, both highly successful economic systems under traditional conditions, have proven particularly vulnerable to increased population pressures and outside efforts to raise productivity beyond its natural limits. Research in Amazonia demonstrates that population pressures and related resource depletion can be created indirectly by official policies that restrict swidden peoples to smaller territories. Resource depletion itself can then become a powerful means of forcing tribal people into participating in the

FIGURE 8.3

This area in Botswana was formerly thornbush desert; now it is devastated by overgrazing related to government intervention that modified traditional cultural patterns. (R. Lee, Anthro-Photo.)

world-market economy—thus leading to further resource depletion. For example, Bodley and Benson (1979) showed how the Shipibo Indians in Peru were forced to further deplete their forest resources by cash cropping in the forest area to replace the resources that had been destroyed earlier by the intensive cash cropping necessitated by the narrow confines of their reserve. In this case, certain species of palm trees that had provided critical housing materials were destroyed by forest clearing and had to be replaced by costly purchased materials. Research by Gross (1979) and others showed similar processes at work among four tribal groups in central Brazil and demonstrated that the degree of market involvement increases directly with increases in resource depletion.

The settling of nomadic herders and the removal of prior controls on herd size have often led to serious overgrazing and erosion problems where these had not previously occurred. There are indications that the desertification problem in the Sahel region of Africa was aggravated by programs designed to settle nomads. The first sign of imbalance in a swidden system appears when the planting cycles are shortened to the point that garden plots are reused before sufficient forest regrowth can occur. If reclearing and planting continue in the same area, the natural patterns of forest succession may be disturbed irreversibly and the soil can be impaired permanently. An extensive tract of tropical rainforest in the lower Amazon of Brazil was reduced to a semiarid desert in just fifty years through such a process (Ackermann, 1964). The soils in the Azande area are also now seriously threatened with laterization and other problems as a result of the government-promoted cotton development scheme (McNeil, 1972).

The dangers of overdevelopment and the vulnerability of local resource systems have long been recognized by both anthropologists and tribal peoples themselves, but the pressures for change have been overwhelming. In 1948 the Maya villagers of Chan Kom complained to Redfield (1962) about the shortening of their swidden cycles, which they correctly attributed to increasing population pressures. Redfield told them, however, that they had no choice but to go "forward with technology" (Redfield, 1962:178). In Assam, swidden cycles were shortened from an average of twelve years to only two or three within just twenty years, and anthropologists warned that the limits of swiddening would soon be reached (Burling, 1963:311–312). In the Pacific, anthropologists warned of population pressures on limited resources as early as the 1930s (Keesing, 1941:64–65). These warnings seemed fully justified, considering the fact that the crowded Tikopians were prompted by population pressures on their tiny island to suggest that infanticide be legalized. The warnings have been dramatically reinforced since then by the doubling of Micronesia's population in just the fourteen years between 1958 and 1972, from 70,600 to 114,645, while consumption levels have soared. By 1985 Micronesia's population had reached 162,321.

The environmental hazards of economic development and rapid population growth have become generally recognized only since worldwide concerns over environmental issues began in the early 1970s. Unfortunately, there is as yet little indication that the leaders of the now developing nations are sufficiently concerned with environmental limitations. On the contrary, governments are forcing tribal peoples into a self-reinforcing spiral of population growth and intensified resource exploitation, which may be stopped only by environmental disaster or the total impoverishment of the tribals.

The reality of ecocide certainly focuses attention on the fundamental contrasts between tribal and industrial systems in their use of natural resources. In many respects the entire "victims of progress" issue hinges on natural resources, who controls them, and how they are managed. Tribal peoples are victimized because they control resources that outsiders demand. The resources exist because tribals managed them conservatively. However, as with the issue of the health consequences of detribalization, some anthropologists minimize the adaptive achievements of tribal groups and seem unwilling to concede that ecocide might be a consequence of cultural change. Critics attack an exaggerated "noble savage" image of tribals living in perfect harmony with nature and having no visible impact on their surroundings. They then show that tribals do in fact modify the environment, and they conclude that there is no significant difference between how tribals and industrial societies treat their environments. For example, Charles Wagley declared that Brazilian Indians such as the Tapirape

> are not "natural men." They have human vices just as we do. . . . They do not live "in tune" with nature any more than I do; in fact, they can often be as destructive of their environment, within their limitations, as some civilized men. The Tapirape are not innocent or childlike in any way.

> Wagley, 1977:302

Anthropologist Terry Rambo demonstrated that the Semang of the Malaysian rain forests have a measurable impact on their environment. In his monograph *Primitive Polluters*, Rambo (1985) reported that the Semang live in smoke-filled houses. They sneeze and spread germs, breathe, and thus emit carbon dioxide. They clear small gardens, contributing "particulate matter" to the air and disturbing the local climate because cleared areas proved measurably warmer and drier than the shady forest. Rambo concluded that his research "demonstrates the essential functional similarity of the environmental interactions of primitive and civilized societies" (1985:78) in contrast to a "noble savage" view (Bodley, 1983) which, according to Rambo (1985:2), mistakenly "claims that traditional peoples almost always live in essential harmony with their environment."

This is surely a false issue. To stress, as I do, that tribals tend to manage their resources for sustained yield within relatively self-sufficient subsistence economies is not to make them either innocent children or natural men. Nor is it to deny that tribals "disrupt" their environment and may never be in absolute "balance" with nature.

The ecocide issue is perhaps most dramatically illustrated by two sets of satellite photos taken over the Brazilian rain forests of Rôndonia (Allard & McIntyre, 1988:780–781). Photos taken in 1973, when Rôndonia was still a tribal domain, show virtually unbroken rain forest. The 1987 satellite photos, taken after just fifteen years of highway construction and "development" by outsiders, show more than 20 percent of the forest destroyed. The surviving Indians were being concentrated by FUNAI (Brazil's national Indian foundation) into what would soon become mere islands of forest in a ravaged landscape. It is irrelevant to quibble about whether tribals are noble, childlike, or innocent, or about the precise meaning of balance with nature, carrying capacity, or adaptation, to recognize that for the past 200 years rapid environmental deterioration on an unprecedented global scale has followed the wresting of control of vast areas of the world from tribal groups by resource-hungry industrial societies.

DEPRIVATION AND DISCRIMINATION

Contact with European culture has given them a knowledge of great wealth, opportunity and privilege, but only very limited avenues by which to acquire these things.

Crocombe, 1968

Unwittingly, tribal peoples have had the burden of perpetual relative deprivation thrust upon them by acceptance—either by themselves or by the governments administering them—of the standards of socioeconomic progress set for them by industrial civilizations. By comparison with the material wealth of industrial societies, tribal societies become, by definition, impoverished. They are then forced to transform their cultures and work to achieve what many economists now acknowledge to be unattainable goals. Even though in many cases the modest GNP goals set by development planners for the developing nations during the "development decade" of the 1960s were often met, the results were hardly noticeable for most of the tribal people involved. Population growth, environmental limitations, inequitable distribution of wealth, and the continued rapid growth of the industrialized nations have all meant that both the absolute and the relative gap between the rich and poor in the world is steadily widening. The prospect that tribal peoples will actually be able to attain the levels of resource consumption to which they are being encouraged to aspire is remote indeed except for those few groups who have retained effective control over strategic mineral resources.

Tribal peoples feel deprivation not only when the economic goals they have been encouraged to seek fail to materialize, but also when they discover that they are powerless, second-class citizens who are discriminated against and exploited by the dominant society. At the same time, they are denied the satisfactions of their traditional cultures, because these have been sacrificed in the process of modernization. Under the impact of major economic change family life is disrupted, traditional social controls are often lost, and many indicators of social anomie such as alcoholism, crime, delinquency, suicide, emotional disorders, and despair may increase. The inevitable frustration resulting from this continual deprivation finds expression in the cargo cults, revitalization movements, and a variety of other political and religious movements that have been widespread among tribal peoples following their disruption by industrial civilization.

· 9 ·

The Self-Determination Revival

Our plea to the world is to help us in our struggle to find a place in the world community where we can exercise our right to self-determination as a distinct people and as a nation.

The Dene Declaration (Watkins, 1977)

THE PREVIOUS CHAPTERS HAVE presented a rather gloomy picture. Throughout, tribal peoples have appeared largely as passive victims, except for episodes of armed resistance. It might, therefore, be easily assumed that their situation is hopeless. Indeed, many observers have confidently predicted the impending extinction of tribal peoples, but such a judgment would be premature. Almost imperceptibly, during the 1970s tribal peoples who had experienced overwhelming external pressures against their traditional cultures began forging new political structures that would help promote a viable accommodation with the national states surrounding them. Ideally, such an accommodation would be characterized by "self-determination" that would safeguard tribal ways of life from outside interference. As native people define it, self-determination would mean a return to full local political, economic, and cultural autonomy. As we shall see, this need not mean isolation from the metropolitan world, but rather that tribal peoples would be allowed to control affairs on their own terms within their own territories. As the preceding chapters have shown, self-determination of this kind has been lost in the push for progress in most parts of the tribal world. Regaining control of their destinies while retaining the vital elements of tribal culture is a difficult struggle, but it is being fought with surprising vigor by a newly emerging "indigenous peoples" movement. The term *indigenous peoples* is introduced here because it is used extensively by individuals and organizations who are involved in the struggle. The term itself will be examined in detail in following sections.

The present self-determination revival by indigenous peoples raises such critical issues as: Who are indigenous peoples? What are their objectives, and how can they be realized? Perhaps the most important questions center on the self-identity of indigenous peoples and the nature of their social, political, and economic institutions. These issues are especially important today, because many conflicting groups are clamoring for recognition, control over resources, and self-determination. This conflict creates a situation in which the uniqueness of indigenous peoples may continue to be overlooked and their claims may be ignored. The present chapter considers these questions in detail.

Who Are Indigenous Peoples?

The most obvious answer to the question, Who are indigenous peoples? is that they are who they say they are. However, the consciousness of sharing a common identity is only now developing among indigenous peoples. Furthermore, indigenous peoples have sometimes been justifiably reluctant to define themselves, because in the past "legal" definitions have been used by governments to divide and manipulate them. In 1977 the second general assembly of the World Council of Indigenous Peoples (WCIP) passed a resolution declaring that only indigenous peoples could define indigenous peoples. Indigenous peoples know who they are, and they know they are unique. Unfortunately, the few formal definitions they have offered have not always been adequate. The official definition used by the WCIP states:

> *Indigenous people shall be people living in countries which have populations composed of different ethnic or racial groups who are descendants of the earliest populations which survive in the area, and who do not, as a group, control the national government of the countries within which they live.*

WCIP information leaflet

This is basically a political definition that says nothing about special cultural characteristics, nor does it distinguish indigenous people from any national ethnic minorities who are "native" to a country. By this definition, if indigenous peoples were to be recognized as independent sovereign nations, controlling their own national governments, they would suddenly cease to be indigenous peoples. Regardless of these difficulties, there is no doubt that the term *indigenous peoples* is now the most widely accepted global term for the distinctive groups we are concerned with here. There are other generic terms that have gained wide regional acceptance by some indigenous peoples, but that are rejected in other parts of the world. The term *Indian* or *Indio* is now widely accepted in the Americas, but the Eskimo peoples now prefer to call themselves *Inuit* and have never considered themselves to be Indians. The term *tribal* is accepted by many native peoples in Amazonia and the Philippines, but may be rejected elsewhere.

Of course, the real issue is not the label used, but the underlying common identity among indigenous peoples. When leaders from diverse cultures meet each other for the first time, they are overwhelmed by the fact that they share the same basic culture in spite of their often conspicuous, but superficial, differences. As will become apparent in the case studies later in this chapter, indigenous peoples throughout the world are independently saying exactly the same things when they describe the elements that make them different from the dominant societies surrounding them. The first shared trait that is invariably mentioned is their relationship to the land. As Julio Carduño, a Mexican Indian leader, declared at the First Congress of South American Indian Movements held in Cuzco in 1980:

> *Perhaps what most unites us is the defense of our land. The land has never been merchandise for us, as it is with capitalism, but it is the support for our cultural universe.*
>
> Carduño, 1980:112–113, my translation

We have noted repeatedly in other chapters that land is communally held by indigenous peoples. The land cannot be sold, even though there may be many different systems for regulating individual access. Native leaders often state that their land system is equitable and that no exact parallel to it exists in any industrial nations, socialist countries included. Indigenous peoples are also united in opposition to technologies and development projects that they consider destructive and unnecessary. They consider themselves more sensitive to the need to protect their land from environmental deterioration than are those who would take the land from them. This view was presented by Carduño at the Cuzco conference in the following terms:

> *There can be no economic interest superior to the necessity of preserving the ecosystem; we do not want a bonanza today at the cost of a desolate future.*
>
> Carduño, 1980:120–121, my translation

There are other shared features of the social and political systems of indigenous peoples that present sharp contrasts to other national systems, minority groups, or political parties. Leaders of the emerging indigenous peoples' self-determination movement see their own societies as classless, community-based, egalitarian, and close to nature. On the other hand, they see the societies around them as highly stratified, centralized, individualistic, antinature, and highly secular. These opposing constellations of traits do, in fact, pinpoint the most crucial differences that anthropologists recognize between the idealized tribal cultures and modern nation-states (see, for example, Diamond, 1968, and Redfield, 1953). Some anthropologists might argue that no society was ever really egalitarian and that all contemporary tribal societies have irrevocably lost whatever ideal features they may have once possessed, but today's indigenous leaders do not agree.

Certainly, not all indigenous peoples accept the idealized view of their traditional culture, nor do they necessarily all support the self-determination movement. Many individuals may find the personal rewards potentially available in the dominant society to be more attractive than the traditional tribal life style. It is significant, however, that those who are prominent in the self-determination movement have usually had extensive experience and opportunities in the dominant society but have rejected it in favor of their own culture, which they consider to be superior. An example of this attitude was demonstrated by a Bolivian Indian leader when he attempted to explain to a journalist in Amsterdam why the Indian movement rejected Marxism. To make his point, he outlined general differences between Indian and Western social systems and discussed the advantages of Indian methods of wealth and power regulation, concluding:

> We think that this [Indian method] is an original way of solving the problem of individual wealth accumulation and political power at the same time, but it seems absurd to westerners. We want to conserve our institutions not only because they are ours, but also because we consider them just.
>
> Portugal, 1980:177, my translation

Objectives of the New Movements

What we want is to have the tools to run our own lives and to participate as equals in the greater life of Canada as a whole. The principal tools are, simply, reasonable Inuit land claims settlements and a Nunavut territorial government.

from the brief of the Nunavut Constitutional Forum
(NCF) to the Royal Commission on the Economic Union
and Development Prospects for Canada, Patterson, 1984:52

In the past government officials, missionaries, anthropologists, and other experts have endlessly debated the best policies for indigenous peoples. The usual solution was to recommend integration into the dominant society, perhaps blending "the best of both worlds." The natives themselves were seldom consulted, because either no one thought the natives knew what was good for them or no one was seriously concerned about their real desires. However, it is now apparent that indigenous leaders of the self-determination movement do have a clear conception of who indigenous peoples are. They also know what needs must be accommodated if their cultures are to remain a viable alternative to the perceived deficits of industrial civilization. The specific objectives of different indigenous groups may vary widely according to local conditions, as will be seen in the case studies that follow, but self-determination is the common theme, and control over traditional lands is always an overriding objective.

There have been many cases in which indigenous peoples would approach government officials with well-reasoned proposals that would permit their cultural autonomy and continued well-being. However, such proposals have seldom been accepted. For example, in 1975 representatives from thirty-four Guajibo communities in the Colombian llanos presented the government with a formal petition for the establishment of a reserve measuring 20,000 square kilometers for the 40,000 Guajibo, the traditional residents of the region. They argued that not only did they know how to take care of the land, but that they also had a rightful claim to it, unlike the twenty colonists who had illegally moved in. They also rejected a previous recommendation for a series of small Guajibo reserves, because such fragmentation would facilitate their eventual destruction (*Unidad Indigena*, 1975, I[1]: 4). In 1976 the Inuit Tapirisat (Eskimo) of Canada presented the Canadian government with a proposal for the establishment of a special territory to be known as *Nunavut*, which means "our land" in the Inuit language. Nunavut would consist of the nearly 2 million square kilometers of traditional Inuit land that was never surrendered by treaty, where the Inuit continue to be the dominant inhabitants. The Inuit wanted full ownership of some 648,000 square kilometers and exclusive hunting and fishing rights over the remainder. As the majority population, they proposed that they should control the regional government as well as the regulation of any resource development of Nunavut, which would ensure their primary objective of self-sufficiency.

In their 1982 letter to the provincial Prime Ministers of Canada, the Inuit Committee on National Issues (ICNI) eloquently presented their position on the constitutional guarantees that they required as the minimum conditions for the recognition of their basic rights and to set the stage for the creation of Nunavut. Specifically, they wanted the following principles to be protected:

> i. The collective recognition of the aboriginal peoples as distinct peoples in Canada due to our occupation of our lands since time immemorial, including the protection of our cultures, histories and lifestyles, and flowing from this principle:
> ii. The recognition of our political rights to self-governing institutions (structures) of various kinds within the Canadian Confederation; and
> iii. The recognition of our economic rights to our lands and waters, their resources and their benefits, as a base for self-sufficiency and the development of native communities and families, including the protection of our traditional livelihoods.

> cited in IWGIA Newsletter, 1983, 33:114

In 1982 the Inuit voted overwhelmingly in a plebescite in favor of the establishment of Nunavut as a politically separate Inuit territory. Shortly thereafter, the Nunavut Constitutional Forum (NCF) and the Canadian federal government agreed in principle to the establishment of Nunavut (Patterson, 1984). The forum made it clear that what they were seeking was not an ethnically or racially based political division, but rather a division based on peoples who were

FIGURE 9.1

Map showing Nunavut Territory as originally proposed in 1976, including some 2 million square kilometers of land spread over an area larger than the eastern third of the United States. (From *Vort land, vort liv* (Our Land, Our Life) by Helge Kleivan. Institute for Eskimology, Copenhagen University, no. 3, 1976. Map drawn by Jørgen Ulrich. Also in IWGIA Newsletter, 1983, 34:31.)

permanent residents of a natural region and who practiced a traditional economy based on renewable resources. Additional and more detailed proposals for the design of Nunavut were presented by Inuit representatives at a constitutional conference held in 1983, in which they emphasized that Nunavut was to be a form of self-government within the Canadian federal tradition. Final agreements on specific boundaries of Nunavut were not completed until 1988.

In both the case of the Guajibo and the Inuit, the governments involved have refused to respond favorably. However, the point is clear: Indigenous peoples do know what they want, but they often have been thwarted in realizing their objectives.

In rare cases, indigenous peoples have successfully been able to *force* governments to accept their proposals. In 1925 the Kuna Indians were able to take advantage of the relative political and military weakness of the Panamanian government and declared themselves an independent nation. The Kuna fought a brief armed rebellion before the government compromised with them in 1930 and accepted the Kuna plan for the establishment of an autonomous Kuna reserve (Falla, 1979a). This reserve still exists today as the *Comarca Kuna*, and the lands within it continue to be communally held by the 28,000 resident Kuna who carefully restrict use of their resources by outsiders (Falla, 1979b). The Kuna run their own internal affairs and send three representatives to the Panamanian national assembly. Since 1980 the Kuna have aligned themselves with international conservation groups, such as the World Wildlife Fund, to turn their territory into an internationally recognized biosphere reserve to afford even greater protection to its vulnerable resources (Nietschmann, 1988; Wright, Houseal, & Leon, 1985). They are especially concerned with defending the rainforest-covered watershed against a potential invasion by settlers. The Comarca Kuna constitutes what is, in effect, a province within Panama, but it remains a uniquely Kuna, highly traditional, and self-sufficient area. The objectives achieved are basically the same as those being sought by the Canadian Inuit and Dene peoples, who are engaged in a strictly political struggle with the Canadian government.

THE POLITICAL STRUGGLE

In many respects, the problems confronting indigenous peoples are political power problems: Indigenous peoples are being destroyed because they lack the political power to adequately defend themselves against dominant societies and to press for their demands. Unfortunately, the obvious solution of seeking political power is not as easy as it might seem. In the past, nonstate peoples have sometimes consolidated in self-defense against invading states, transforming themselves into states, only to lose their unique features in the process. Fortunately, stateless societies have devised many ingenious ways of regulating political power. Today, indigenous peoples are designing political structures that permit the consolidation of a power base to successfully confront states without sacrificing their egalitarian and communal characteristics. On the other hand, tribal societies are often numerically weak and face the difficult task of combining with ethnically different, often hostile, neighboring groups. To further complicate matters, they must win allies in the dominant society. Regardless of the difficulties, in recent years there has been a steady emergence of regional, national, and international indigenous political organizations that have been working with increasing success for the self-determination of indigenous peoples.

Genuine native political organizations can accomplish many critical tasks. Perhaps the most important task is the double role of keeping the traditional heritage strong and organizing often widely dispersed and demoralized peoples into a united force to confront the common external threat. Acting in concert, indigenous peoples can press their demands with much greater visibility and effectiveness. Simply bringing local cases to national and international attention is an important function, because many of the most serious assaults on native peoples are illegal, according to national legislation and widely recognized international agreements. Under the embarrassing glare of international publicity, national governments have, in certain cases, been forced to take action on behalf of native peoples. It is also likely that most of the recent improvements that have taken place in official policies have been a direct result of the steadily increasing political power of indigenous peoples.

The unifying role of native political organizations is often carried out by holding periodic local and regional assemblies where common problems are discussed and resolutions passed. Many organizations have increasingly come to rely on their own published newspapers, magazines, and newsletters. In a few cases, groups have operated their own radio broadcasting systems and have gained control over their own formal educational institutions. Native political organizations vary widely in the details of their structures and exist at different levels. Some may be small, local groups representing single homogeneous ethnic groups. Others are regional federations, perhaps united on the basis of a more remote cultural heritage. In many countries there are now national-level indigenous peoples organizations, and more recently, a World Council of Indigenous Peoples (WCIP) has been formed.

Although the basic objectives of these new political organizations are remarkably similar throughout the world, the context of the political struggle varies considerably from country to country. This makes it difficult to generalize about strategies and prospects. In order to give a clearer picture of the complexities of this ongoing struggle, case studies will be presented in the following sections illustrating examples from Ecuador, Colombia, Canada, Australia, and the Philippines. These cases by no means exhaust the field—there are many other important indigenous political organizations, particularly in North, Central, and South America, that will not be discussed. The cases examined, however, do provide a reasonable sample of the problems that indigenous organizations face and how they are dealing with them. In the South American examples that are examined, Indian political organizations confront powerful local elites who are often closely allied with civil and military forces within national governments. These forces are often hostile to the acquisition of political power by any native groups. Here, the indigenous struggle can easily be understood as part of a larger class struggle, although the Indians generally do not regard themselves as part of the class system and are often suspicious of alliances with leftist groups. In the Canadian and Australian examples, the governments may be supportive of native political organizations, but they also have a conflicting interest in encouraging large corporations to extract resources from tribal lands. Here, however, there is no pronounced class struggle and there may be considerable popular support for native peoples. The Philippines example represents a case where emerging tribal organizations faced a hostile dictatorship that was allied with multinational corporations. Meanwhile, the country is divided by a strongly polarized national class system and ongoing armed liberation movements.

THE SHUAR SOLUTION

A culture that evolves by itself and finds in itself new solutions for new problems, is more alive than ever.

Federación de Centros Shuar, 1976:130, my translation

The Shuar are a forest-dwelling group in Ecuador, who by their own estimate numbered over 26,000 people in 1975. Traditionally, they were self-sufficient cultivators and hunters, living in dispersed extended families. Together with other Jivaroan-speaking groups in neighboring Peru, they were widely known as "headhunters" and for their successful resistance to foreign domination since the arrival of the Spanish in 1540. The Shuar still retained control over much of their traditional territory and their basic culture remained viable well into the present century. However, by 1959 they were outnumbered by colonists and were rapidly losing their most valuable subsistence lands. Their entire way of life was threatened with disintegration.

At this point the Shuar in the most heavily invaded areas set about developing what they called an "original self-solution" to the crisis. They concluded that their situation had been irrevocably altered by circumstances, but felt that they could still make a satisfying adjustment. The basic objective was to retain control over their own futures—they sought self-determination. They realized that the key to self-determination lay in retaining an adequate community land base, which would require effective participation in the government colonization program. If the Shuar sought individual land titles, only a few would succeed, given the pro-colonist bias in the entitlement process. In the end the Shuar community would be destroyed. The solution was the creation in 1964 of a fully independent, but officially recognized, corporate body—a federation, based on regional associations of many local Shuar communities. The federation became a legal entity, the *Federación de Centros Shuar*, that as of 1978 contained some 20,000 members organized into 160 local centers and 13 regional associations (Zallez & Gortaire, 1978). According to the Federation's official statutes, the basic objectives of the organization are to promote the social, economic, and moral advancement of its members and to coordinate development efforts with official government agencies. There are elected officials with carefully specified duties and five specialized commissions to deal with such matters as health, education, and land.

The Federation quickly opted for a system of community land titles through the appropriate government body IERAC (*Instituto Ecuatoriano de Reforma Agraria y Colonización*) and promoted cooperative cattle ranching as the new economic base. Cattle ranching was especially important because land was titled on the basis of actual use and the legitimate requirement for pastureland was greater than for other forms of land use. The Federation obtained financial and technical assistance from various national and international agencies; by 1975, 95,704 hectares were securely in community titles. By 1978 the cattle herd had grown to more than 15,000 head and had become the primary source of outside income.

With the approval and support of the Ecuadorian ministry of education, and with the cooperation of the Salesian mission, the Federation has developed an education system suited to local needs and supportive of the traditional culture. Much of the instruction utilizes the Shuar language and Shuar teachers. In order to minimize the family disruption caused by boarding schools, and to spread educational opportunities as widely as possible, the Federation established its own system of radio-broadcast bilingual education beginning in 1972. The program has successfully reduced the elementary school role of the mission-operated boarding schools, which have now been converted into technical schools for advanced training. The Federation has operated its own radio station since 1968, broadcasting in both Shuar and Spanish. In addition, since 1972 it has published a bilingual newspaper, *Chicham*, the official organ of the Shuar Federation. The story of the Shuar and their confrontation with the national society is also presented in a motion picture, *The Sound of Rushing Water*, produced by the Shuar themselves.

The Federation solution is in many ways unique in Amazonia. The Shuar are the only native group to have retained such effective control over its own future. The initiative for the major adaptive changes that have occurred in the Shuar system as well as the administration of the entire program has been carried out by the Shuar themselves. Of course, the Federation itself was a response to uninvited outside pressures, and its early formation was facilitated by the Salesian missionaries who had been in the area since 1893, but there is no doubt that the Shuar have created a distinctly *Shuar* solution to the problem. The Federation has not yet become fully self-sufficient, but it has drawn on a broad base of financial support so that no single outside interest has been able to assert undesired influence. Technical volunteers from many countries have been recruited on a temporary basis, but they have not dominated any programs.

The Shuar are proud of the Federation and of the gains they have made. They recognize that they have had to make enormous changes in their culture, but they feel that they are still Shuar. Certainly, many traditional patterns have been abandoned with few regrets, and many material elements are disappearing or have been converted to the tourist trade. But the Federation has succeeded in strengthening the Shuar language and cultural identity and in securing a viable resource base. The Shuar are actively promoting selected qualities that they feel represent the essence of their culture and that clearly distinguish them from their non-Indian neighbors. These qualities include: communal land tenure, cooperative production and distribution, a basically egalitarian economy, kin-based local communities with maximum autonomy, and a variety of distinctive cultural markers.

The Federation has not existed without problems. Understandably, the colonists have resented its successes. In 1969 the Federation's central office was burned down, presumably by colonists, and Federation leaders have been jailed and tortured for crimes for which they were never convicted (Zallez & Gortaire, 1978:78; see also IWGIA Newsletter, 1978–1979, nos. 20–23). Although the Ecuadorian government officially recognizes and cooperates with the Federation, actual support for their programs has been sporadic, and outside interests have consistently been favored by government agencies over the needs of the Shuar. The government has also forcefully attempted to prevent the Shuar from promoting the political organization of other Ecuadorian Indians and generally seems opposed to the idea of Ecuador becoming a multiethnic nation (see Whitten, 1976). The Federation has also been criticized by leftist organizations for accepting aid from capitalists, while some missionaries have accused Federation leaders of being communists. In the long run, the Federation faces other problems as well. Economic differentiation related to cattle ranching and the gradual emergence of an educated and salaried elite may be difficult to contain within the traditional egalitarian ideal to which the Federation still aspires. Furthermore, the present Shuar land base, which is broken up into discontinuous islands, may prove in a short time to be inadequate for the needs of a growing population.

INDIAN UNITY IN COLOMBIA

Without unity we will never have the force to defend our land and the future of our children.

Unidad Indigena, 1975 1(1):1

Since 1971 at least five major regional Indian organizations have emerged in Colombia. As with the Shuar in Ecuador, the primary focus of all of these organizations has been to fight for control of traditional Indian lands, for traditional forms of organization, and for their language and culture. These new organizations include: CRIC, the Regional Indian Council of the Cauca in the southern Andean region; UNDICH, the Union of Chocó Indians of the western lowlands; COIA, the Arhuaco Indian Congress of the Sierra Nevada of northern Colombia; CRIVA, the Regional Indian Council of the Vaupes in the forested eastern lowlands; and UNUMA of the eastern llano Guajibo peoples. The activities of these organizations, as well as other more localized groups, are covered by a nationally distributed newspaper, *Unidad Indigena*. The First National Indigenous Congress was held in 1982 near Bogotá. It was attended by 2,500 people representing twenty-five indigenous groups from Colombia, plus many international guests, especially from neighboring countries. The congress established the first permanent national-level Indian organization in Colombia, the *Organización Nacional Indígena de Colombia* (ONIC), which was dedicated to indigenous autonomy and the defense of indigenous communal territory and resources (IWGIA Newsletter, 1982, 30:60–64, 31/32:30–38). An official statement issued by the congress's commission on land and settlers defined the most critical issue facing Indian groups in Colombia:

Indian land and all of its resources belong to the community and should be placed totally under the control of the community's internal authority; land should never be divided up as private property.

IWGIA Newsletter, 1982, 30:61

These organizations have effectively raised Indian pride in their own identity, promoted widespread awareness of common problems, and they have presented realistic proposals to the Colombian government from a position of considerable strength. Significant gains have been made in some areas, but serious opposition has also been aroused. The example of CRIC will be discussed in detail because it was the earliest organization to be established in Colombia and has become a model for other groups.

The Colombian department of Cauca in the southwest corner of Colombia contains one of the densest Indian concentrations in the country. Reliable figures are unavailable, but there may now be over 200,000 Chibcha-speaking Paez and Guambiano Indians in a department that counted a total population of over 600,000 people in 1968. This is a mountainous region of large coffee plantations, where in 1970 80 percent of the agricultural land was held by a mere 14 percent of the landowners (DANE, 1978:106–107, table 41). The Indians were conquered by the Spanish in the sixteenth century and were allocated communally held reservations, or *resguardos*, and their own form of internal self-government, the *cabildo* system. The reservations were to be permanently removed from the land market, and it seems that the Indians enjoyed a relatively secure existence in spite of the colonial oppression that they faced in the form of labor and tribute payments. However, in the nineteenth century, the reserves began to be invaded by colonists and the government initiated termination proceedings. Throughout the present century, many reserves have been eliminated entirely and the protesting Indians have been crowded into smaller and smaller reserves that, in many cases, have become inadequate to their needs. The Indians fought protracted legal battles for the defense of these fragmented lands, but little was achieved.

The picture began to change dramatically in 1971 when 2,000 Indians from ten reserves held a mass meeting and organized CRIC (*Consejo Regional Indigena del Cauca*) to coordinate the Indian struggle throughout the Cauca region. The new organization was formed as a federation, and the governing body consisted of representatives from each of the reserves. Annual congresses were convened and by 1973, forty-five local reserves had joined. CRIC's original objectives were specified in the following seven points (Cartilla del CRIC no. 1, cited Corry, 1976:43–47; see also IWGIA Newsletter, 1980, 24:19–26), which remain the basis of its program:

1. To recuperate the reservation lands
2. To increase the size of the reservations
3. To strengthen the Indian Councils (cabildos)

4. To stop the payment of illegal land rents
5. To make known the laws concerning Indians and to insist on their proper application
6. To defend the history, language, and customs of the Indians
7. To train Indian teachers to teach in the Indian language in ways that are applicable to the present situation of the people

In an unequivocal answer to those who might suggest that they have been too heavily acculturated by 400 years of reservation life to still be considered Indians, they emphatically state, "We are Indians, and we believe that it is good to be an Indian" (Corry, 1976:43). The Cauca Indians have much in common with the local peasantry, and indeed both see the large landowners as enemies, but the Indians are specific about what makes them unique. They of course point to their ancestry, language, dress, and customs, but they also emphasize their economic egalitarianism:

> We are Indians because we believe that the things of the world are made for everyone. It is like saying that since we are all equal, the means of living should also be equal. . . . Because of this, we believe that the land, just as the air, the water and all the other things which keep us alive should not be only for the few. The land should not be owned, but should be communal. . . . This is why we like the reservations. Because there, the lands must all be shared out between all the members of the community.
>
> Cartilla del CRIC no. 1, cited Corry, 1976:43

The primary struggle has, of course, been over land. The CRIC strategy has been to reorganize the councils that have been terminated and to campaign for the restoration of the old reserves or for the extension of existing reserves by legal appeals through INCORA (*Instituto Colombiano de la Reforma Agraria*), the government agrarian reform office. When legal means fail, the Indians nonviolently occupy the lands they claim and begin to cultivate them. Arrests usually follow, but in many cases their legitimate claims are recognized. Within three years 5,000 hectares had been recovered and the "rents" charged Indians on lands illegally expropriated from them were eventually abolished.

The early successes of CRIC resulted in countermeasures from the local power structure. At first the landowners threatened CRIC leaders and attempted to control the cabildos. When these measures failed, the government moved to block Indian assemblies. Finally, in 1974, assassinations began and critical areas of the Cauca were militarized. Key CRIC leaders were arrested under the pretext that CRIC was a subversive organization linked to the M-19 leftist guerrillas. By 1979, thirty CRIC leaders, including the CRIC president, were imprisoned. In 1982 CRIC claimed that eighty-two of its leaders had been killed by state, church, and economic interests opposed to its objectives. Leftist, antigovernment guerrilla forces also claimed responsibility for killing seven CRIC members who they considered "counterrevolutionaries." The violence in

Cauca continued in 1987, when twenty-two Indian communities were reportedly attacked and 239 indigenous people were arrested (IWGIA Yearbook 1987:23).

THE DENE NATION: LAND, NOT MONEY

The Dene Indians of the Canadian Northwest Territories are one of the best examples of the self-determination revival in North America. These Athapaskan-speaking peoples, who number about 17,000, are scattered throughout some 725,000 square kilometers of the great Mackenzie Valley (McCullum, McCullum, & Olthuis, 1977:40). In this area, just as their ancestors did for thousands of years before them, they continue to rely on moose, caribou, and fish for much of their subsistence. Since approximately 1790, when they began to be drawn into the fur trade, their economic self-reliance has been gradually reduced. However, their egalitarian regional economy, based on kinship reciprocity, has remained strong. When the world fur market declined after World War II, the Canadian government responded to the "crisis" by attempting to push the Dene into full dependence on the stratified, highly individualistic wage-labor economy. In order to receive their welfare checks and to keep their children in school, the Dene were encouraged to settle in towns. This sedentary life made traditional subsistence pursuits more difficult (Asch, 1977). By the late 1960s, Dene society and culture was showing obvious signs of stress, but even more serious threats loomed when in 1968 oil was discovered at Prudhoe Bay in Alaska. The Canadian government immediately proposed converting the Mackenzie Valley into an "energy corridor" for pipelines to move Arctic oil and gas to consumers in the United States and southern Canada. The Dene then had real fears that their entire way of life was in jeopardy.

In 1970, under the slogan "Land and Unity," the Dene formed the Indian Brotherhood of the Northwest Territories, combining all of the scattered tribes into a single political organization capable of mounting an effective struggle for recognition of their rights to the land and an independent existence. Their first major political act, in 1973, was the filing of a legal caveat with the Territorial court that registered their prior claim to the land in order to block any further development without their approval. They were able to demonstrate that the treaties of 1899 and 1921, which supposedly cancelled their land rights, were fraudulent, and they obtained a favorable ruling on the caveat. The pipeline companies and the Department of Indian and Northern Affairs were appalled at the decision, which was overturned by the Supreme Court in 1976 on a technicality, but it did serve to demonstrate the validity of the native claim.

The Dene political movement gradually began to take shape. In 1974 more than 250 native people from throughout the Mackenzie Valley met at Fort Good Hope. They had before them the unfortunate example of the Alaska natives, who had been forced to accept the poorly conceived Native Claims Settlement

Act of 1971 in order to clear the way for the Alaska pipeline. At Fort Good Hope the Dene agreed emphatically that they wanted their rights recognized, not extinguished—they wanted "land, not money." Their position was clarified the following year at a second assembly of 250 Dene at Fort Simpson, at which a formal Dene Declaration was drawn up. In this eloquent statement, the Dene pointed out that they were a majority within the Northwest Territories, yet they had not been allowed to control their own future. They declared themselves to be a distinct people and a "nation." They also called for recognition of their right to self-determination as native peoples within the Canadian nation. They were not, of course, seeking independent nation-state status. Their proposal was reasonable in terms of the Canadian Constitution (Russell, 1977), but they were immediately accused of being separatists, racists, or "socialists."

In order to fully document their claim to the land, in 1974–1976 the Dene carried out an extensive two-year research project into their own land-use practices. They interviewed one-third of the Dene hunters and trappers from throughout their territory and plotted on large-scale maps the areas they utilized. This work revealed a maze of trails and traplines in an area that, to outsiders, would look like only wilderness. This demonstrated beyond any doubt that the Dene were indeed still a hunting people. Whether considered in terms of the numbers of people involved, the cash value of the resources obtained, or the actual contribution to the diet, traditional use of the land was absolutely vital for the Dene (Nahanni, 1977; Rushforth, 1977).

In spite of the mounting native resistance to the proposed pipeline, the major energy companies pressed ahead with their plans. In order to satisfy all the legal requirements that blocked final approval of the pipeline, the Canadian government commissioned a formal study of the project and its possible implications for the north. The inquiry was conducted by British Columbia Supreme Court Justice Thomas R. Berger, who took the unprecedented step of seeking direct testimony and written documents from the Dene people. For several months in 1975–1976 he visited every major town and settlement in the Mackenzie Valley and heard from nearly a thousand people. In his final report, issued in 1977, Berger expressed strong support for native self-determination and argued that the pipeline should be delayed for at least ten years to allow sufficient time for a just settlement of native claims. The Dene had presented a compelling case.

In fact, the Canadian government was taking seriously the Dene demand for self-determination. In 1976 the Minister of Indian Affairs asked the Dene to prepare a formal position paper so that negotiations on their land claim could begin. In this "Agreement-in-Principle," the Dene appealed to international law and United Nations declarations in support of their right to self-determination. They listed sixteen principles as a basis for negotiations, including the following:

1. The Dene have the right to recognition, self-determination, and ongoing growth as a People and as a Nation.

2. The Dene, as Aboriginal People, have the right to retain ownership of so much of their traditional lands, and under such terms, as to ensure their

independence and self-reliance, traditionally, economically and socially. (Watkins, 1977)

The Agreement-in-Principle claimed that it was the Dene's place to define themselves and thereby avoided the divisiveness of a formal definition of who they were. They stated simply, "The Dene know who they are." Who the Dene are is implicit in their concept of self-determination. Self-determination for the Dene means following the Dene system and not the dominant system of southern Canada. As George Barnaby, vice-president of the Indian Brotherhood of the Northwest Territories, explained, the Dene system means a cooperative community life based on sharing, joint decision making, and communal land ownership (Barnaby, Kurszewski, & Cheezie, 1977:120–121).

In 1981 the Dene struggle for land and political autonomy moved closer to victory with the formation of the Aboriginal Rights Coalition, which brought together all aboriginal groups in Canada, including the various Inuit, Indian, and Metis (mixed French and Indian) organizations to press for explicit inclusion of aboriginal rights in the Canadian Constitution, which was being rewritten as part of Canada's formal break of its colonial ties to Britain (Jull, 1982). From 1983 to 1987 four nationally televised conferences were held involving government officials and native leaders to work out the details of a constitutional arrangement for native self-government (Jull, 1987). These meetings prepared the way for a final agreement in principle, which was signed in September of 1988 by William Erasmus, president of the Dene Nation, and Canadian Prime Minister Brian Mulroney. Under the terms of this agreement, the Dene receive full title to some 10,000 square kilometers of land, with both surface and subsurface mineral rights. They receive surface rights and significant mineral royalties over another 170,000 square kilometers, as well as traditional land use rights to more than 1 million square kilometers and a 500-million-dollar cash settlement. The precise details of Dene self-government were still to be worked out, but clearly this was a major achievement, and it has been called the largest land transfer in Canadian history.

LAND RIGHTS AND THE OUTSTATION MOVEMENT IN AUSTRALIA

What is happening is an Aboriginal revival, a reversal—if you like—of frontiers. No longer is the government pushing Aboriginals back. It is Aboriginals who today are pushing Governments back.

Australia, DAA 1977, Aboriginal
Affairs Minister, R. I. Viner, Perth, 1977

Australian Aborigines have refused to either die out or be assimilated. Today they are struggling with increasing success to gain legal control over their lands, and they are abandoning government settlements in favor of traditionally oriented communities in the bush. The catalyst for the present revival was the full-scale assault in the mid-1960s by multinational mining corporations on the aboriginal reserves in Arnhem Land and Cape York Peninsula. These regions in the Northern Territory and northern Queensland contained large populations of Aborigines who still lived on their ancestral lands. Unfortunately, the land also contained outstanding bauxite deposits. The Aborigines were opposed to mining because they knew it would mean destruction of their traditional economy and of their sacred sites, as well as a disruption of their societies. However, the government approved the mining projects, completely disregarding aboriginal protests. Ultimately, the mining did proceed, but the Aborigines did not give up. Their resistance attracted the attention of Aborigines and white supporters throughout Australia and resulted in a major land rights political struggle.

In 1968 the Yirrkala people of the Gove peninsula in Arnhem Land initiated legal proceedings in order to establish their aboriginal claim, arguing that the government and the mining companies had illegally appropriated their lands. In 1971 the court finally ruled against them, but this decision only served to draw attention to the blatant injustice of official Australian policies toward aboriginal land claims, which intensified the opposition to those policies. Aborigines began to organize public demonstrations on an unprecedented scale to demand changes in the law. Early in 1972 an "Aboriginal Embassy" was established in a tent in front of the parliament building in Canberra. It was torn down by police, only to be reerected, and remained for six months as an irritating symbol to the Australian government of their injustices to Aborigines. Finally, in December of 1972 the Labour party came to power on a pro-Aborigine platform, and genuine changes in official policy began to take shape.

The first concrete action on the part of the new government was the establishment in 1973 of an Aboriginal Land Rights Commission under Justice A. E. Woodward to determine how to implement a just land policy. The Woodward Commission reports, which came out in 1973 and 1974, strongly recommended that Aborigines in the Northern Territory be given title to their reserved lands and that they be able to prohibit mining on those lands. It also recommended that the Aborigines be allowed to claim unalienated crown lands outside of the established reserves if they could demonstrate traditional ties, and it called for the establishment of aboriginal-run land councils to implement the new policies. Officially there was at last to be an end to injustice, repression, and the old assimilation policy. According to the new Australian prime minister, E. G. Whitlaw, the primary objective of the new policy would be

> to restore to the Aboriginal people of Australia their lost power of self-determination in economic, social and political affairs.

> cited Pittock, 1975:30

The Labour government did propose a progressive aboriginal land rights bill, but before it could be approved they were thrown out of office and replaced by a much more cautious government which proceeded to rewrite and significantly weaken the land rights bill. Angered over the modifications, Aborigines organized a National Aboriginal Land Rights Conference in Sydney in August of 1976 where they presented a formal declaration outlining their conditions for a satisfactory land right settlement as follows:

1. Acknowledgment that all Aborigines, wherever they live, share a claim to land, which was totally the Aborigines' land prior to the arrival of White settlers who stole it from them.
2. That to remedy this injustice, Aborigines must be granted freehold control of all lands they rightfully claim, and total compensation for those lands previously taken away.
3. That the return of all lands to the Aboriginal people must include total control of minerals, forests, fishing, coastal waters, and all other aspects of the land, together with the right to control their own destiny on the land. (pamphlet, National Aboriginal Land Rights Conference, Sydney, 1976)

When the Aboriginal Land Rights (Northern Territory) Act of 1976 became law in January of 1977, it rejected most of the above demands. However, this act still represented at least a partial victory for Aborigines and can be seen as a major concession coming from a government that for nearly 200 years had stubbornly refused to recognize the legitimacy of any aboriginal land claims. The act created a legal basis for defending existing reserves and for extending them in some cases. Under the act, the Aborigines organized representative land councils in the Northern Territory and have worked vigorously to help local communities document their land claims. The councils have negotiated with mining companies and the government to minimize the detrimental impact of development projects on their lands. Unfortunately, under the present terms of the Land Rights Act, state and territorial governments retain considerable control over the administration of aboriginal land and the Aborigines cannot prevent mining that is considered to be in the "national interest." The two aboriginal land councils in the Northern Territory are officially recognized and are supported by a percentage of the royalties from mining on reserve lands. Aborigines in Queensland and Western Australia have also now organized their own unofficial land councils, and they are pressing for legal control over their lands as well.

After passage of the Land Rights Act, there were attempts to establish nationally endorsed land rights legislation as a model for the other Australian states, but by 1986 the federal government decided to permit the individual states to continue making their own land policies. At the same time, there were moves by mining and pastoral interests to weaken the Northern Territory Land Rights Act of 1976 with amendments to reduce aboriginal control over mining and aboriginal benefits from mining royalties and to halt the conversion of pastoral leases to aboriginal lands (IWGIA Yearbook 1986:37). Along with these apparent setbacks, there have been some positive moves, however. In

FIGURE 9.2

Malak Malak claimants erect a sacred site
sign on the Kilfoyle waterhole in the Daly
River land claim area, 1979. (Arthur B.
Palmer, Northern Land Council, Darwin,
Australia.)

anticipation of the 1988 bicentennial year, as early as 1983 the federal government indicated that it was ready to acknowledge that Australia was not in fact
terra nullius when Europeans arrived, and throughout 1988 negotiations were
under way between the government and Aborigines over the details of a treaty
recognizing the pre-European aboriginal occupation of Australia.

As they have gradually regained some control over the land, and as the government has softened its official emphasis on assimilation as the only alternative,
Aborigines have begun to reassert their traditional culture and independence in
a dramatic way. The most visible manifestation of this revival is the "Outstation
Movement." By 1978, throughout the country there were 148 outstations, or
decentralized communities, where small groups of Aborigines were reestablishing the traditional life on their own ancestral lands away from the crowded,
dependent conditions of the missions and government posts (Australia, Department of Aboriginal Affairs, 1978). In 1986 there were 13,400 Aborigines living
in 699 such communities, which were becoming identified as "homeland cen-
tres" (Australia, Parliament of the Commonwealth, 1987:xvi). These new communities have sought to be maximally self-sufficient, and wherever possible
they rely heavily on wild food resources, but many still receive support from the
government and maintain radio and transportation links with central stations.

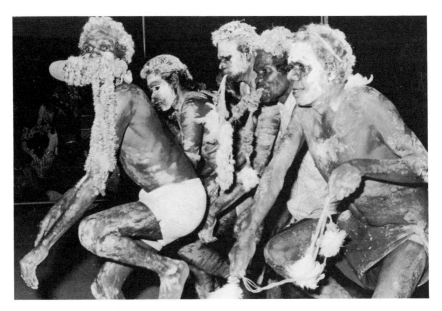

FIGURE 9.3

Yirrkala men from eastern Arnhem Land preparing a dog (dingo) hero dance for land at the formation of the Kimberley Land Council, Noonkanbah, Western Australia, 1978. (Arthur B. Palmer, Northern Land Council, Darwin, Australia.)

The important thing is that in the outstations Aborigines are again in control of their daily life, and they are securely on their own lands to which they have profound spiritual bonds. The advantages of life in the outstations have been seen immediately in terms of improved health conditions, but the aboriginal social system is also gaining renewed strength and there has been an enthusiastic revival of ceremonial life. So far this new movement has been so successful that in some areas half of the aboriginal population has already moved to outstations.

Intense Pressure Over Kakadu Uranium

Although the Land Rights Act of 1976 gives the aboriginal land councils the right to negotiate on behalf of traditional owners before mining can proceed on aboriginal land, and the Aborigines have limited veto power over mining, subject to national interests, the pressures on Aborigines to give unwilling "consent" can be overwhelming. The irony of this situation is that the land councils themselves are ultimately dependent on mining royalties and are thus placed in an ambiguous position as spokesmen for Aborigines opposed to mining. The government attitude was made clear in the 1977 Fox Commission report on the Ranger uranium mine, which declared that aboriginal opposition "should not be allowed to prevail." In the case of the Jabiluka uranium lease along the eastern border of Kakadu National Park, ten aboriginal owners finally gave consent to mining in 1982, after a ten-day "bargaining session" ending an intense series of negotiations between representatives of the Pancon-Getty Oil consortium and government officials, the land council, and local Aborigines, lasting over a year. During the negotiations, Aborigines were shuttled by helicopter from their camps to "urgent" meetings and had little choice but to listen to hours of intense haggling. Given that the Jabiluka project was projected to produce 8 billion dollars worth of uranium yellowcake and 150 million dollars in gold over twenty-seven years, it is hardly surprising that the interested parties were not prepared to accept an aboriginal veto (Niklaus, 1983:6–15).

PHILIPPINE TRIBALS: NO MORE RETREAT

Today there are over 4 million tribal people in the Philippines, representing some forty major groups, who seek to maintain their independent identities. Many of these groups have successfully retained their independence by gradually retreating into the mountains, but now, after more than 400 years of colonial domination, they have nowhere else to go. They are being forced to adopt new forms of self-defense because their final refuges are being invaded by powerful national and international interests. The tribal peoples are strong numerically, as they constitute some ten percent of the total national population, but they are widely scattered and separated by differences of language and culture, making a common defense difficult. However, in response to new external threats to their survival, they have begun to bury their internal differences and are mounting a major resistance movement.

The most serious threats facing these groups today are dams, mining, and agribusiness, all of which would displace them from their lands. Since 1973 the Philippine government's National Power Corporation (NPC) has been attempting to implement its planned construction of twenty-one hydroelectric projects, which would flood tribal lands in Mindanao and northern Luzon. These projects directly support the efforts of multinational companies, such as DelMonte, who are turning tribal lands into giant pineapple plantations. The tribal peoples quite correctly see their land and cultures as inseparable, and understandably they do not want them sacrificed for the benefit of a wealthy few. The official government program for tribal peoples is to crowd them into carefully controlled "Service Centers" in order to free tribal lands for development. Since 1968 this resettlement process has been methodically carried out by PANAMIN (Presidential Assistant on National Minorities), the special government agency established for that purpose. By 1979 an estimated 2.6 million tribal people were being "assisted" by PANAMIN (Rocamora, 1979:2a).

So far the tribal peoples have utilized a variety of approaches to prevent the loss of their lands. At first they sent delegations with petitions directly to Philippine President Marcos. When these appeals were rejected they held organizational meetings, issued formal declarations, and turned to more active resistance. Their basic demands were simple and are eloquently expressed in the formal declaration prepared by the Mangyan people of Mindoro at a meeting of tribal representatives in 1976:

1. We want land for our tribe, enough for all of us, a piece of land that is titled and secure, that others cannot steal. . . . We will not retreat anymore.

2. We want our own way of life. We are willing to live side-by-side with others but we want to live our own culture and traditions. (cited Rocamora, 1979:9–10a)

The 500,000 Igorots (Kalinga and Bontoc) in northern Luzon were traditional enemies, but in 1975 they signed a formal peace treaty and combined to fight together against the government's plan to build four major dams on the Chico River in their territory (Drucker, 1985; Razon, 1976; Rocamora, 1979a, b; Winnacker, 1979). These dams would have destroyed a highly productive engineering system of terraces to manage water and soil that has been called a "wonder of the world" and that in this case supported some 90,000 people. The allied Igorot tribes agreed to reject all overtures from PANAMIN and the NPC, and refused all cooperation with the construction effort. At first the Igorots managed to stall construction by dismantling survey camps, but the workers kept returning. Finally, when antigovernment guerrillas belonging to the New People's Army (NPA) came to the support of the Igorots and began to encourage them to violent action, the Philippine army was called in. The entire zone was militarized and Philippine army units moved to block further protests. Many tribal leaders were arrested and entire villages were forcibly relocated, but resistance to the dams continued. The Igorots appealed to President Marcos and even attempted to prevent funding of the projects by presenting their case to an International Monetary Fund–World Bank conference in Manila, but all of their efforts only succeeded in gaining time while Marcos remained intransigent. Tribal resistance continued to grow, however, and in 1984 more than 300 representatives of twenty-three local tribal organizations from throughout the mountains of Luzon met together and formed the Cordillera People's Alliance to create an even stronger political defense of their homeland. Ultimately, the Igorot resistance contributed to the fall of Marcos in 1986 and opened the possibility of genuine tribal autonomy under the terms of the new constitution sponsored by the Aquino government. However, the uncertain political and military situation in the country makes the long-term prospect for autonomy in the tribal areas problematic. Following the collapse of the Chico project, the World Bank, which had originally funded it, was forced to reassess its view of tribal peoples and development issues; this will perhaps lead them to be more cautious with such projects in the future.

THE INTERNATIONAL ARENA

So far we have examined representative regional and national level indigenous political movements in several countries. In this section we move to the international level, where indigenous peoples have become increasingly active in their struggle for self-determination. International indigenous political organizations, combining related indigenous peoples separated only by national boundaries, have existed for some times. For example, the Nordic Sami Council, uniting the Sami of Norway, Sweden, and Finland, was founded in 1953. However, coordinated, large-scale political action by diverse indigenous peoples from many different countries is a recent phenomenon. Since the widespread establishment of regional native organizations, which began in earnest only in the early 1970s, it has been an obvious step for indigenous leaders to convene international conferences of representatives of these national organizations and finally to establish permanent international organizations.

Perhaps the first major, multiethnic international conference organized and run by indigenous peoples was the First Circumpolar Arctic People's Conference held in Copenhagen, Denmark in November of 1973. This conference brought together Indian, Inuit (Eskimo), and Sami (Lapp) representatives from some 16 indigenous organizations in Alaska, Canada, Greenland, Norway, Finland, and Sweden. In their official resolutions they agreed to cooperate in the preservation of their cultures and claimed a common identity in their special relationship to the land, which cross-cut their cultural differences. As they declared:

> *We are autochthonous peoples, that is, we are an integral part of the very lands and waters we have traditionally used and occupied. Our identity and culture is firmly rooted in these lands and waters. It is this relationship which constitutes the very unique features of our cultural identity in contrast to the cultures of other peoples within each of the countries from which we come.*
>
> Boye, 1974:69

The delegates called upon national governments to recognize and respect their unique claims of collective ownership of their traditional lands and waters, and stressed:

> *There must not be any displacement or interference with our rights by government and/or industry, nor can there be disturbance of our lands.*
>
> Boye, 1974:70

A few months later in 1974 another international, multiethnic conference, the American Indian Parliament of the Southern Cone, was convened by indigenous peoples in Paraguay for the purpose of defining common problems and proposing solutions. Representatives from fifteen Indian groups from Argentina, Bolivia, Brazil, Venezuela, and Paraguay attended the week-long conference. The official conclusions of the parliament emphasized the common Indian identity rooted in a cultural heritage that was thousands of years old and which has existed independently of any affiliations with present nation-states. Specific statements were issued on a variety of topics including land, labor, education, language, health, and political organization. The basis of the Indians' position in regard to land closely resembled the view presented earlier by the Arctic peoples and was expressed in their uncompromising statement of principle:

> The land is of the Indian. The Indian is the earth itself. The Indian is the owner of the land, with property titles or without them.
>
> cited Chase-Sardi & Colombres, 1975:240

More specifically, they stated that Indian land should be recognized as communally held and Indian communities should be legally recognized, self-governing, corporate entities. They felt that the natural resources of their lands should be exploited only by themselves for their own benefit. They wanted an educational system that promoted their own cultural values and languages. In regard to their own political mobilization, they stressed the need for greater unity and the rapid formation of more regional federations, but they warned against possible manipulation of their new organizations by alien political interests or by false native leaders who were promoted by government authorities. They felt that any outside aid that they accepted should be without ideological preconditions. They also emphasized that divisions promoted by religious sects must not hinder their political unity, and they warned specifically against the dangers of any trend toward the emergence of internal stratification within Indian communities.

Even before the First Circumpolar Arctic People's Conference, preliminary plans were being worked out by the National Indian Brotherhood of Canada for the establishment of a permanent international organization of indigenous peoples having official status as a Non-Governmental Organization (NGO) of the United Nations. The advantage of such an organization was that it would be in a position to present the case of indigenous people before the world community much more effectively than any existing national indigenous organizations. This new organization, the World Council of Indigenous Peoples (WCIP), was formally inaugurated in 1975 at its first general assembly hosted by the Sheshaht (Nootka) Indians on their tribal lands on Vancouver Island, British Columbia (Sanders, 1977). Fifty-two delegates representing indigenous organizations from nineteen countries attended. In addition to the numerous Indians from North and South America, there were also indigenous peoples from Australia, New Zealand, Greenland, and Scandinavia. A formal charter was adopted by the assembly that opened its membership to organizations of indigenous people who were working, ". . . to further their economic self-sufficiency and to obtain self-determination." The principal objectives of the WCIP included the following points:

1. To ensure political, economic, and social justice to indigenous peoples
2. To establish and strengthen the concepts of indigenous and cultural rights

Policy for the World Council is formulated by the general assemblies and is carried out by the executive council, which is composed of single representatives from major world regions such as Canada, Central America, South America, Europe and Greenland, and the South Pacific. The World Council has obtained financial support from a wide variety of sources including international humanitarian organizations, religious bodies, and national governments. Since gaining NGO status it has also sought funding directly from the United Nations.

The World Council held its second general assembly in Swedish Samiland in 1977. This assembly issued a final report containing what is the most comprehensive and sophisticated statement of rights and principles yet published by any organization of indigenous peoples (see Appendix D). The report (WCIP, 1977), which appeared in the Sami language, Swedish, and English, includes a major declaration listing fundamental principles, resolutions, and fourteen basic rights. The fundamental principle stressed at the outset was the just claim of indigenous peoples to their lands. This was followed by the "irrevocable and inborn" right to self-determination. The other rights for the most part amplified these issues of land and self-determination.

The World Council gradually expanded the scope of its organization to include more and more indigenous groups in various parts of the world. For example, in 1980 the Ainu of Japan joined the council, and CISA, the Indian Council of South America, was officially organized as the regional organization for South America with eighteen representatives from nine countries. Some 300 indigenous representatives from twenty-three countries attended the Fourth Assembly of the WCIP, which was hosted in Panama in 1984 by the Kuna, Guaymi, and Embera Indians. The Fourth Assembly issued a Declaration of Principles of Indigenous Rights (see Appendix E).

The activities of indigenous political organizations have clearly generated a response at the United Nations. It is to be expected that official international conventions will increasingly reflect the positions now being expressed by indigenous peoples themselves. In 1977 more than fifty leaders of indigenous organizations were given a unique opportunity to present their position when they were invited to attend the International Conference on Discrimination Against Indigenous Populations in the Americas, organized in Geneva by the special United Nations NGO Committee on Human Rights. The conference was attended by delegates from forty-six national and international organizations and by observers from twenty-seven national governments in addition to the special indigenous peoples delegations. At its conclusion, the conference adopted a number of resolutions strongly supporting indigenous peoples. The international response to the legitimate demands of indigenous peoples was even stronger in the declaration and programme of action presented by the 123 nations attending the United Nations World Conference to Combat Racism and

Racial Discrimination held in Geneva in 1978 and approved by the United Nations General Assembly. The declaration specifically stated in Article 21:

> *The Conference endorses the right of indigenous peoples to maintain their traditional structure of economy and culture, including their own language, and also recognizes the special relationship of indigenous peoples to their land and stresses that their land, land rights and natural resources should not be taken away from them.*

The full text of the proposed programme of action in favor of indigenous peoples is presented in Appendix C.

In 1981, 130 indigenous representatives attended a similar NGO Geneva Conference on Indigenous Peoples and their Land and recommended the establishment of the Working Group on Indigenous Peoples as a formal UN mechanism for developing international standards for the treatment of indigenous peoples. The Working Group was promptly established by the UN Sub-Commission on Prevention of Discrimination and Protection of Minorities and held its first meeting in Geneva in 1982. It was attended by representatives of the WCIP and indigenous representatives from North, Central, and South America, as well as Australia. By 1987 the Working Group had held five meetings. In 1986 it produced ten Draft Principles on the Rights of Indigenous Populations (see Appendix F). The long-term objective of the Working Group is to see a Universal Declaration on Indigenous Rights ratified by 1992, the 500th anniversary of Columbus's landing in the New World (IWGIA Yearbook 1987:87). A survey report on the current conditions of indigenous peoples throughout the world has been published by a researcher from the Anti-Slavery Society who has been involved with the Working Group (Burger, 1987). A related report has also been issued by the Independent Commission on International Humanitarian Issues (1987). The Independent Commission consists of a 27-member international panel of distinguished individuals who were convened in 1983 under UN sponsorship. They operate as private individuals, on global humanitarian issues such as war, terrorism, famine, and the problems of indigenous peoples.

Revision of the ILO's Convention 107

The International Labour Organization (ILO) is a UN-affiliated organization whose members are governments. When member governments ratify particular ILO conventions, it means that they have agreed to abide by the specified standards or face possible censure.

Until the recent political activism of indigenous organizations, the ILO's Convention 107 "concerning the protection and integration of indigenous and other tribal and semi-tribal populations of independent countries," which was adopted in 1957, remained as the primary international standard for humane policies toward indigenous peoples. Convention 107 contained positive elements, but still reflected the integrationist and ethnocentric assumptions typical of the colonial era. Indigenous leaders were especially critical of Article 12, which permits the removal of tribals from their territories in the interests of national development. The indigenous delegates to the UN Working Group, who were in a position to directly influence UN policy, urged revision of Convention 107. In 1986 the ILO agreed that change was in order and convened a committee of experts to begin the revision process. The pro-indigenous peoples' experts on the committee wanted the new Convention 107 to endorse self-determination and fought hard to have the rights of indigenous peoples to land and resources strengthened and to reduce the right of national governments to intervene in the name of "national interests." The final recommendations will be a compromise between conflicting interests, but it appears that they will support the minimum interests of indigenous peoples.

· 10 ·

Human Rights and the Politics of Ethnocide

> *Not because they are indigenous peoples, but because they are human beings with indigenous cultures, and with unique ways of being human, should their defense and protection be a matter of the highest-priority concern for all people the world over who care about human rights.*

> Bay, 1984

THE DESTRUCTION OF INDEPENDENT tribal societies was an immense human tragedy that was brought about by political decisions which were both inhumane and genocidal. Millions died in the hundred years before 1920, when tribals were forced to surrender nearly half of the globe. Why was this allowed to happen? Was it the inevitable outcome of evolutionary processes with no viable alternatives? What was the role and responsibility of government administrators, missionaries, and anthropologists? This chapter will examine the response of those organizations and individuals within the expanding industrial societies who were most concerned with the fate of tribals. We will see that ethnocide was caused by political decisions which denied the human rights of tribal peoples to an independent existence. Those who accepted ethnocide as inevitable were unable to prevent massive tribal depopulation, and their humanitarian efforts to minimize the damage diverted attention from the real political issues and delayed the human rights struggle of indigenous peoples.

The problem of tribal destruction was debated by politicians, religious

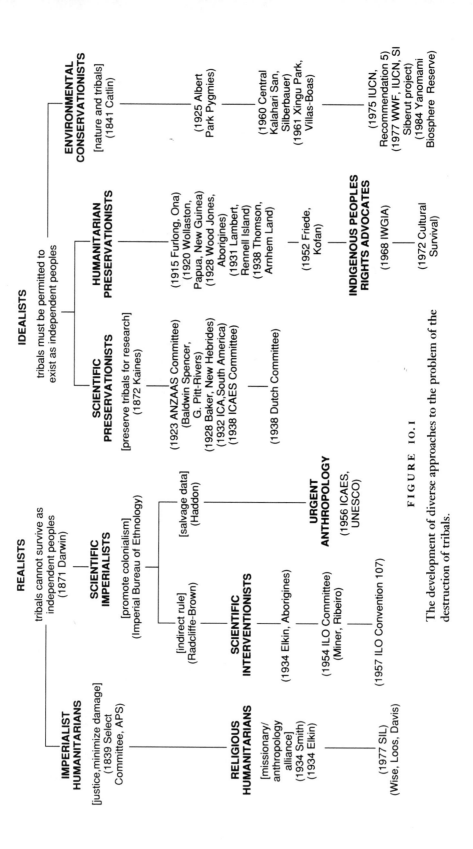

REALISTS
tribals cannot survive as independent peoples (1871 Darwin)

IMPERIALIST HUMANITARIANS
[justice, minimize damage] (1839 Select Committee, APS)

SCIENTIFIC IMPERIALISTS
[promote colonialism] (Imperial Bureau of Ethnology)

[salvage data] (Haddon)

[indirect rule] (Radcliffe-Brown)

URGENT ANTHROPOLOGY
(1956 ICAES, UNESCO)

SCIENTIFIC INTERVENTIONISTS
(1934 Elkin, Aborigines)
(1954 ILO Committee) (Miner, Ribeiro)
(1957 ILO Convention 107)

RELIGIOUS HUMANITARIANS
[missionary/ anthropology alliance] (1934 Smith) (1934 Elkin)
(1977 SIL) (Wise, Loos, Davis)

IDEALISTS
tribals must be permitted to exist as independent peoples

SCIENTIFIC PRESERVATIONISTS
[preserve tribals for research] (1872 Kaines)
(1923 ANZAAS Committee) (Baldwin Spencer, G. Pitt-Rivers)
(1928 Baker, New Hebrides) (1932 ICA, South America) (1938 ICAES Committee)
(1938 Dutch Committee)

HUMANITARIAN PRESERVATIONISTS
(1915 Furlong, Ona) (1920 Wollaston, Papua, New Guinea) (1928 Wood Jones, Aborigines) (1931 Lambert, Rennell Island) (1938 Thomson, Arnhem Land)
(1952 Friede, Kofan)

INDIGENOUS PEOPLES RIGHTS ADVOCATES
(1968 IWGIA)
(1972 Cultural Survival)

ENVIRONMENTAL CONSERVATIONISTS
[nature and tribals] (1841 Catlin)
(1925 Albert Park Pygmies)
(1960 Central Kalahari San, Silberbauer) (1961 Xingu Park, Villas-Boas)
(1975 IUCN, Recommendation 5) (1977 WWF, IUCN, SI Siberut project) (1984 Yanomami Biosphere Reserve)

FIGURE 10.1

The development of diverse approaches to the problem of the destruction of tribals.

leaders, and scientists for 150 years from the perspective of two conflicting philosophical camps: the "realists," who felt that ethnocide was inevitable, and the
"idealists," who argued that tribal survival was possible (see Figure 10.1). Realists accepted the "reality" of national expansion. They assumed that tribals
would ultimately be unable to survive as independent peoples and would either
become extinct or be integrated into the dominant national society while losing
much of their cultural distinctiveness. Idealists were both more critical of the
frontier process and more optimistic about the possibility of tribals maintaining
their political and cultural integrity.

THE REALISTS: HUMANITARIAN IMPERIALISTS AND SCIENTISTS

The prevailing realist view that the demise of tribals was inevitable was a self-
serving political opinion, not a well-founded scientific judgment. This "myth of
inevitability," however, supported government policies of expansion into tribal
territories. Unfortunately, the idealist position was largely ignored during the
critical early decades of this century because the debate mistakenly focused on
tribal "protection" and "preservation" rather than political "self-determination."
Realist perspectives dominated policy making until 1968 when idealist organizations began to successfully redefine the tribal survival problem as an issue of
community human rights and came to the support of the emerging indigenous
political organizations. This shift coincided with global concerns over war, oppression, poverty, and environmental deterioration. Clearly, tribals would not
be the only victims of uncontrolled industrial expansion.

The following sections begin by demonstrating that well into the twentieth
century the scientific community accepted as inevitable the fact that colonial expansion was destroying tribal peoples. We will see that initially scientists were
more concerned with the loss of valuable data on tribals than with the inhu-
manity of ethnocide. Next, the rise of applied anthropology will be linked to the
efforts by realist anthropologists to minimize the damage to tribal societies while
supporting imperialist expansion into tribal areas. Finally, detailed case studies
of three realist organizations will be presented: the Aborigines Protection Society, the Summer Institute of Linguistics, and the World Bank.

Vanishing Data and the Reality of Genocide

Regardless of the inherent vitality of tribal peoples, the overwhelming historical
reality, which was well established early in the nineteenth century, was that
tribal peoples died and their cultures disintegrated when Europeans invaded
tribal territory. The British Parliamentary Select Committee on Aborigines acknowledged this fact in their official reports of 1836–1837. Even Charles Darwin included a discussion of the "extinction of savage tribes" in *The Descent of*

Man and attributed it to "competition" with civilized races (1871:228–231). Initially, anthropologists saw the impending end of tribals in terms of vanishing data to be salvaged and then as an opportunity to make anthropology an applied science.

From the 1870s on, the extinction of tribals was a frequent theme in the anthropology section of the British Association for the Advancement of Science and at the meetings of the Royal Anthropological Institute, where it was assumed that the Pacific Islanders, the Andamanese, the Bushmen, and the Australian Aborigines, among others, all faced "utter extinction" and would soon follow the Tasmanians, who were considered extinct by 1876. Many of these dire predictions proved wrong, however: Not all tribals died out (even the Tasmanians survived), and the resilience of these cultures and the human capacity for resistance were often vastly underrated, as Chapter 9 demonstrated. But the point here is that genocide and ethnocide were occurring on an unprecedented scale, as the physical anthropologist W. H. Flower made clear before the British Association in 1881:

> We live in an age in which, in a far greater degree than any previous one, the destruction of races, both by annihilation and absorption, is going on.
>
> Flower, 1882:688

Perhaps the most striking demonstration that anthropologists were fully aware of the scope of the destruction of tribal peoples was their frantic attempt to save the vanishing data, which became a major theme at professional meetings beginning in the 1870s. As Colonel A. H. Lane Fox Pitt-Rivers declared in his address to the anthropology section of the British Association in 1871, vital data are "rapidly disappearing from the face of the earth" (1872:171). He joined E. B. Tylor, John Lubbock, and others to prepare the original version of "Notes and Queries" as a guide to salvage anthropology.

Although some authorities attributed the extermination of tribals to degeneration, most agreed that it was an inevitable result of colonial expansion. It is indeed curious that so few anthropologists challenged the underlying assumption that tribals could not continue to exist as autonomous peoples. Thus, while everyone assumed that unlimited colonialism would doom all tribals, few anthropologists were willing to urge the obvious step of stabilizing the frontiers and thereby preventing the destruction. The reasons for this failure are complex, but they do not relieve those involved from responsibility.

Scientific Imperialists and Applied Anthropology

The realists had their roots in the philosophy of nineteenth-century social darwinism, which assumed that European expansion was natural and inevitable and would ultimately benefit the whole world. Several realist subgroups can be distinguished: The imperialist humanitarians began with the British Parliamentary Select Committee members, who criticized the destructiveness of tribal policy in the 1830s and founded the Aborigines Protection Society in 1839. These humanitarians wanted justice for dispossessed tribals and hoped to minimize the harm done to them. This approach eventually led to alliances among anthropologists, missionaries, and governments, such as Brazil's Indian Protectorate Service (1910) and the Summer Institute of Linguistics (1934).

Another realist subgroup, the scientific imperialists, dates from the founding of anthropology as a scientific discipline and was exemplified by the unsuccessful nineteenth century efforts of the Royal Anthropological Institute (RAI) to establish an Imperial Bureau of Ethnology as a support for the colonial enterprise and to serve as a repository for vanishing data. The scientific imperialists eventually split into two main branches: the scientific interventionists, who were applied anthropologists seeking to combine scientific respect for tribal culture with economic development and integration of the tribals into the national society; and the salvage anthropologists, whose primary concern was to save vanishing data. British anthropologists, especially, were eager to support the expanding empire and could be labeled "scientific imperialists."

The response of anthropologists to the crisis of tribal peoples, aside from the rush to save vanishing data, was to develop the field of applied anthropology. The term *applied anthropology* was coined by RAI president Lane Fox Pitt-Rivers in 1881 to classify a paper entitled "On the Laws Affecting the Relations between Civilized and Savage Life . . . ," which was read before the RAI by colonial administrator Sir Bartle Frere (1881). Sir Frere felt that natural law required "savages" to surrender their political autonomy and become integrated into the dominant society in order to survive.

Some early observers of the extermination of tribal societies recognized that the problem was in the seemingly irreconcilable differences between tribal and civilized societies. Although unwilling to condemn colonial expansion itself, they felt that the damage to tribals could be minimized, as Flower expressed in his presidential address to the RAI in 1883:

> And when we have to do with people still more widely removed from ourselves, African Negroes, American Indians, Australian or Pacific Islanders, it seems almost impossible to find any common ground of union or modus vivendi; the mere contact of races generally ends in the extermination of one of them. If such disastrous consequences cannot be altogether averted, we have it still in our power to do much to mitigate their evils.
>
> Flower, 1884:493

This gloomy optimism was echoed a year later by A. L. P. Cameron in his notes about the vanishing tribes in Australia's New South Wales. He saw the destruction of the tribes as unavoidable:

> Experience everywhere proves that races in a state of savagery, and even those races which are beginning to emerge from it, are unable to withstand the advance of European civilization. But it is to be hoped that something will be done without delay to at

least ameliorate the condition of the tribes now fading from the earth under the influence of our presence.

Cameron, 1885:370

Early applied anthropologists were confident that they were doing science, not politics. Reverend Edwin W. Smith, missionary president of the RAI, argued that anthropology should be a "coldly neutral," value-free science when in the service of "practical undertakings," yet it was not to be yoked to "politics, to religion, to nationalism, [or] to philosophy" (1934:xxxiv–xxxv). Value-based policy opinions were not to be passed off as science. However, for Smith, anthropology was "not an enemy of progress," and he did not advocate preserving tribal people.

Realist Humanitarians: The Aborigines Protection Society

Throughout the nineteenth century since its founding in 1839, the Aborigines Protection Society (APS), was the only major humanitarian organization to lobby for just policies toward tribals. The APS favored limited tribal land rights, but not the political autonomy of tribal peoples, and supported the conquest of tribal areas as long as it was carried out justly, although "justice" for the APS apparently only meant protection from direct violence. The motives of the APS were both humanitarian and practical, and while it did not advocate the independent existence of tribal peoples, this organization set the standard of enlightened policy toward tribals. Operating at the height of the colonial era, the APS did much to reduce the worst abuses against tribal peoples. However, its benevolent policies were frequently ignored by colonial authorities, and it was unable to prevent the extermination of millions of tribal peoples. Even if the APS had argued for the right of tribals to freely follow their own way of life, it probably would have found few supporters in a rapidly developing industrial world that still accepted the legitimacy of imperial expansion by wars of conquest. In 1839 the International Red Cross did not yet exist, and in Europe there was no Geneva Convention to limit the atrocities of war.

The APS was founded by a group of British philanthropists who had succeeded in abolishing slavery in the British Empire by 1833 and realized that a similar political struggle was needed on behalf of native peoples to ensure that they were not also victimized by colonial expansion. But unfortunately at this critical juncture, the wrong issue was raised. In 1835 Thomas Buxton, one of the APS founders and a member of the British Parliament, succeeded in having the House of Commons Select Committee on Aborigines appointed, with the objective of ensuring that tribal peoples on the expanding frontiers of empire were treated justly. This attempt to combine colonial expansionism with justice toward tribal peoples has dominated the realist approach to the "native problem" up to the present time. Over the years, few observers have even suggested that the real question is not how to secure the progress of industrial nations while at the same time extending justice and humanity to tribal peoples. Rather:

Is forcing "civilization" onto tribal peoples a just and humane process in and of itself? In retrospect, it is not surprising that in the 1830s the problem of tribal peoples was not viewed in these terms—the concept of "human rights" and "self-determination" of peoples had simply not reached such a stage.

The original objective of the APS was to "assist in protecting the defense-less and promoting the advancement of uncivilized tribes." Here again, as with the Select Committee, the right of tribals to maintain their independent existence was not recognized as an issue. The "advancement" of tribes meant that they were to lose their political independence, participate in the economic life of the colonies, and adopt the Christian religion of their conquerors. The primary issue raised by the APS was that this was to occur *humanely*. The objection was to "unjust invasion," not to the right of political conquest of tribes by states. The right of tribes to maintain control over their lands, often in specially de-marcated reserves, was frequently argued by the APS, but the right to remain "uncivilized" was not considered. It is not surprising that the APS merely continued the program of the Select Committee because the first APS president, Thomas Buxton, was also chair of the Select Committee and four other members of the Select Committee became members of the executive committee of the APS. The religious element in the APS is conspicuous in the fact that several prominent members of the Society of Friends were incorporated in the executive committee.

The APS listed some 281 members in 1839, including twenty-seven religious ministers and representatives from twelve European countries and the United States. Regular public meetings were held in London, and the society's activities were frequently reported in the press. Certainly, the APS was highly successful in focusing public attention on the condition and needs of tribal peoples, mainly through the publication and distribution of inexpensive pamphlets.

The APS proposed new policies and by means of written petitions and personal meetings, directly influenced the adoption of legislation, or the intervention of government officials, on behalf of tribal peoples. It also functioned as a watchdog to see that the laws it helped formulate were followed and that infractions were punished.

One of the primary architects and most active agents of the APS was Thomas Hodgkin, who was also a founder of the society. Under his guidance, the APS attempted with varying degrees of success to intervene on behalf of tribals in Canada, southern Africa, Australia, and New Zealand. Because colonial rule in Australia had barely begun in 1839, when the APS was founded, the society was in a favorable position to influence policy to benefit the Aborigines. The petitions of the APS, and its detailed publications on conditions in Australia, were instrumental in the appointment of Protectors of Natives, who were able to buffer the Aborigines from some of the worst types of frontier violence. When the extension of the sheep industry was depriving Aborigines of their subsistence and driving them to desperation and ultimate extermination, the APS advocated the establishment of aboriginal reserves in 1850, which would combine schools, missions, and farms.

The economic utility of preserving tribal peoples, but not their cultures, remained a dominant theme for the APS because this was the best way to convince both the public and the government that it made sense to protect Aborigines. If tribals were to be preserved, they had to become useful farmers, stockkeepers, seamen, and domestic servants. It was thought better to protect than to destroy them, because "self-interest is on the side of justice and mercy" (APS 9th Annual Report, 1846:28).

Throughout the remainder of the nineteenth century the APS concentrated much of its attention on problems in Africa. It lobbied for international agreements by the colonial nations to reduce frontier abuses as Africa was partitioned at the end of the nineteenth century. But these efforts did not achieve the positive results intended, especially in view of the atrocities committed in the Congo Free State. In Australia, the influence of the APS declined as the colonies became more self-governing, and in many areas, such as Tasmania and New South Wales, the Aborigines became less of a problem because so many had been exterminated. In the Pacific the APS attempted, with only limited success, to gain international agreements to limit the availability of guns and alcohol and to regulate the activities of traders and labor recruiters who operated as slavers.

By the end of the century, the APS came to view itself as a combination appellate court for mistreated natives and an advisory body for colonial administrators. In spite of the terrible attrition of tribal peoples that continued to mark the advance of colonial frontiers even with the best efforts of the APS to ameliorate conditions, the organization was still not prepared to challenge the legitimacy of colonial expansion. On the contrary, the APS often found it necessary to apologize for its incessant criticism of colonial practice. The APS was, after all, merely setting the standard of humane imperialism—it was not an anti-imperialist organization.

The Aborigines Protection Society eventually merged with the Anti-Slavery Society, which continues to be concerned with indigenous peoples and now can be considered a general human rights organization. As the era of colonial empire building passed, Christian missionary organizations began to play a prominent role as self-styled defenders of the welfare of tribal groups. The following section will examine the realist philosophy of one such organization, the Summer Institute of Linguistics.

Jungle Realities: The SIL Philosophy

The SIL (Summer Institute of Linguistics) is an organization of Bible translators and linguists founded in 1934 by the American missionary-linguist William Cameron Townsend and based on his realist humanitarian philosophy that Christianity, introduced through the Bible in the native language, provides the best means for helping "needy and oppressed" tribal peoples. The SIL is composed of two corporate entities: the Wycliffe Bible Translators (WBT), which presents its religious missionary role to the home churches in the United States and Europe that provide most of the dual organizations' financial support;

and the SIL proper, which operates in the field. The SIL has become perhaps the largest organization directly concerned with the welfare of tribal peoples throughout the world.

With the rise of indigenous self-determination movements in the 1970s, the SIL came under increasing criticism by native groups and their idealist supporters who objected to the SIL role in promoting the economic penetration of tribal areas by outsiders, while offering Christianity and the promise of economic progress as compensation (Hvalkof & Aaby, 1981; Stoll, 1982). In 1976 the SIL defended its intervention philosophy before the 42nd International Congress of Americanists meeting in Paris. The SIL argument (Kietzman, 1977; Wise, Loos, & Davis, 1977) was that the introduction of Christianity would help native peoples adapt to the "inevitable contact and change" more easily while retaining their ethnic identities. The implication was that those who condemned missionary intervention were adopting an unrealistic and romantic attitude that apparently ignored the fact that cultures change and that most tribal groups had already experienced either direct or indirect contacts with outsiders.

Of course, the reality that culture change is a "normal and inevitable" occurrence is not a matter of dispute. What is at issue is the degree to which contact and change is imposed upon tribal peoples by the political and economic policies of the dominant society. The SIL accepts the "reality" of existing policies by arguing that "contact and change" is inevitable and that it is the responsibility of Christian missionaries to make it less destructive and to help tribals to adapt to this "reality." The SIL philosophy is clearly not a spirited defense of the self-determination approach.

According to the SIL, native groups face a wave of outsiders, from oil prospectors and tourists to missionaries and travelers. They also acknowledge the "reality" that these "contacts" are often destructive and that not only is "culture change" occurring, but that the natives are being deprived of their territories and resources and being politically marginalized. However, this is an unavoidable process in the SIL view, because even groups that retreat into remote areas containing nothing of value for the dominant society will eventually be surrounded by civilization. Furthermore, even if they are successful in evading civilization for a time, the natives may seek contact themselves out of a desire to obtain manufactured goods. However, this desire for industrial goods may not mean that they also seek externally imposed culture change, would welcome missionaries, or would abandon their political autonomy.

The SIL philosophy also stresses that the natives might not always want to maintain all aspects of their culture and quotes a Candoshi Indian's statement that the Candoshi would not wish to continue headhunting. Furthermore, the natives might be eager to learn about the outside world. Again, this is not the issue. The real point is that these should be matters for the tribals to work out, without the pressure of outside intervention, whether from oil companies or missionaries. The SIL is unwilling to take a strong position against intrusion into tribal territories because of its own interest in evangelism. The position it does take appears to support native culture:

Not desiring to force the members of a marginal group to adjust to other forms, nor obligating them to maintain their status quo (if that were possible), it is necessary to find an alternative to help them to retain their identity within a viable, strong, united, and just culture, whose values can survive in the face of culture contact.

Wise, Loos, & Davis, 1977:502

This solution assumes that tribals must adapt to externally imposed "culture contact," which means that the underlying political and economic policies imposing such "contact" go unchallenged. It also implies that something was wrong with the tribal culture that outsiders can and should correct. The SIL actually offered guidelines for distinguishing between "positive" and "negative" tribal culture traits. While official SIL policy is to maintain political neutrality, considering itself a "guest" in each country that it works, it argues that intervention in a tribal culture by anthropologists or missionaries, for the purpose of reducing "negative" culture traits, is appropriate and professionally ethical. Ideally, the SIL argues, this kind of intervention would not destroy the culture; rather, it would judiciously work within the culture.

In response to its critics, the SIL stated that it was not acting paternalistically—that it was creating neither dependency nor domination. It was merely providing tools with which the tribals could accommodate themselves in their own way to the "new sociological realities" that they must face. Its role was to promote "fruitful cultural interchange," not cultural domination.

In some respects, the SIL philosophy attempts to represent itself as both realist and idealist. It accepts the inevitability of conquest but denies that ethnocide must follow. Indeed, cultural destruction is not always complete. In the SIL view, ethnocide is not a valid concept, and it would lead to pessimism if one equated ethnocide with culture change imposed by the inevitable progress of civilization. According to Kietzman (1977), an SIL member, the term *ethnocide* is ambiguous, because many tribals survive as ethnic groups even though they undergo large-scale cultural change. Kietzman is interested in identifying those factors that make *ethnic* survival possible, because in line with the SIL philosophy, he considers the advance of civilization and the consequent transformation of tribal cultures to be unstoppable:

It will be impossible to divert the sweep of a commercially oriented, energy-deficient civilization through the Amazon basin. Nationalism and pressures of population growth impel exploitation of underpopulated areas.

Kietzman, 1977:528

or:

The course of Brazilian national development makes it inevitable that all tribes will be brought into permanent contact with Brazilian society.

1977:530

Of course, Kietzman considers any talk of "isolating" tribals "impractical" and "authoritarian," but he feels that there must be ways of helping threatened Indian groups to adapt "in an orderly manner." Successful adaptation for Kietzman was phrased in terms of "integration" as Ribeiro originally defined it in 1957:

> *Specifically, tribal peoples adapt by developing greater resistance to disease and divesting themselves of their linguistic and cultural uniqueness.*
>
> Ribeiro, 1957:21

Kietzman points out that many of the "integrated" tribes in Brazil in fact managed to retain their languages and some distinctive cultural traits. In his final list of policy recommendations designed to give the tribals a chance at "gradual and voluntary accommodation to new ways" (1977:535), Kietzman emphasized the need to safeguard tribal territory and to permit the Indians to determine their pace of change.

Although missionary organizations remain a dominant influence on tribal groups in many parts of the world, since 1960 international lending agencies have come to play a more strategic role by providing financial support for government projects designed to develop tribal areas. The following section examines the realist policy position of the World Bank, the single most influential such agency.

The World Bank Policy

> *How can the government harmonize its interest in the development of a rich ore body or a major hydro potential with the need to safeguard the rights of the tribal people in the project area? These are matters for judgements guided by the principle that Bank assistance should help prevent or mitigate harm, and provide adequate time and conditions for acculturation.*
>
> The World Bank: Operational Manual Statement, cited in *IWGIA Yearbook 1986*, pp. 149–153

The World Bank, or the International Bank for Reconstruction and Development, a UN affiliate founded in 1945, has had an enormous impact on tribal peoples because it is one of the world's largest funding agencies for large-scale development programs. For example, in 1983 it approved more than 14 billion dollars in financial assistance to some eighty countries. The Bank is owned by its 144 member countries and loans money to governments for the primary purpose of promoting economic growth and improving living standards. Unfortunately, many of the projects that it has supported, such as hydroelectric development in India and the Philippines, transmigration in Indonesia, and agricultural development, colonization, and highway construction in Brazil, have forced tribal populations off their lands and have even led to loss of life. Such programs, as noted in previous chapters, have generated armed resistance by tribals, and they have caused international criticism of the World Bank itself. Already under attack for the environmental damage that Bank-funded projects caused, the Bank responded to its critics in 1982 by issuing a public document presenting what it considered to be idealistic policy guidelines for funding projects that might affect tribals (Goodland, 1982).

Publication of a formal policy on tribals and development by such a powerful multinational lending agency as the World Bank was a clear measure of the growing strength of indigenous political organizations. However, close inspection of the Bank's policy statement reveals serious contradictions. Even though it contains some idealist language, it falls within the realist, albeit humanitarian, perspective. While the document declares emphatically that the Bank will not support projects that tribals reject, and it endorses what it calls "cultural autonomy" and "freedom of choice" by tribals in development matters, it is clear that the Bank believes that ultimately tribals will be "developed" and must surrender their independent existence.

Publicly, the Bank acknowledges that national development projects have often had disastrous consequences for tribals, but it argues that such failures were due to improperly designed projects, and the Bank fails to admit any incompatibility between short-run national development goals and the long-term interests of specific tribal groups. The Bank may call for the demarcation of tribal lands, but it also has guidelines for "forced removals" in cases where national interests must override tribal land rights. In reality, the Bank seems unwilling to insist upon special rights to tribal groups that might perpetuate their existence as independent communities. Instead, the emphasis is on "interim safeguards" in order to minimize the damage "until the tribe adapts sufficiently" or on the need to "minimize the imposition of different social or economic systems until such time as the tribal society is sufficiently robust and resilient to tolerate the effects of change" (Goodland, 1982:27, 28).

This kind of realism accepts the continuing necessity of national expansion, while proclaiming humanitarian concerns for the tribals who are harmed in the process. In the Bank's view, political self-determination and economic autonomy are not "realistic" goals for tribals, because such goals might give them control over their natural resources. It is significant that the Bank's policy states that the most favorable outcome for tribals is to become "accepted ethnic minorities" (Goodland, 1982:27) and carefully avoids linking "ethnicity" to any special community-level human rights or unique political status.

The Bank apparently recognized the contradictions between the idealist passages within its policy statement and its actual policy in practice. Bank spokesmen quickly denied that the statement was a "policy statement," preferring instead to call it a "working paper." By 1984 editions of the document began to appear with the disclaimer that it was "unofficial" and did "not necessarily represent the Bank's official policy." In 1986 a spokesman for the World Bank told the Committee of Experts working on the revision of the ILO's Convention 107 that on tribal matters the Bank followed secret internal policy guidelines, not its own public policy. In fact, the Bank admitted that it did not feel tribals had the right to block development projects because this would give the tribals special privileges. The Bank's internal guidelines, which have now "unofficially" come to light (*IWGIA Yearbook 1986*, pp. 149–154), reveal an underlying realist political philosophy that tribals represent a "stage" of "acculturation," which they will outgrow in time. Conflicts between tribal and national interests are acknowledged, but they are to be resolved in favor of the state, with the harm to tribals "mitigated."

The World Bank has been sensitive to recent criticism of its lending policies, especially since environmentalist and pro-indigenous peoples groups mounted a campaign aimed at the U.S. congressional committee that oversees appropriations for the American contribution to the Bank (for example, see Bodley, 1983). The United States dramatically reduced its support for the Bank in 1987, which forced the Bank to reassess its policies. An immediate outcome was a reduction in Indonesia's transmigration program.

THE IDEALIST PRESERVATIONISTS

In contrast to the pro-expansionist conservatism of the humanitarian and anthropological organizations, a minority of well-informed individuals argued the unpopular and unprofitable position that tribal cultures were still viable and could be saved—if the appropriate authorities had the will to do so. At least three main groups shared the common theme that tribals should be left alone, free of outside intrusion: scientific preservationists, humanitarian preservationists, and environmental conservationists (see Figure 10.2). Scientific preservationists wanted tribals preserved for scientific purposes, usually in order to save the vanishing data. Humanitarian preservationists wanted tribals left alone because they felt this was the only way to prevent the ultimate destruction of these peoples. Environmental conservationists wanted to preserve both tribal cultures and their natural environments. The following sections will review the development of each of these approaches.

Human Zoos: The Scientific Preservationists

In 1872 Joseph Kaines, a member of the Royal Anthropological Institute, told the British Association for the Advancement of Science that anthropologists have the "duty" of working to preserve disappearing tribals because the development of their science depended on the survival of tribes. At first the idea of tribal preservation attracted little interest, because of the prevailing opinion that tribals were inevitably doomed to extinction. However, between the world wars, from about 1920 to 1938, there were many specific proposals for the preservation of tribals for scientific purposes, although they were seldom implemented because there were few economic advantages in preservation and there

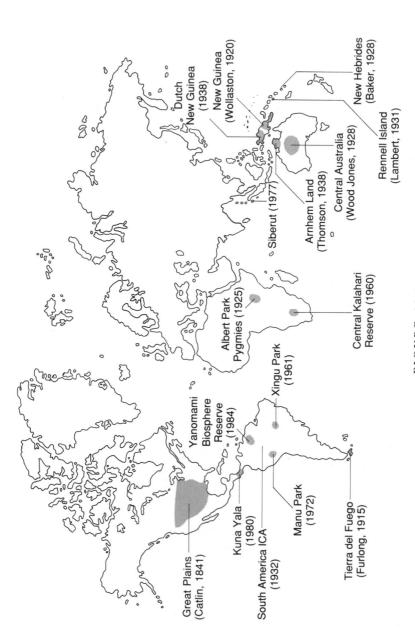

FIGURE 10.2

Idealist preservationist proposals discussed in text.

was invariably opposition by development interests. Several such proposals are examined below.

A tribal conservation proposal was presented to the Australian Association for the Advancement of Science (ANZAAS) by a group of anthropologists in 1923. ANZAAS passed a resolution calling for the segregation of certain select, but unspecified, areas in the Pacific containing "uncontaminated" tribal peoples in order to preserve them for study. A Committee on Vital Statistics of Primitive Races was set up in order to monitor demographic conditions within designated tribal areas. Vast reserves were created by the Australian government in the 1920s, but these areas were not sanctuaries where Aborigines would be free to live independently.

In 1928 British zoologist John R. Baker (1928, 1929) proposed a quarantine of the 600 native residents of the island of Gaua in the New Hebrides to determine if they could escape depopulation and preserve their culture by avoiding European influence. Baker ironically observed that interesting animals were legally protected, whereas "anthropological treasures" were allowed to disappear, but he did not link his proposal directly with environmental conservation. Dr. S. M. Lambert, health officer for the Commonwealth Health Service in the western Pacific, advocated a similar quarantine for Rennell Island, in the Solomons, in order to "preserve in its entirety" its valuable, and "almost untouched" Polynesian culture (Lambert, 1931).

A tribal conservation policy was also proposed by the International Congress of Americanists (ICA), a scholarly organization composed primarily of anthropologists specializing in the Americas. In 1932 the ICA passed a resolution calling for "conservation" of Indian peoples in South America for scientific purposes. The resolution envisioned the creation of "indigenous reserves" under the patronage of the ICA: "in order to obtain, in view of ethnological interest, the conservation of South American indigenous races, with their languages, and where possible, with their own customs" (ICA, 1934, 25:xlv). The resolution further recommended that conservation of tribal peoples be a permanent theme in successive congresses in order to monitor its advance throughout South America, but it appears that none of the ICA proposals were ever carried out.

A similar tribal conservation theme emerged at the 1938 International Congress of Anthropological and Ethnological Sciences in Copenhagen where a research committee was established "For the Study of Governmental Measures for the Conservation of Aboriginal Peoples Whose Ways of Life Are of Scientific Interest." This committee included such prominent anthropologists as A. R. Radcliffe-Brown, Alfred Kroeber, Paul Rivet, Diamond Jenness, and Donald Thomson, but its efforts were interrupted by World War II. When the committee reconvened in 1946, it shifted its emphasis to salvage ethnology and applied anthropology rather than tribal conservation. None of these early conservation proposals gained any permanent support, however; in fact, some were later repudiated.

In 1938 the Nederlandsche Commissie voor Internationale Natuurbescherming (Dutch International Nature Protection Committee) proposed the creation of a temporary tribal sanctuary in Dutch New Guinea. The committee felt that long-term tribal "preservation" was probably unethical and certainly impossible, because modernization was inevitable, and they specifically rejected any "human zoo" approach. Their final recommendations were presented as temporary "conservation" measures to strictly regulate culture contact in order to minimize depopulation and destabilization and to give anthropologists a chance to study the tribes before they disappeared (Bijlmer, 1953; Nederlandsche Commissie voor Internationale Natuurbescherming, 1937).

Leave Them Alone: Humanitarian Preservationists

Humanitarian preservationists were not interested in preserving tribal peoples as research objects; instead, they argued that tribals should be left alone. Ultimately, this approach evolved into the humanitarian philosophy of today's advocates for the human rights of indigenous peoples. Initially, scientific organizations were often reluctant to endorse such an approach on purely humanitarian grounds, but many individuals did, and a sampling of their views is presented below.

Charles Wellington Furlong, lieutenant colonel and resident of Boston, who visited the surviving hunting and gathering tribes of Tierra del Fuego in 1907–1908, had great admiration for the ability of the "splendid" Ona tribe to deal successfully with an extremely harsh environment (1915:438). While their more exposed neighbors, the Alacaluf and Yahgan, were on the brink of extinction due to devastating contacts with civilization, Furlong found the outlook for the Ona more hopeful because of the natural protection provided by their remote environment, which held little appeal for outsiders. The Ona occupied the interior of the great island of Tierra del Fuego as well as the coast, and the southern half of the island was blanketed with impenetrable forests, bogs, and snow-covered mountains. Under the disruptive effects of European sheep farming and missionary work, the Ona population plummeted from 3,000 in the early 1880s to 500 by 1910.

As a solution, Furlong recommended that the governments of Chile and Argentina, who divided the island of Tierra del Fuego in two, should permanently reserve the Ona's present natural refuge for their "sole use," especially because it appeared to have little development potential. He also urged that the reserve be restocked with wild guanacos (related to the camel and llama) from the mainland in order to maintain the Ona's primary subsistence resource. Although he realized that this was a "dim hope," Furlong felt that such a policy would be a credit to Chile and Argentina, and if carried out, "This little remnant of people would be saved and the tribe preserved" (1915:444).

Australian physical anthropologist Frederic Wood Jones took an antimissionary, pro-humanitarian preservationist stance toward tribal Aborigines in his 1926 presidential address before the anthropology section of the ANZAAS. He quoted the complete text of Wollaston's 1920 plea to the Royal Geographical Society that interior New Guinea be left as an independent tribal area. Wollaston

(1920) had recommended that the New Guinea interior be left "as a native reserve where these people can live their own life" with no outside interference.

Wood Jones accepted as a scientifically respectable verdict that such reserves would be the only way to guarantee "the racial survival for such people as the Australian Aborigine" (1928:509). He argued that it was land appropriation and prolonged contact with civilization that doomed Aborigines to a "lingering but certain death." Missionary welfare and schooling were inadequate compensation, which he called "euthanasia." Wood Jones rejected the notion that the extinction of the Aborigine was inevitable. In a departure from the reservation system earlier proposed by Baldwin Spencer (1913), which provided for missionaries, schooling, and the interests of settlers, Wood Jones instead advocated "real reserves" that would allow continuation of tribal culture and traditions.

However, in reviewing the recent history of reserve policy in Australia, he was forced to conclude that while the government bowed to public opinion and pressure from international scientific organizations and established "reserves" for Aborigines in central Australia, in fact these were only "fictions and frauds" because they existed only on paper and were revoked whenever outside economic interests demanded entry. Wood Jones declared, "There are no real reserves in Australia where the Aborigine is free to live, what everyone is agreed on calling, a life uncontaminated by the white man" (1928:513).

A similar preservation policy was advocated by anthropologist Donald Thomson, who was commissioned by the Australian federal government in 1934 to investigate conditions in the Arnhem Land aboriginal reserve and make policy recommendations after the Aborigines killed five Japanese fishermen and a policeman. Alone and unarmed, Thomson contacted the hostile groups and spent nearly two years with them from 1935–1937. He concluded that the 1,500 independent Aborigines who remained in Arnhem Land were "on the road to extinction" and had acted in self-defense in killing intruders. Thomson felt that it was still possible for the Aborigines to remain self-sufficient if given a chance and that the government would be directly responsible if they were allowed to die. The most remarkable aspect of Thomson's report was the "positive action" that he recommended: He felt that the Aborigines should be left in occupation of their own territory and steps should be taken to "preserve their culture intact." Specifically, Thomson (1938) called for: (1) "absolute segregation" of the Arnhem Land reserve; (2) complete preservation of the social structure "in toto"; (3) complete preservation of the nomadic settlement pattern; (4) protective patrols to prevent outside intrusion; and (5) medical intervention to eliminate yaws, leprosy, and introduced diseases.

Perhaps the most important of Thomson's recommendations was his call for absolute segregation, which would exclude labor recruiters, stockmen, and missionaries from the reserve. He felt this measure was essential because of the cultural and physical vulnerability of the Aborigines. Thomson's proposals were apparently interrupted by World War II and found little support in Australia's anthropological community at the time. However, missionary development was in fact limited, and serious mineral development did not begin in Arnhem Land until the 1960s. The absence of roads and the general remoteness of this region helped maintain a de facto isolation of Arnhem Land from the rest of Australia.

Another statement of support for the right of tribal peoples to an independent existence was presented by Colombian anthropologist Juan Friede at the 30th ICA meeting at Cambridge in 1952. Friede discussed the situation of the Kofan, a threatened tribal group living in the upper Amazon of Colombia. At the end of his paper he declared:

> *The only solution, in my view, would be to recognize for the Kofan, as also for the other indigenous groups of Colombia, their rights as racial minorities, rights to utilize their language and to follow their customs, designating to them at the same time land and rivers with plain guarantees that no whites (settlers, traders, administrators, or missionaries) would establish themselves in their territory.*

Friede, 1952:218

There was no suggestion in Friede's "solution" that Indians be preserved so that they could be studied. He saw it as simply a matter of ensuring their basic human rights. At the ICA meeting held two years later in Sao Paulo (1954), the human rights approach was strongly endorsed in a resolution on Brazilian Indians. Herbert Baldus, senior Brazilian ethnologist and secretary general of the ICA executive commission, and Paulo Duarte addressed their resolution to the president of Brazil (ICA 1955, 31(1):lxix–lxx). They noted that the future survival of many Indian groups in Brazil was threatened because their lands were being invaded in complete disregard for their constitutional rights. Baldus and Duarte endorsed proposals placed before the Brazilian Parliament by the Indian Protectorate Service that were designed to increase the legal protection of Indian lands, requesting funds to demarcate tribal lands and to create the Xingu Indian Park. The park was created in 1961, but the Indian Protectorate Service became an agent of Indian dispossession and was disbanded in 1968 (see Chapter 2).

The emphasis in this resolution was on "survival of Indian tribes"—there was no mention of their acculturation or integration into the national society as an objective. Likewise, the resolution was not linked to any concern for the scientific value of vanishing data. It was strictly a matter of ensuring human rights. The Xingu project was specifically endorsed because it would permit the maintenance of the intertribal system, which if broken "would condemn the tribes to extermination."

Environmentalists and Tribal Sanctuaries

In 1841, after spending eight years traveling through the still uncivilized American West and visiting forty-eight tribes, the American artist George Catlin concluded that there was little hope for the half a million Indians still enjoying "their primitive state." However, he recognized that the government "could shield them from destruction," and he proposed the establishment of a vast na-

FIGURE 10.3

George Catlin (1796–1872), the American artist-ethnologist who painted this portrait of a Crow warrior, was one of the first to advocate the creation of cultural-environmental preservation parks. (*Smithsonian Report for 1964.*)

tional park covering the Great Plains from Mexico to Canada, to preserve both Indian and bison for future generations. In 1872, the year Catlin died, the U.S. government established the first national park at Yellowstone, but by this time nearly all of the tribes had been engulfed by the frontier.

Perhaps the first link between tribal peoples and nature conservation since Catlin involved the Pygmies and Albert Park, Africa's first national park, created in 1925 by the Belgian government. Although the original purpose of Albert Park was to preserve the mountain gorilla, it was enlarged from 92 to 781 square miles in 1929 "to save in their ancestral way of living some of the primitive African Pygmies, a race now threatened by extinction" (Akeley, 1931:296). Subsistence hunting by the Pygmies using "primitive weapons" was permitted in the buffer zones surrounding the gorilla sanctuary in the center of the park. The inclusion of the Pygmies in the park was clearly for the purpose of conserving a vulnerable anthropological resource, not in recognition of their human rights or because the Pygmies were conservationists.

In spite of frequent opposition to sanctuary approaches, at least two large reserves, the 52,347-square-kilometer Central Kalahari Game Reserve in Botswana and the 22,000-square-kilometer Xingu National Park in Brazil, were established in the early 1960s for the dual purpose of nature conservation and the protection of tribal peoples. However, it was not until Catlin's idealism was revived by conservationists such as Nash (1968) and Dasmann (1976), and the international environmental movement gained strength, that the concept of tribal sanctuaries became more acceptable.

The United Nations 1972 Stockholm Conference on the Human Environment called for the strict protection of wilderness areas representing diverse biomes, while defending the right of tribal peoples to pursue their traditional activities within such protected zones. Belgian anthropologist Andre-Marcel d'Ans (1972, 1980; Jungius, 1976), as director of the Anthropological Programme of Peru's Manu National Park from 1969–1971, laid the groundwork for the park's present enlightened approach with his policy toward the Machiguenga Indians, who were living in the park. He argued that exploitation of park resources for outside interests should be prohibited while the Indians were to be guaranteed freedom to hunt, gather, fish, and garden for their own needs.

The American conservationist Raymond Dasmann was a leading figure in drawing world attention to the importance of tribal peoples for environmental planning. In 1973 Dasmann raised the issue of tribals before the IUCN (International Union for the Conservation of Nature and Natural Resources), stressing the importance of preserving human cultural diversity and observing that what the tribals needed was "protection of the opportunity to carry out traditional ways of life" (Dasmann, 1973:29). In 1974 he pointed out that tribals were dependent on local resources and tended to manage them for sustained yield and that they were "natural" conservationists living in de facto nature preserves. Dasmann advocated granting tribal groups legal title to, and full control over, their traditional lands, including the right "to exclude all visitors, including missionaries and anthropologists" (1975:135).

Dasmann's perspective was incorporated in Recommendation 5, on "Protection of Traditional Ways of Life," by the 12th General Assembly of the IUCN, meeting in Zaire in 1975. The assembly stressed the conservation importance of traditional cultural practices and recommended that indigenous groups be allowed to retain ownership and use rights over their traditional lands even when the lands were incorporated into conservation areas. Shortly thereafter, the IUCN World Directory of National Parks and Other Protected Areas included a special classification for "protected anthropological areas" covering

areas set aside to provide for the continuance of ways of life endangered by the expansion of industrial civilization and its technology. They are areas occupied by people practising ways of life of anthropological or historical importance and are intended to provide for the continuance of those ways of life for so long as there are people willing to practice them and capable of doing so.

IUCN, 1977

One of the subcategories of protected anthropological areas included "natural biotic areas" to cover cases in which the impact of human activities on the environment was considered to be minor, as, for example, the San Bushmen in the Central Kalahari Game Reserve of Botswana and the Indians in the Xingu Indian Park in Brazil. Tourism in such areas was to be restricted. "Cultivated landscapes" was a subcategory applied to environments more obviously modified by traditional farming or pastoral peoples. Here the intent was to encourage the continuation of traditional activities, but tourism was considered more acceptable.

Implementation of such proposals was slow. The IUCN's 1977 World Directory lists several parks that were being used by tribal groups, but these were not actually designated as protected anthropological areas, and the tribals were often referred to as a "disturbance," as in the case of the Pygmies within the Odzala National Park in the Congo or the pastoralists in Ethiopia's Awash National Park.

The 1982 United Nations List of National Parks and Protected Areas, also compiled by the IUCN, continues to endorse the possibility of protection of tribal groups and provides Category VII, "anthropological reserves/natural biotic areas," where "the influence or technology of modern man has not significantly interfered with or been absorbed by the traditional ways of life of the inhabitants." Here, tribals are considered to be part of the natural environment, and the areas are to be managed to maintain habitat "for traditional societies so as to provide for their continuance within their own cultural *mores*" (IUCN, 1982). The IUCN justified the creation of such anthropological reserves in terms of the uniqueness of tribal cultures and their potential importance for anthropological research and the preservation of genetic diversity in the form of unique local cultigens. Significantly, the 1982 Directory lists no existing Category VII reserves.

The UN-endorsed World Conservation Strategy calls on development planners to include special provisions for local cultures in their planning and to make use of the specialized environmental knowledge of local cultures (IUCN, 1980). A meeting of the IUCN Commission on Environmental Planning in 1982 recommended that specific material on conservation and tribal peoples be compiled (Pitt, 1983). At about the same time, Klee (1980) published a survey of conservation, or "resource management," practices by traditional peoples from throughout the world, and the government of Papua New Guinea sponsored a conference on traditional conservation in Papua New Guinea (Morauta, Pernetta, & Heaney, 1982).

Biosphere Reserves

The UN Biosphere Reserve program, originally proposed in 1971 as part of UNESCO's Man and the Biosphere (MAB) program, further legitimated the conservation role of tribal peoples and the protection of tribal ways of life. Biosphere reserves were to comprise a global network of specially protected areas designed to preserve ecosystems, and according to the formal criteria adopted in 1974 by MAB Project No. 8, they were to include "man-modified landscapes." Biosphere reserves were different from standard nature reserves, because they were to be used to promote research toward the sustained human use of such ecosystems.

In 1977 the IUCN, the World Wildlife Fund, Survival International, and the Indonesian government began to design a biosphere reserve for Siberut Island, the largest of the Mentawai Islands off the west coast of Sumatra (McNeely, 1982). Siberut was occupied by some 18,000 tribal peoples, who were maintaining an effective balance with their resource base. It was recommended that the entire island be designated as a biosphere reserve, and forms of development that would not disturb the traditional use of the land were to be promoted. However, it seems that logging and agricultural development were the Indonesian government's highest priority, and over half of the island was designated as a "development zone" into which the tribals and transmigrants from overcrowded areas of Indonesia were to be moved, over the objections of Survival International. Only one-fourth of the area was designated for traditional use but not traditional settlement, and the government actually encouraged various forms of disruptive cultural intervention including resettlement. As Sumardja explained, the objective of the Siberut project was to "elevate the people well above the Neolithic level and bring them as gracefully as possible into the 20th century" (1984:8). Thus, the intent of this biosphere reserve was apparently not to maintain an environment where a tribal group could continue a traditional way of life.

One of the most promising applications of the biosphere reserve approach to the protection of a tribal population is Venezuela's Yanomami Biosphere Reserve as proposed by the IVIC, the Instituto Venezolano de Investigaciones Cientificas, in 1984 (Arvelo-Jimenez, 1984). This plan envisions the creation of a 37,285-square-kilometer biosphere reserve in southern Venezuela in order to protect the Orinoco watershed, the rainforest ecosystem, and 10,000 Yanomami Indians. It is argued that the Yanomami themselves and their unique cultural system are vital to the successful protection of the area because they have utilized the region's natural resources without degrading them. Furthermore, their presence along an otherwise unprotected frontier would discourage potential Brazilian political intervention. The creation of the Yanomami Biosphere

Reserve, it is argued, would constitute a definitive exercise of Venezuelan sovereignty in a previously neglected and vulnerable corner of their national territory.

The Yanomami Reserve would be divided into restricted, multiple use, buffer, and frontier patrol zones. Significantly, especially in comparison with the Siberut plan, nearly 75 percent of the total area, or some 27,000 square kilometers, falls within the restricted zone, which would be for undisturbed use by the Yanomami. The multiple use zone, totaling only 10 percent of the reserve area, was drawn to contain the various national institutions already present, including missionary, medical, and military posts, and would permit future tourist or recreational use. Any such uses already established within the restricted zone were to be relocated to the multiple use zone. The 10 percent buffer zone surrounding the multiple use area would permit research and restricted public access. The patrol zone paralleled Venezuela's frontier with Brazil and was limited to military security functions. The entire reserve area was to be administered by Venezuela's Ministry of Defense and the Ministry of Environment and Renewable Natural Resources. Six years after the proposal for the Yanomami Biosphere Reserve was presented to the Venezuelan government, it still had not been implemented, and it could be delayed indefinitely while the likelihood of invasion and development by outsiders increases, disrupting the integrity of the Yanomami. Napoleon Chagnon, the American anthropologist who is well known for his work on the Yanomami, or Yanomamo as they are called in his monograph (Chagnon, 1983), has recently established an organization to help defend the Yanomamo (see Appendix A).

Many other biosphere reserves involving tribal peoples already exist, such as the Rio Platano Biosphere Reserve in Honduras, La Amistad in Costa Rica and Panama, and the Manu Park in Peru. Other reserves are planned, as in Panama, where the Kuna Indians have proposed the creation of a reserve, Kuna Yala, as a buffer zone to protect their homeland from unwanted development (Wright, Houseal, & Leon, 1985).

The alliance between tribals and environmentalists holds great promise, but many problems remain. Although the two groups have common interests, environmentalists might balk at supporting the increasing demands of tribals for full political autonomy or full entitlement to traditional territory (Clad, 1985). Such autonomy or entitlement might imply the right of tribals to abandon traditional conservation practices in favor of new technologies and an expanded role in the market economy. Also, if traditional resource management practices have already been abandoned, the environmentalist's assumption that tribals are natural "conservationists" might be misplaced. From the tribal viewpoint, environmentalists and protected areas might be seen as unwelcome intrusions.

Ideally, such issues might be resolved by placing maximum emphasis on the collective human rights of tribal peoples to maintain their cultures (Bay, 1984) and giving them full authority to manage their own resources. Some of the options in this regard have been discussed by Brownrigg (1985), who notes that protected areas could be established within tribal lands and managed by tribal peoples in their own interests. In other cases, a national conservation agency might control an area occupied by tribals. Here, the tribals would not be legally designated as the owners, but instead could be recognized as "guardians" of the area. Administration would need to allow for population growth and culture change by giving tribals increased access to resources as their needs increased. Gardner and Nelson (1981) have explored in great detail the different policy options that have been applied to native peoples in national parks by government agencies in Australia, Canada, and the United States. Nietschmann (1984) has pointed out that not only are local people often the best managers of their resources, but they are also often the best able to defend their resources against misuse by outsiders if they have the legal authority to do so.

Dasmann has frequently stressed (1982, 1983:6) that reserves in themselves can never be large enough to protect either endangered species or peoples and cultures if they are contained within poorly managed national or global ecosystems. Ideally, the careful management practices of reserved areas would become models of appropriate conservation of natural resources and ecosystems for larger societies. In the long run, only in this way would the future of tribal cultures and the ecosystems sustaining them be secure.

You Can't Leave Them Alone: The Realists Prevail

Of the many conflicts between the proponents of different solutions to the problem of tribal exterminations and ethnocide, the most unfortunate was that in which the realists lumped all of the idealists with the scientific preservationists and accused them of seeking to establish human zoos as a way to preserve their tribal data.

The attack on the idealists was led by Rev. E. W. Smith in his 1934 RAI presidential address when he declared that anthropology did not advocate preserving tribal people in human zoos, or "refurbishing" disintegrated tribes. He accused the idealists of believing tribals to be racially incapable of progress, but Smith ignored the real political issue of state domination of tribal cultures. The political opinion that Smith passed off as science was that there was no basis for allowing tribals to remain independent. He argued not only that tribals were capable of progress, which was not the relevant issue, but that once tribals came into contact with "a more advanced culture," change was "inescapable." In Smith's view, this was a scientific anthropological law. He cited the renowned British scientist, Sir Julian Huxley, to support his argument that "human zoos" were impossible. But here again it was obviously a political not a scientific issue, and Huxley, referring to Africa, had actually stated that tribal preservation was not possible because it was not British policy:

> It can never be our aim . . . merely to preserve a human zoo. . . . It cannot be our
> aim, for it would not work. Our mere presence in Africa makes it in the long run

impossible: the fact that we are encouraging native production and native education, permitting the entry of white capital, missionaries, and science into Africa, makes it doubly impossible.

Huxley, 1931:137

It is significant that Smith also overlooked Huxley's "scientific" observation that many African tribals were being exterminated by civilization and his suggestion that in such cases it made sense to leave them alone. Huxley's opinion on tribal preservation was:

It can never be our aim, save perhaps with a few out-of-the-way peoples whose fate in unrestricted contact with Western ideas would be simply to wilt, degenerate and disappear (the Congo Pygmies seem to be an African example), merely to preserve a human zoo, an Anthropological Garden.

Huxley, 1931:137

Another central figure in the rejection of idealist approaches was A. P. Elkin, a Sydney anthropologist and Christian minister, who followed the functionalist colonial anthropology of Radcliffe-Brown and Malinowski. Elkin was an influential and outspoken advocate of "justice" for Aborigines, but his main concern was to ensure humane treatment for Aborigines as individuals; he was not interested in safeguarding aboriginal lands or maintaining the independence of native peoples. In direct opposition to Thomson, who advocated leaving Aborigines alone, Elkin stressed the need for "raising of the Aborigines in the scale of culture" and declared, "To leave them alone is impossible" (Elkin, 1935:207). Elkin's realism must have stemmed partly from the fact that his research program was supported by the Australian government and the Rockefeller Foundation, which supported realist policies. Furthermore, Elkin's immediate predecessor, Radcliffe-Brown, had ominously endorsed the realist position when he declared that "the Australian Aborigines, even if not doomed to extinction as a race, seem at any rate doomed to have their cultures destroyed" (1930:3). Within this context, Elkin's position made good political sense. In his 1934 summary of the "future of Aborigines" written for *Oceania*, Elkin declared:

It should be stated quite clearly and definitely that anthropologists connected with the Department in the University of Sydney have no desire to preserve any of the aboriginal tribes of Australia or of the islands in their pristine condition as "museum specimens" for the purpose of investigation; this charge is too often made against anthropologists.

Elkin, 1934:2

The "human zoo" charge, and the related accusations of racism, romanticism, and antiprogress, effectively halted the idealist preservationist movement by 1938. It soon became almost impossible for anthropologists to argue for "preservation" on any grounds, and when the ICAES Committee on the

Conservation of Aboriginal Peoples reconvened in 1946, attention was shifted to the dual realist program of data salvage and applied anthropology.

The clearest indication of the political strength of the realist position can be seen in the International Labor Organization (ILO) Convention 107 (1957), which endorsed integration and development over tribal autonomy. In 1954 the ILO convened a Committee of Experts to debate policy prior to the drafting of Convention 107. According to Horace Miner (1955), the Committee was divided between the "protectionists," led by Brazilian anthropologist Darcy Ribeiro, who favored respect for tribal culture and a slow integration of tribals into the dominant society, and Asian representatives who argued for rapid integration. In the end the realist position won. As Miner explained, "The realist recognizes the inevitability of increasing encroachment of civilization on the remaining outposts of preliterate culture" (1955:441). The realists battled among themselves over the rate of change, with the applied anthropologists generally favoring greater caution and respect for native culture and the religious humanitarians pushing for more rapid integration, but neither saw any possibility of leaving tribals alone.

INDIGENOUS PEOPLES RIGHTS ADVOCATES

We exist to help tribal peoples protect their rights; the simplest, unarguable rights of all people . . . and, moreover, to support their right to determine, themselves, their own future and that of their children—tribal self-determination.

Corry, 1976:11, for Survival International

The idealist perspective had only limited impact as long as it emphasized "preservation" and was represented only by isolated individuals and sporadic resolutions by scientific organizations. However, when it was revealed in 1967 that Brazil's Indian Protectorate Service, a government organization devoted to realist humanitarian principles, was engaged in a systematic genocidal program, idealist anthropologists were shocked into action. In 1968 at the 38th International Americanist Congress in Stuttgart, Germany, a group of anthropologists led by Norwegian Helga Kleivan, formed IWGIA, the International Work Group for Indigenous Affairs. IWGIA is a human rights organization, headquartered in Copenhagen, Denmark, which supports the right of indigenous peoples to maintain their independent existence. Since 1968 a number of similar advocacy organizations have been formed that share IWGIA's objectives, such as: Cultural Survival, founded in 1972 in Cambridge, Massachusetts; Survival International, founded in London in 1969; Survival International USA; and the Gesellschaft für bedrohte Völker (Society for Threatened Peoples) in Germany.

Cultural Survival, one of the most prominent pro-indigenous peoples organizations in the United States, founded and directed by Harvard anthropologist David Maybury-Lewis, seeks to inform the public about the problems of indigenous peoples and to influence policy makers to undertake actions favorable to indigenous peoples. It publishes a journal, the *Cultural Survival Quarterly*, and an extensive series of occasional papers and special reports. It has supported many special assistance projects, often designed by indigenous peoples themselves, to improve their prospects for survival.

The primary objective of such organizations is to help indigenous peoples gain self-determination and international recognition of their human rights. For example, IWGIA describes its purpose as "establishing the indigenous peoples' right to self-determination" and "helping to secure the future of indigenous people in concurrence with their own efforts and desires" (IWGIA leaflet, 1980). The overall strategy of these organizations seems to be threefold:

1. To focus international attention on the contemporary situation of indigenous peoples
2. To pressure governments to respect the internationally recognized rights of indigenous peoples
3. To provide financial assistance to indigenous peoples in support of their self-determination struggle

In pursuit of their objectives, these organizations maintain constant communication with each other, with more specialized regional organizations, and with indigenous organizations. Together they form a wide network composed of indigenous leaders, anthropologists, and other fieldworkers, who are all in close touch with events that influence tribal peoples throughout the world. It is now possible to respond almost immediately to any crisis situation, and a powerful coalition of informed opinion can be mobilized to influence government authorities to act responsibly in the expressed interests of indigenous peoples.

For example, in 1978 the international organizations learned that the Brazilian government was quietly preparing to "emancipate" Amazon Indians and thereby terminate their legally protected status. An international protest movement was immediately mounted, and the government was forced to withdraw the decree. Since then the Anthropology Resource Center (ARC) in Boston, IWGIA, and Survival International have coordinated an international campaign, together with other international organizations and twenty-seven pro-Indian organizations in Brazil, in support of a proposal to create a 6.4-million-hectare reserve for the Yanomamo Indians to counteract a government plan to isolate them in twenty-one small reserves.

Most international organizations have focused heavily on the issue of protecting tribal land rights. For example, Survival International lists land rights as its first essential priority. Another organization, CIMRA (Colonialism and Indigenous Minorities Research and Action), also London based, has campaigned heavily in favor of aboriginal land rights in Australia. As part of its campaign, CIMRA offers the following action proposals to concerned individuals who agree that something should be done to help Aborigines, but ask, "Yes, but what can I do?":

1. "Support . . . Aborigine land rights movements."
2. "Protest . . . to foreign corporations mining Aborigine land."
3. "Lobby . . . the Australian Government." (CIMRA, 1979:27)

These recommendations are followed by names and addresses of aboriginal organizations, mining companies, and government offices that can be contacted.

International Development Action (IDA), founded in Australia in 1970 as a research organization, focused on tribal land rights as a development issue. IDA called itself a "development education group" and was funded by Australian religious charities, development aid, and student and educational organizations. One of its early projects was an extended study of the role of multinational mining corporations in the expropriation of aboriginal lands on the Cape York Peninsula of Queensland, Australia. This research was carried out in close cooperation with the Aborigines, and the results were published in a series of monographs (Roberts, 1975; Roberts, 1978; Roberts & McLean, 1976; Roberts, Parsons, & Russell, 1975). More recently, IDA investigated the Purari hydroelectric scheme that would uproot thousands of Papua New Guinea tribal peoples so that massive amounts of electricity could be generated to enable Japanese companies to produce aluminum from the bauxite taken from tribal lands in the nearby Cape York Penninsula of Australia. The Purari project has not been approved, partly due to the protests raised against it. IDA's New Guinea work was a joint effort between IDA and the Purari Action Group, a native New Guinea organization opposing the development project.

In their efforts to focus world attention on the problems of indigenous peoples, the international organizations arrange press conferences, sponsor lectures, and carry out ambitious publication programs. IWGIA, for example, has published over sixty documents reporting on conditions in Central and South America, Canada, Australia, India, and the Philippines. In addition, it publishes a newsletter in English and Spanish. These materials are distributed to some two thousand social scientists throughout the world, to indigenous organizations, and governments, special United Nations organizations, and to other interested international organizations. Organizations such as IWGIA operate on small budgets with limited staffs. They support themselves through grants from philanthropic organizations and governments (IWGIA is heavily supported by Scandinavian governments) and from private donations and subscriptions.

Increasingly, these unique organizations have become important sources of funds to meet requests from indigenous political organizations or to carry out specific projects in support of self-determination for indigenous peoples. Although the total amount of this aid is still very modest, it represents a significant shift from traditional international aid, which often supports massive, inappropriate programs that may adversely affect indigenous peoples. Ideally, the kinds of projects being sponsored by these new organizations are small in scale and are usually initiated and directed by the native peoples themselves. For example, IWGIA has channeled funds to support conferences organized by indigenous peoples and to help free imprisoned indigenous political leaders. Together with Survival International, IWGIA has helped to finance the operation of Indian organizations in Colombia and Ecuador. Most of the funds ultimately originate from large foundations, charities, and church aid organizations.

CONCLUSION

Paradoxically, tribals were destroyed because global technological evolution outstripped social and political evolution in the twentieth century. A more humanistically evolved global culture would control its exploitation of resources while accommodating the existence of autonomous micropolities such as tribes and would permit great ethnic and cultural diversity.

The end of tribal autonomy is as momentous an event for humanity as is the rise of the Industrial Age, yet it has only recently begun to receive much attention. Now, important questions are being raised about the evolving global industrial system: Can the world be made safe for ethnic and cultural diversity, local autonomy, and social equality? Can natural ecosystems be maintained? In many respects, the disappearance of tribal cultures is an early warning device, because as tribal cultures have disappeared, the natural ecosystems that they occupied have become endangered and poverty, social inequality, and global insecurity have increased. Today, only a few thousand independent tribals remain, and the debate goes on over how to deal with them. A broader discussion of these issues will benefit these remnant groups, but will also be significant for the estimated 200 million indigenous peoples who are now struggling to regain control over their lives and resources.

Appendix A

Support Organizations

There are many organizations concerned with indigenous peoples and the defense of their rights. An extensive list of such organizations with addresses may be found in *Cultural Survival Quarterly* 9(2):B1–B8, 1985. Listed below are addresses of four of the best-known organizations:

Cultural Survival
11 Divinity Avenue
Cambridge, Massachusetts 02138

IWGIA
Fiolstraede 10
DK-1171 Copenhagen K
Denmark

Survival International
29 Craven Street
London WC2N 5NG
England

Survival International-USA
2121 Decatur Place, NW
Washington, D.C. 20008

In 1989 anthropologist Napoleon Chagnon founded an organization devoted exclusively to defending the rights of the Yanomamo Indians in Venezuela:

Yanomamö Survival Fund
P.O. Box 3684
Santa Barbara, California 93105

Appendix B

World Council of Churches Programme to Combat Racism PCR 1/71 (E) Declaration of Barbados*

FOR THE LIBERATION OF THE INDIANS

The anthropologists participating in the Symposium on Inter-Ethnic Conflict in South America, meeting in Barbados, January 25–30, 1971, after analyzing the formal reports of the tribal populations' situation in several countries, drafted and agreed to make public the following statement. In this manner, we hope to define and clarify this critical problem of the American continent and to contribute to the Indian struggle for liberation.

The Indians of America remain dominated by a colonial situation which originated with the conquest and which persists today within many Latin American nations. The result of this colonial structure is that lands inhabited by Indians are judged to be free and unoccupied territory open to conquest and colonization. Colonial domination of the aboriginal groups, however, is only a reflection of the more generalized system of the Latin American states' external dependence upon the imperialist metropolitan powers. The internal order of our dependent countries leads them to act as colonizing powers in their relations

* The Barbados Symposium was sponsored jointly by the Programme to Combat Racism and the Churches Commission on International Affairs of the World Council of Churches, together with the Ethnology Department of the University of Berne (Switzerland). The views expressed are those of the members of the Symposium, and not necessarily those of the co-sponsors of the Symposium.

211

with the indigenous peoples. This places the several nations in the dual role of the exploited and the exploiters, and this in turn projects not only a false image of Indian society and its historical development, but also a distorted vision of what constitutes the present national society.

We have seen that this situation manifests itself in repeated acts of aggression directed against the aboriginal groups and cultures. There occur both active interventions to "protect" Indian society as well as massacres and forced migrations from the homelands. These acts and policies are not unknown to the armed forces and other governmental agencies in several countries. Even the official "Indian policies" of the Latin-American states are explicitly directed towards the destruction of aboriginal culture. These policies are employed to manipulate and control Indian populations in order to consolidate the status of existing social groups and classes, and only diminish the possibility that Indian society may free itself from colonial domination and settle its own future.

As a consequence, we feel the several States, the religious missions and social scientists, primarily anthropologists, must assume the unavoidable responsibilities for immediate action to halt this aggression and contribute significantly to the process of Indian liberation.

The Responsibility of the State

Irrelevant are those Indian policy proposals that do not seek a radical break with the existing social situation; namely, the termination of colonial relationships, internal and external; breaking down of the class system of human exploitation and ethnic domination; a displacement of economic and political power from a limited group or an oligarchic minority to the popular majority; the creation of a truly multi-ethnic state in which each ethnic group possesses the right to self-determination and the free selection of available social and cultural alternatives.

Our analysis of the Indian policy of the several Latin American nation states reveals a common failure of this policy by its omissions and by its actions. The several states avoid granting protection to the Indian groups' rights to land and to be left alone, and fail to apply the law strictly with regard to areas of national expansion. Similarly, the states sanction policies which have been and continue to be colonial and class oriented.

This failure implicates the State in direct responsibility for and connivance with the many crimes of genocide and ethnocide that we have been able to verify. These crimes tend to be repeated and responsibility must rest with the State which remains reluctant to take the following essential measures:

1. Guaranteeing to all the Indian populations by virtue of their ethnic distinction, the right to be and to remain themselves, living according to their own customs and moral order, free to develop their own culture.

2. Recognition that Indian groups possess rights prior to those of other national constituencies. The State must recognize and guarantee each Indian

society's territory in land, legalizing it as perpetual, inalienable collective property, sufficiently extensive to provide for population growth.

3. Sanctioning of Indian groups' rights to organize and to govern in accordance with their own traditions. Such a policy would not exclude members of Indian society from exercising full citizenship, but would in turn exempt them from compliance with those obligations that jeopardize their cultural integrity.

4. Extending to Indian society the same economic, social, educational and health assistance as the rest of the national population receives. Moreover, the State has an obligation to attend to those many deficiencies and needs that stem from Indians' submission of the colonial situation. Above all the State must impede their further exploitation by other sectors of the national society, including the official agents of their protection.

5. Establishing contacts with still isolated tribal groups is the States' responsibility, given the dangers—biological, social and ecological—that their first contact with agents of the national society represents.

6. Protection from the crimes and outrages, not always the direct responsibility of civil or military personnel, intrinsic to the expansion process of the national frontier.

7. Definition of the national public authority responsible for relations with Indian groups inhabiting its territory; this obligation cannot be transferred or delegated at any time or under any circumstances.

Responsibility of the Religious Missions

Evangelization, the work of the religious missions in Latin America, also reflects and complements the reigning colonial situation with the values of which it is imbued. The missionary presence has always implied the imposition of criteria and patterns of thought and behavior alien to the colonized Indian societies. A religious pretext has too often justified the economic and human exploitation of the aboriginal population.

The inherent ethnocentric aspect of the evangelization process is also a component of the colonialist ideology and is based on the following characteristics:

1. Its essentially discriminatory nature implicit in the hostile relationship to Indian culture conceived as pagan and heretical

2. Its vicarial aspect, implying the reidentification of the Indian and his consequent submission in exchange for future supernatural compensations

3. Its spurious quality given the common situation of missionaries seeking only some form of personal salvation, material or spiritual

4. The fact that the missions have become a great land and labor enterprise, in conjunction with the dominant imperial interests

As a result of this analysis we conclude that the suspension of all missionary activity is the most appropriate policy on behalf of both Indian society as well as the moral integrity of the churches involved. Until this objective can be realized the missions must support and contribute to Indian liberation in the following manner:

1. Overcome the intrinsic Herodianism of the evangelical process, itself a mechanism of colonialization, Europeanization and alienation of Indian society.

2. Assume a position of true respect for Indian culture, ending the long and shameful history of despotism and intolerance characteristic of missionary work, which rarely manifests sensitivity to aboriginal religious sentiments and values.

3. Halt both the theft of Indian property by religious missionaries who appropriate labor, lands and natural resources as their own, and the indifference in the face of Indian expropriation by third parties.

4. Extinguish the sumptuous and lavish spirit of the missions themselves, expressed in various forms but all too often based on exploitation of Indian labor.

5. Stop the competition among religious groups and confessions for Indian souls—a common occurrence leading to the buying and selling of believers and internal strife provoked by conflicting religious loyalties.

6. Suppress the secular practice of removing Indian children from their families for long periods in boarding schools where they are imbued with values not their own, converting them in this way into marginal individuals, incapable of living either in the larger national society or their native communities.

7. Break with the pseudo-moralist isolation which imposes a false puritanical ethic, incapacitating the Indian for coping with the national society—an ethic which the churches have been unable to impose on that same national society.

8. Abandon those blackmail procedures implicit in the offering of goods and services to Indian society in return for total submission.

9. Suspend immediately all practices of population displacement or concentration in order to evangelize and assimilate more effectively, a process that often provokes an increase in morbidity, mortality and family disorganization among Indian communities.

10. End the criminal practice of serving as intermediaries for the exploitation of Indian labor.

To the degree that the religious missions do not assume these minimal obligations they, too, must be held responsible by default for crimes of ethnocide and connivance with genocide.

Finally, we recognize that, recently, dissident elements within the churches are engaging in a conscious and radical self-evaluation of the evangelical process. The denunciation of the historical failure of the missionary task is now a common conclusion of such critical analyses.

The Responsibility of Anthropology

Anthropology took form within and became an instrument of colonial domination, openly or surreptitiously; it has often rationalized and justified in scientific language the domination of some people by others. The discipline has continued to supply information and methods of action useful for maintaining, reaffirming and disguising social relations of a colonial nature. Latin America has been and is no exception, and with growing frequency we note nefarious Indian action programs and the dissemination of stereotypes and myths distorting and masking the Indian situation—all pretending to have their basis in alleged scientific anthropological research.

A false awareness of this situation has led many anthropologists to adopt equivocal positions. These might be classed in the following types:

1. A *scientism* which negates any relationship between academic research and the future of those peoples who form the object of such investigation, thus eschewing political responsibility which the relation contains and implies

2. A *hypocrisy* manifest in the rhetorical protestation based on first principles which skillfully avoids any commitment in a concrete situation

3. An *opportunism* that although it may recognize the present painful situation of the Indian, at the same time rejects any possibility of transforming action by proposing the need "to do something" within the established order. This latter position, of course, only reaffirms and continues the system.

The anthropology now required in Latin America is not that which relates to Indians as objects of study, but rather that which perceives the colonial situation and commits itself to the struggle for liberation. In this context we see anthropology providing on the one hand, the colonized peoples those data and interpretations both about themselves and their colonizers useful for their own fight for freedom, and on the other hand, a redefinition of the distorted image of Indian communities extant in the national society, thereby unmasking its colonial nature with its supportive ideology.

In order to realize the above objectives, anthropologists have an obligation to take advantage of all junctures within the present order to take action on behalf of the Indian communities. Anthropologists must denounce systematically by any and all means cases of genocide and those practices conducive to ethnocide. At the same time, it is imperative to generate new concepts and explanatory categories from the local and national social reality in order to overcome the subordinate situation of the anthropologist regarded as the mere "verifier" of alien theories.

The Indian as an Agent of His Own Destiny

That Indians organize and lead their own liberation movement is essential, or it ceases to be liberating. When non-Indians pretend to represent Indians, even on occasion assuming the leadership of the latter's groups, a new colonial situation is established. This is yet another expropriation of the Indian populations' inalienable right to determine their future.

Within this perspective, it is important to emphasize in all its historical significance, the growing ethnic consciousness observable at present among Indian societies throughout the continent. More peoples are assuming direct control over their defense against the ethnocidal and genocidal policies of the national society. In this conflict, by no means novel, we can perceive the beginnings of a Pan-Latin-American movement and some cases too, of explicit solidarity with still other oppressed social groups.

We wish to reaffirm here the right of Indian populations to experiment with and adopt their own self-governing development and defense programs. These policies should not be forced to correspond with national economic and socio-political exigencies of the moment. Rather, the transformation of national society is not possible if there remain groups, such as Indians, who do not feel free to command their own destiny. Then, too, the maintenance of Indian society's cultural and social integrity, regardless of its relative numerical insignificance, offers alternative approaches to the traditional well-trodden paths of the national society.

Barbados, 30 January 1971

Nelly Arvelo-Jiménez—Venezuela

Miguel Alberto Bartolomé—Argentina

Guillermo Bonfil Batalla—Mexico

Victor Daniel Bonilla—Colombia

Gonzalo Castillo-Cárdenas—Colombia

Miguel Chase-Sardi—Paraguay

Georg Grünberg—Switzerland

Darcy Ribeiro—Brazil

Scott S. Robinson—USA

Stefano Varese—Peru

Esteban Emilio Mosonyi—Venezuela

Appendix C

United Nations Declaration and Programme of Action to Combat Racism and Racial Discrimination, Geneva, 1978

DECLARATION, ARTICLE 21: *The Conference endorses the right of indigenous peoples to maintain their traditional structure of economy and culture, including their own language, and also recognizes the special relationship of indigenous peoples to their land and stresses that their land, land rights and natural resources should not be taken away from them;*

PROGRAMME OF ACTION

Measures at the National Level (Articles 8–11)

8. The Conference urges States to recognize the following rights of indigenous peoples:

    (a) To call themselves by their proper name and to express freely their ethnic, cultural and other characteristics;

    (b) To have an official status and to form their own representative organization;

    (c) To carry on within their areas of settlement their traditional structure of economy and way of life; this should in no way affect their right to participate freely on an equal basis in the economic, social and political development of the country;

(d) To maintain and use their own language, wherever possible, for administration and education;

(e) To receive education and information in their own language, with due regard to their needs as expressed by themselves, and to disseminate information regarding their needs and problems.

9. Funds should be made available by the authorities for investments, the uses of which are to be determined with the participation of the indigenous peoples themselves, in the economic life of the areas concerned, as well as in all spheres of cultural activity.

10. The Conference urges States to allow indigenous peoples within their territories to develop cultural and social links with their own kith and kin everywhere with strict respect for the sovereignty, territorial integrity and political independence and non-interference in the internal affairs of those countries in which the indigenous peoples live.

11. The Conference further urges States to facilitate and support the establishment of representative international organizations for indigenous peoples, through which they can share experiences and promote common interests.

Appendix D

World Council of Indigenous Peoples Second General Assembly Kiruna, Sweden, August 24–27, 1977

DECLARATION ON HUMAN RIGHTS

The Indigenous Delegates present at the Second General Assembly of the World Council of Indigenous Peoples, assembling at Kiruna, Samiland, Sweden, have studied the Universal Declaration of the United Nations on Human Rights and other international agreements and, having analysed our present situation as aboriginals, we submit to the opinion of the world the following:

Declaration

We have surveyed those areas [that] were invaded by the Europeans. To make their intrusion they used various means: direct or indirect violence, fraud and manipulation. These were the methods they used to occupy the land of the indigenous populations and acquire titles to such property which was rightfully owned by the aboriginals. These infamous conditions still prevail as of today, without any consideration to the fundamental declarations of the United Nations on Human Rights.

The most important ones are the Declaration of the General Assembly of 1948 and United Nations Convention on the Abolishment of all forms of Racial Discrimination.

Here is not the question of ordinary political persecution, but of the white man's use of medieval methods to encroach upon and exterminate the indigenous peoples and take over their lands. This is possible thanks to the complicity between the land owners, the multinational companies, and the governments.

Through our own members and individuals as well as international organizations, the World Council of Indigenous Peoples has received documented reports, at the First as well as at the Second General Assembly, of daily violations against indigenous groups and individuals. These are violations aimed at the most elementary needs which are denied and the human rights such as we understand them and as they have been explained by the official agencies of the United Nations.

This applies in particular to the greater part of South America, where the conditions have been described as especially severe. Outright massacres have taken place, in the style of those enacted by the conquerors and usurpers, in the 15th and 16th centuries. People have been imprisoned without legal cause, they have been tortured and murdered. In this way almost all the articles in the Convention of 1948 have been violated.

Even participation in the World Council for Indigenous Peoples has constituted grounds for imprisonment, torture, loss of civil rights, and expulsion.

No less serious is the inclination of certain states to deny the indigenous population, in groups or as individuals, the right to land and water. These are the fundamental resources for human life and prerequisites to an indigenous development of their own institutions, culture and language. All this also constitutes principles which have been manifested in international conventions:

1. International Convention on Economic, Social and Cultural Rights
2. The International Labour Organization's Convention No. 107
3. International Convention on Civil and Political Rights

Fundamental Principle

The World Council of Indigenous Peoples upholds, as a fundamental principle, that the Indigenous Peoples are the rightful owners of the land, whether they hold formal title deeds, issued by the colonists and usurpers, or not. It is, anyway, up to the colonists, usurpers, and intruders to submit evidence to their title, and this should be required on the part of the aboriginals. This principle should be considered as a fundamental element of legal justice.

I. All those Conventions and Declarations on the Human Rights which have been approved in the United Nations or in other international bodies by the representatives of the National Government, are not adhered to because the United Nations has no mandatory power nor are the member states particularly keen on realising them in practice. These conventions, furthermore, do not take account of the true situation and rights of the Indigenous Peoples.

II. We, therefore, wish to make clear those irrevocable and inborn rights which are due to us in our capacity as Aboriginals:

1. Right to self-determination;
2. Right to maintain our culture, language and traditions in freedom;
3. Right to have the World Council of Indigenous Peoples as a United Nations member, representing our people;
4. Right to recover the land which rightfully and according to millenary tradition belongs to us, but has been robbed from us by the foreign intruders;
5. Right to occupy land collectively with sole rights as something irrevocable and nontransferable;
6. Right to organize ourselves and administer our land and natural resources;
7. Right to demand from the governments of the countries sufficient land to improve the conditions of the Indigenous communities and promote their development under their own tutorship;
8. Right to make use of the natural resources existent in the areas of the indigenous peoples, such as forests, rivers, ore deposits and the riches of the sea, and a right for the indigenous people to take part in the project and construction work and the use of it;
9. Right to demand the states that such laws are passed, that will be of benefit to the Indigenous People, particularly for the protection of their right to land ownership, recognizing representative aboriginal organizations and their full involvement in the process of making laws;
10. Right to secure requisite funds for the Indigenous Peoples from the individual countries to be used for agrarian and natural resources development;
11. Right to acquire a share in the funds accruing from the member states to the United Nations, either through a project or directly, and right to exchange technical and scientific information between the Indigenous Populations of different countries;
12. Right to subsidies from governmental or international economic institutions through the granting of long-term credit at low interest;
13. Right to respect our Indigenous culture in all its modes of expression, for the protection of which appropriate by-laws should be passed;
14. Right to an appropriate education in accordance with our culture and our traditions, without any foreign elements and within the framework of an educational system which recognizes the values of our culture and acknowledges an official status to our language at all educational levels.

The Second General Assembly of the World Council of Indigenous Peoples addresses itself to all the peoples of the world, to individuals and to nations, to the United Nations and all its agencies, and to other international organizations, with an urgent appeal that all the violent actions and measures against indigenous peoples, as related above, be immediately brought to an end.

The World Council of Indigenous Peoples requests all its members to exert strong pressure wherever possible on the agencies in their respective countries, to make those agencies co-operate with international organizations to ensure that the inhuman conditions of Aboriginals are abolished.

The World Council of Indigenous Peoples urges the United Nations to establish a special fund for the support of groups or individual Aboriginals, so that they may be able to bring their cases to national or international courts and that they may be able to develop their areas, economic and culture.

The World Council of Indigenous Peoples should also work for the establishment of an international university for Indigenous Peoples having its seat in, for instance, the capital of Collasuyo (Bolivia).

WCIP
August 24–27, 1977
Kiruna, Samiland, Sweden

Appendix E

Declaration of Principles of Indigenous Rights, Fourth Assembly, World Council of Indigenous Peoples, Panama, September 1984*

DECLARATION OF PRINCIPLES OF INDIGENOUS RIGHTS

Principle 1. All indigenous peoples have the right of self-determination. By virtue of this right they may freely determine their political status and freely pursue their economic, social, religious and cultural development.

Principle 2. All states within which an indigenous people lives shall recognize the population, territory and institutions of the indigenous people.

Principle 3. The cultures of the indigenous peoples are part of the cultural heritage of mankind.

Principle 4. The traditions and customs of indigenous people must be respected by the states, and recognised as a fundamental source of law.

Principle 5. All indigenous peoples have the right to determine the person or groups of persons who are included within its population.

Principle 6. Each indigenous people has the right to determine the form, structure and authority of its institutions.

* *IWGIA Newsletter* no. 40 (Dec. 1984): 129–130

Principle 7. The institutions of indigenous peoples and their decisions, like those of states, must be in conformity with internationally accepted human rights both collective and individual.

Principle 8. Indigenous peoples and their members are entitled to participate in the political life of the state.

Principle 9. Indigenous people shall have exclusive rights to their traditional lands and its resources; where the lands and resources of the indigenous peoples have been taken away without their free and informed consent such lands and resources shall be returned.

Principle 10. The land rights of an indigenous people include surface and sub-surface rights, full rights to interior and coastal waters and rights to adequate and exclusive coastal economic zones within the limits of international law.

Principle 11. All indigenous peoples may, for their own needs, freely use their natural wealth and resources in accordance with Principles 9 and 10.

Principle 12. No action or course of conduct may be undertaken which, directly or indirectly, may result in the destruction of land, air, water, sea ice, wildlife, habitat or natural resources without the free and informed consent of the indigenous peoples affected.

Principle 13. The original rights to their material culture, including archaeological sites, artifacts, designs, technology and works of art, lie with the indigenous people.

Principle 14. The indigenous peoples have the right to receive education in their own language or to establish their own educational institutions. The languages of the indigenous peoples are to be respected by the states in all dealings between the indigenous people and the state on the basis of equality and non-discrimination.

Principle 15. The indigenous peoples and their authorities have the right to be previously consulted and to authorize the realization of all technological and scientific investigations to be conducted within their territories and to be informed and have full access to the results of the investigation.

Principle 16. Indigenous peoples have the right, in accordance with their traditions, to move freely and conduct traditional activities and maintain kinship relationships across international boundaries.

Principle 17. Treaties between indigenous nations or peoples and representatives of states freely entered into, shall be given full effect under national and international law.

Appendix F

Draft Principles on the Rights of Indigenous Populations, UN Working Group on Indigenous Populations, 1986*

1. The right to the full and effective enjoyment of the fundamental rights and freedoms universally recognized in existing international instruments, particularly in the Charter of the United Nations and the International Bill of Human Rights.

2. The right to be free and equal to all other human beings in dignity and rights, and to be free from discrimination of any kind.

3. The collective right to exist and to be protected against genocide, as well as the individual right to life, physical integrity, liberty, and security of person.

4. The right to manifest, teach, practise and observe their own religious traditions and ceremonies, and to maintain, protect, and have access to sites for these purposes.

5. The right to all forms of education, including the right to have access to education in their own languages, and to establish their own educational institutions.

6. The right to preserve their cultural identity and traditions, and to pursue their own cultural development.

7. The right to promote intercultural information and education, recognizing the dignity and diversity of their cultures.

* *IWGIA Yearbook 1986*, pp. 93–94

8. The right to determine, plan and implement all health, housing, and other social and economic programmes affecting them.

9. The right to special State measures for the immediate, effective and continuing improvement of their social and economic conditions, with their consent, that reflect their own priorities.

10. The right to be secure in the enjoyment of their own traditional means of subsistence, and to engage freely in their traditional and other economic activities, without adverse discrimination.

Bibliography

Aborigines Protection Society, London. Annual Report vols. 1–10, 1837–1847.

Ackermann, F. L. 1964. *Geologia e Fisiografia da Região Bragantina, Estado do Pará*. Manaus, Brazil: Conselho Nacional de Pesquisas, Instituto Nacional de Pesquisas da Amazônia.

Akeley, Mary L. Jobe. 1931. Africa's first national park. *Scientific American*, Nov., 295–298.

Allan, William. 1965. *The African Husbandman*. New York: Barnes and Noble.

Allard, William Albert, and Loren McIntyre. 1988. Rondonia's settlers invade Brazil's imperiled rain forest. *National Geographic* 174(6):772–799.

Anderson, Douglas D., Ray Bane, Richard K. Nelson, Wanni W. Anderson, and Nita Sheldon. 1977. *Kuunanmiit Subsistence: Traditional Eskimo Life in the Latter Twentieth Century*. Washington, D.C.: National Park Service, U.S. Department of the Interior.

Andrist, Ralph K. 1969. *The Long Death: The Last Days of the Plains Indian*. New York: Collier Books.

Anonymous. 1945. Indians shoot at plane. *Life* 18 (March 19):70–72.

———. 1963–1964. Statement on ethics of the society for applied anthropology. *Human Organization* 22:237.

———. 1972. Columbia trial reveals life ("Everyone kills Indians") on plains. *Akwesasne Notes* 4(4):26.

Arcand, Bernard. 1972. *The Urgent Situation of the Cuiva Indians of Colombia*. IWGIA Document no. 7. Copenhagen: IWGIA.

Arensberg, Conrad M., and Arthur H. Niehoff. 1964. *Introducing Social Change: A Manual for Americans Overseas*. Chicago: Aldine.

Arhem, Kaj. 1985. *The Maasai and the State: The Impact of Rural Development Policies on a Pastoral People in Tanzania*. IWGIA Document no. 52. Copenhagen: IWGIA.

Arnold, Robert. 1978. *Alaska Native Land Claims*. Anchorage: The Alaska Native Foundation.

Arvelo-Jiménez, Nelly. 1984. *La Reserva de Biosfera Yanomami: Una Autentica Estrategia para el Ecodesarrollo Nacional (Borrador de Trabajo)*. Caracas: Instituto Venezolano de Investigaciones Científicas.

Asch, Michael. 1977. The Dene economy. In *Dene Nation—The Colony Within*, ed. Mel Watkins, pp. 47–61. Toronto: University of Toronto Press.

Australia, Commonwealth Bureau of Census and Statistics. 1970. *Official Yearbook of the Commonwealth of Australia*, no. 56. Canberra.

Australia, DAA (Department of Aboriginal Affairs). 1977. Address by the Minister for Aboriginal Affairs the Honourable R. I. Viner at the Announcement of the Poll Results for the National Aboriginal Conference Elections, Perth, 28 November 1977. Pamphlet.

———. 1978. Statement by the Honorable R. I. Viner, M. P., Minister for Aboriginal Affairs, on Aboriginal Policies & Achievements in Aboriginal Affairs, House of Representatives, 24 November 1978. Pamphlet.

Australia, Department of Territories, Territory of Papua. *Report for 1964–1965*.

———. *Report for 1967–1968*.

Australia, Parliament of the Commonwealth. 1987. *Return to Country: The Aboriginal Homelands Movement in Australia*. House of Representatives Standing Committee on Aboriginal Affairs. Canberra.

Awad, Mohamed. 1962. Nomadism in the Arab lands of the Middle East. In *The Problems of the Arid Zone*, pp. 325–339. Paris: UNESCO.

Bailey, Robert. 1982. Development in the Ituri Forest of Zaire. *Cultural Survival Quarterly* 6(2):23–25.

Baker, John R. 1928. Depopulation in Espiritu Santo, New Hebrides. *Journal of the Royal Anthropological Institute* 58:279–303.

———. 1929. The Northern New Hebrides. *The Geographical Journal* 73(4): 305–325.

Barber, James. 1967. *Rhodesia: The Road to Rebellion*. London: Oxford University Press.

Barnaby, Georgy, George Kurszewski, and Gerry Cheezie. 1977. The political system and the Dene. In *Dene Nation—The Colony Within*, ed. Mel Watkins, pp. 120–129. Toronto: University of Toronto Press.

Barnett, Homer G. 1956. *Anthropology in Administration*. New York: Row, Peterson.

Barth, Fredrik. 1962. Nomadism in the mountain and plateau areas of South West Asia. In *The Problems of the Arid Zone*, pp. 341–355. Paris: UNESCO.

Bartolomé, Miguel Alberto. 1972. The situation of the Indians in the Argentine: The Chaco area and Misiones Province. In *The Situation of the Indian in South America*, ed. W. Dostal, pp. 218–251. Geneva: World Council of Churches.

Bascom, William R. 1965. Ponape: A Pacific economy in transition. *Anthropological Records* 22. Berkeley: University of California Press.

Bauer, Peter T., and Basil S. Yamey. 1957. *The Economics of Under-Developed Countries*. Cambridge Economic Handbooks. Chicago: University of Chicago Press.

Bay, Christian. 1984. Human rights on the periphery: No room in the ark for the Yanomami? *Development Dialogue* 1(2):23–41.

Bennett, Gordon. 1978. *Aboriginal Rights in International Law*. Occasional Paper no. 37, Royal Anthropological Institute of Great Britain & Ireland.

Bennett, Gordon, Audrey Colson, and Stuart Wavell. 1978. *The Damned: The Plight of the Akawaio Indians of Guyana*. Survival International Document no. 7.

Berger, Thomas R. 1985. *Village Journey: The Report of the Alaska Native Review Commission*. New York: Hill and Wong.

Berkhofer, Robert F. 1965. *Salvation and the Savage: An Analysis of Protestant Missions and American Indian Response, 1787–1862*. Lexington: University of Kentucky Press.

Beshir, Mohamed Omer. 1968. *The Southern Sudan: Background to Conflict*. New York: Praeger.

Bijlmer, H. J. T. 1953. Protection of native societies. *Proceedings of the Seventh Pacific Science Congress* 7:131–134.

Billington, Ray A. 1963. The frontier in American thought and character. In *The New World Looks at its History*, ed. Archibald R. Lewis and Thomas F. McGann. Austin: University of Texas Press.

Birdsell, Joseph B. 1971. Ecology, spacing mechanisms, and adaptive behavior in aboriginal land tenure. In *Land Tenure in the Pacific*, ed. Ron Crocombe, pp. 334–361. Melbourne: Oxford University Press.

Bodley, John H. 1970. *Campa Socio-Economic Adaptation*. Ann Arbor: University Microfilms.

———. 1983. The World Bank tribal policy: Criticisms and recommendations. *Congressional Record*, serial no. 98–37, pp. 515–521. (Reprinted in Bodley, 1988.)

———. 1985. *Anthropology and Contemporary Human Problems*. Palo Alto, Calif., and London: Mayfield.

———. 1988. *Tribal Peoples and Development Issues: A Global Overview*. Mountain View, Calif.: Mayfield.

Bodley, John H., and Foley C. Benson. 1979. Cultural ecology of Amazonian palms. *Reports of Investigations*, no. 56. Pullman: Laboratory of Anthropology, Washington State University.

Bonilla, Victor D. 1972. The destruction of the Colombian Indian groups. In *The Situation of the Indian in South America*, ed. W. Dostal, pp. 56–75. Geneva: World Council of Churches.

Bowman, James D. 1965. They like white men—broiled. (Associated Press.) *Eugene Register-Guard*, 7 October, p. 28.

Boye, Ellen. 1974. Samarbejde rundt om Nordpolen. *Grönland*, pp. 65–70. Copenhagen.

Bremaud, O., and J. Pagot. 1962. Grazing lands, nomadism and transhumance in the Sahel. In *The Problems of the Arid Zone*, pp. 311–324. Paris: UNESCO.

Brokensha, David. 1966. *Applied Anthropology in English-Speaking Africa*. Society for Applied Anthropology, Monograph no. 8.

Brownrigg, Leslie A. 1985. Native cultures and protected areas: Management options. In *Culture and Conservation: The Human Dimension in Environmental Planning*, ed. Jeffrey A. McNeely and David Pitt, pp. 33–44. London: Croom Helm.

Buell, Raymond L. 1928. *The Native Problem in Africa*. 2 vols. New York: Macmillan.

Bugotu, F. 1968. The culture clash: A Melanesian's view. *New Guinea* 3(2):65–70.

Bunce, George E. 1972. Aggravation of vitamin A deficiency following distribution of non-fortified skim milk: An example of nutrient interaction. In *The Careless Technology: Ecology and International Development*, ed. M. T. Farvar and John P. Milton, pp. 53–60. Garden City, N.Y.: Natural History Press.

Burger, Julian. 1987. *Report from the Frontier: The State of the World's Indigenous Peoples*. London: Zed Press; Cambridge, Mass.: Cultural Survival.

Burling, Robbins. 1963. *Rengsanggri: Family and Kinship in a Garo Village*. Philadelphia: University of Pennsylvania Press.

———. 1967. Tribesmen and lowlanders of Assam. In *Southeast Asian Tribes, Minorities, and Nations*, ed. Peter Kunstadter, pp. 215–229. Princeton, N.J.: Princeton University Press.

Cameron, A. L. P. 1885. Notes on some tribes of New South Wales. *Journal of the Royal Anthropological Institute* 14:344–370.

Cana, Frank R. 1946. German South-West Africa. *Encyclopedia Britannica*, vol. 10, pp. 230–231.

Capot-Rey, R. 1962. The present state of nomadism in the Sahara. In *The Problems of the Arid Zone*, pp. 301–310. Paris: UNESCO.

Carduño, Julio. 1980. Carta abierta a los Hermanos Indios de America. In *Primer Congreso de Movimientos Indios de Sudamerica*, pp. 103–129. Paris: Ediciones Mitka.

Castillo-Cárdenas, Gonzalo. 1972. The Indian struggle for freedom in Colombia. In *The Situation of the Indian in South America*, ed. W. Dostal, pp. 76–104. Geneva: World Council of Churches.

Catlin, George. 1841. *Letters and Notes on the Manners, Customs, and Conditions of the North American Indian*. London: Tosswill and Myers.

Cavalli-Sforza, Luigi Luca, ed. 1986. *African Pygmies*. New York: Academic Press.

Chagnon, Napoleon A. 1983. *Yanomamö: The Fierce People*. New York: Holt, Rinehart and Winston.

Chase-Sardi, Miguel. 1972. The present situation of the Indians in Paraguay. In *The Situation of the Indian in South America*, ed. W. Dostal, pp. 173–217. Geneva: World Council of Churches.

Chase-Sardi, Miguel, and Adolfo Colombres. 1975. *Por la Liberación del Indigena*. Buenos Aires: Ediciones del Sol.

Chatterjee, Suhas. 1967. Language and literacy in the North-Eastern regions. In *A Common Perspective for North-East India*, ed. Rathin Mittra and Barun Das Gupta, pp. 19–23. Calcutta: Pannalal Das Gupta.

Chaumeil, J. P. 1984. *Between Zoo and Slavery: The Yagua of Eastern Peru and Their Present Situation*. IWGIA Document no. 49. Copenhagen: IWGIA.

Chirif, Alberto. 1975. En torno a la titulación de las comunidades nativas y a los recursos forestales y de fauna silvestre. In *Marginacion y Futuro*, Sistema Nacional de Apoyo a la Movilizacion Social, Direccion General de Organizaciones Rurales, Serie: Communidades Nativas, pp. 66–76. Lima.

CIMRA (Colonialism and Indigenous Minorities Research and Action). 1979. Yes, but what can I do? *New Internationalist*, no. 77 (July):27.

Clad, James C. 1985. Conservation and indigenous peoples: A study of convergent interests. In *Culture and Conservation: The Human Dimension in Environmental Planning*, ed. Jeffrey A. McNeely and David Pitt, pp. 45–62. London: Croom Helm. (Reprinted in Bodley, 1988.)

Clyde, Paul H. 1935. *Japan's Pacific Mandate*. New York: Macmillan.

Cole, Monica M. 1966. *South Africa*. London: Methuen.

Collier, John. 1947. *The Indians of the Americas*. New York: W. W. Norton.

Conrad, Joseph. 1971. *Heart of Darkness*. Edited by Robert Kimbrough. New York: W. W. Norton.

Cook, Sherburne F. 1955. The epidemic of 1830–33 in California and Oregon. *University of California Publications in American Archaeology and Ethnology* 43:303–326.

Cooper, John M. 1946. The Patagonian and Pampean hunters. In *Handbook of South American Indians*, ed. Julian H. Steward, pp. 127–168. Vol. I. Bureau of American Ethnology. Bulletin no. 143. Washington, D.C.: Smithsonian Institution.

Coppens, Walter. 1972. *The Anatomy of a Land Invasion Scheme in Yekuana Territory, Venezuela*. IWGIA Document no. 9. Copenhagen: IWGIA.

Cornevin, Robert. 1969. The Germans in Africa before 1918. In *The History and Politics of Colonialism 1870–1914*, ed. L. H. Gann and Peter Duignan. Vol. 1, *Colonialism in Africa 1870–1960*. Cambridge: Cambridge University Press.

Corris, Peter. 1968. *Aborigines and Europeans in Western Victoria*. Occasional Papers in Aboriginal Studies no. 12, Ethnohistory Series no. 1. Canberra: Australian Institute of Aboriginal Studies.

Corry, Stephen. 1976. *Towards Indian Self-Determination in Colombia*. Survival International Document no. 2.

Cowan, James. 1922–23. *The New Zealand Wars*. Wellington: R. E. Owen, Government Printer.

Crawford, J. R. 1967. *Witchcraft and Sorcery in Rhodesia*. London: Oxford University Press (for International African Institute).

Crocombe, Ron. 1968. Bougainville!: Copper, R. R. A. and secessionism. *New Guinea* 3(3):39–49.

Crocombe, Ron, ed. 1971. *Land Tenure in the Pacific*. Melbourne: Oxford University Press.

Crocombe, Ron, and Robin Hide. 1971. New Guinea: Unity in diversity. In *Land Tenure in the Pacific*, ed. R. Crocombe, pp. 292–333. Melbourne: Oxford University Press.

Cunnison, Ian George. 1966. *Bagara Arabs: Power and Lineage in a Sudanese Nomad Tribe*. Oxford: Clarendon Press.

———. 1967. *Nomads in the Nineteen-Sixties*. Hull, England: Hull University.

DANE (Departemento Administrativo Nacional de Estadística). 1978. *Elementos para el Estudio de los Resguardos Indígenas del Cauca.* Bogotá.

d'Ans, Andre-Marcel. 1972. Les tribus indigenes du Parc National du Manu. International Congress of Americanists 39(4):95–100.

———. 1980. Begegnung in Peru. In *Ist Gott Amerikaner?* ed. Søren Hvalkoff and Peter Aaby, pp. 309–351. Göttingen, Germany: Lamuv Verlag.

Darwin, Charles. 1871. *The Descent of Man.* New York: D. Appleton and Company.

Dasmann, R. F. 1973. Sanctuaries for life styles? *IUCN Bulletin,* n.s. 4(8):29.

———. 1975. *The Conservation Alternative.* New York: John Wiley and Sons.

———. 1975. Difficult marginal environments and the traditional societies which exploit them. *News From Survival International,* no. 11 (July):11–15.

———. 1976. National parks, nature conservation, and "future primitive." *The Ecologist* 6(5):164–178. (Reprinted in Bodley, 1988.)

———. 1982. *The Relationship Between Protected Areas and Indigenous Peoples.* Paper presented at World National Parks Congress, Bali, Indonesia.

———. 1983. *Biosphere Reserves and Human Needs.* First International Biosphere Reserve Congress. Minsk, Byelorussia, USSR.

Davis, A. E., and T. D. Bolin. 1972. Lactose intolerance in Southeast Asia. In *The Careless Technology: Ecology and International Development,* ed. M. T. Farvar and John P. Milton, pp. 61–68. Garden City, N.Y.: Natural History Press.

Davis, Shelton H. 1977. *Victims of the Miracle: Development and the Indians of Brazil.* Cambridge: Cambridge University Press.

———. 1980. Brazilian Indian policy: The present situation. *ARC Bulletin* 3:2–3.

De'Ath, Colin, and Gregory Michalenko. 1980. High technology and original peoples: The case of deforestation in Papua New Guinea and Canada. *Impact of Science on Society* 30(3). (Reprinted in Bodley, 1988:166–180.)

De Marco, Roland R. 1943. *The Italianization of African Natives: Government Native Education in the Italian Colonies 1890–1937.* Teacher's College, Columbia University Contributions to Education, no. 880. New York.

Denevan, William M. 1976. Epilogue. In *The Native Population of the Americas in 1492,* ed. William M. Denevan, pp. 289–292. Madison: University of Wisconsin Press.

Dennett, Glenn, and John Connell. 1988. Acculturation and health in the highlands of Papua New Guinea. *Current Anthropology* 29(2):273–299.

Diamond, Stanley. 1960. Introduction: The uses of the primitive. In *Primitive Views of the World,* ed. Stanley Diamond, pp. v–xxix. New York: Columbia University Press.

———. 1968. The search for the primitive. In *The Concept of the Primitive,* ed. Ashley Montagu, pp. 96–147. New York: Free Press.

Diao, Richard K. 1967. The national minorities of China and their relations with the Chinese Communist regime. In *Southeast Asian Tribes, Minorities, and Nations,* ed. Peter Kunstadter, pp. 169–201. Princeton, N.J.: Princeton University Press.

Dilley, M. R. 1966. *British Policy in Kenya Colony.* New York: Barnes and Noble.

Dobyns, Henry F. 1966. Estimating Aboriginal American population: An appraisal of techniques with a new hemispheric estimate. *Current Anthropology* 7(4):395–449.

Docker, Edward W. 1970. *The Blackbirders: The Recruiting of South Seas Labour for Queensland, 1863–1907*. Sydney: Angus and Robertson.

Dostal, W., ed. 1972. *The Situation of the Indian in South America*. Geneva: World Council of Churches.

Drucker, Charles. 1985. Dam the Chico: Hydropower development and tribal resistance. *The Ecologist* 15(4):149–157. (Reprinted in Bodley, 1988:151–165.)

Dyson-Hudson, Neville. 1962. Factors inhibiting change in an African pastoral society. *Transactions of the New York Academy of Sciences*, series II, vol. 24, pp. 771–801.

Dyson-Hudson, Rada, and Neville Dyson-Hudson. 1969. Subsistence herding in Uganda. *Scientific American* 220(2):76–89.

Eiselen, W. M. 1934. Christianity and the religious life of the Bantu. In *Western Civilization and the Natives of South Africa*, ed. I. Schapera, pp. 65–82. London: George Routledge and Sons.

Elkin, A. P. 1934. Anthropology and the future of the Australian Aborigines. *Oceania* 5(1):1–18.

———. 1935. Presidential address: Anthropology in Australia, past and present. *Report of the 22nd Meeting of ANZAAS* 22:196–207.

———. 1951. Reaction and interaction: A food gathering people and European settlement in Australia. *American Anthropologist* 53:164–186.

Elwin, Verrier. 1939. *The Baiga*. London: John Murray.

———. 1959. *A Philosophy for NEFA*. 2d ed. Shillong, India: J. N. Chowdhury.

———. 1969. *The Nagas in the Nineteenth Century*. London: Oxford University Press.

Fabre, D. G. 1963. *Más Allá del Rio das Mortes*. Buenos Aires: Ediciones Selectas.

Falla, Ricardo. 1979a. *Historia Kuna—Historia Rebelde*. Serie El Indio Panameño no. 4. Panamá: Ediciones "CCS" (Centro de Capacitacion Social).

———. 1979b. *El Tesoro de San Blas*. Serie El Indio Panameño no. 5. Panama: Ediciones "CCS" (Centro de Capacitacion Social).

Federacion de Centros Shuar. 1976. *Solución Original a un Problema Actual*. Sucua, Ecuador.

Fenbury, David. 1968. Those Mokolkols!: New Britain's bloody axemen. *New Guinea* 3(2):33–50.

Fey, Harold E., and D'Arcy McNickle. 1970. *Indians and Other Americans: Two Ways of Life Meet*. New York: Harper and Row.

Flower, W. H. 1882. Chairman's Address for Anthropology. *British Association for the Advancement of Science, Report for 1881* 51:688.

———. 1884. President's address on the aims and prospects of the study of anthropology. *Journal of the Royal Anthropological Institute* 13:488–507.

Forde, Daryll. 1953. Applied anthropology in government: British Africa. In *Anthropology Today*, ed. A. L. Kroeber, pp. 841–865. Chicago: University of Chicago Press.

Formosa, Bureau of Aboriginal Affairs. 1911. *Report on the Control of the Aborigines of Formosa*. Taihoku.

Foster, George M. 1969. *Applied Anthropology*. Boston: Little, Brown.

Frere, Sir H. Bartle. 1881. On the laws affecting the relations between civilized and savage life, as bearing on the dealings of colonists with Aborigines. *Journal of the Royal Anthropological Institute* 11:313–354.

Friede, Juan. 1952. Los Cofan: Una tribu de la alta Amazonia Colombiana. *Proceedings, International Congress of Americanists* 30:202–219.

Fuentes, Hildebrando. 1908. *Loreto—Apuntes Geográficos, Históricos, Estadísticos, Politicos y Sociales*. Vol. II. Lima: Imprenta de la Revista.

Furlong, Charles Wellington. 1915. The Haush and Ona, primitive tribes of Tierra del Fuego. *Proceedings, International Congress of Americanists.* 19:432–444.

Furneaux, Rupert. 1963. *The Zulu War: Isandhlwana and Rorke's Drift*. Philadelphia and New York: J. B. Lippincott.

Gardner, J. E., and J. G. Nelson. 1981. National parks and native peoples in Northern Canada, Alaska, and Northern Australia. *Environmental Conservation* 8(3):207–215. (Reprinted in Bodley, 1988.)

Garra, Lobodon. 1969. *A Sangre y Lanza*. Buenos Aires: Edicíones Anaconda.

Ghurye, G. S. 1963. *The Scheduled Tribes*. 3d ed. Bombay: G. R. Bhatkal.

Goldschmidt, Walter R. 1952. The interrelations between cultural factors and the acquisition of new technical skills. In *The Progress of Underdeveloped Areas*, ed. Bert F. Hoselitz, pp. 135–151. Chicago: University of Chicago Press.

Goodenough, Ward H. 1963. *Cooperation in Change*. New York: John Wiley and Sons.

Goodland, Robert. 1982. *Tribal Peoples and Economic Development: Human Ecologic Considerations*. Washington, D.C.: World Bank.

Goulet, Denis. 1971. *The Cruel Choice: A New Concept in the Theory of Development*. New York: Atheneum.

Graburn, N. H. 1976. *Ethnic and Tourist Arts: Cultural Expressions from the Fourth World*. Berkeley: University of California Press.

Graham, A. C. 1971. China, Europe and the origins of the modern science. *Asia Major* 16 (parts 1–2):178–196.

Gray, Andrew. 1987. *The Amerindians of South America*. Report no. 15. London: Minority Rights Group.

Great Britain, Parliamentary Papers. 1836. "Report From the Select Committee on Aborigines (British Settlements)." Imperial Blue Book no. VII, 538.

Grosart, Ian. 1972. Direct administration. In *Encyclopedia of Papua and New Guinea*, ed. Peter Ryan, vol. I, pp. 266–269. Melbourne: Melbourne University Press.

Gross, Daniel R., and Barbara A. Underwood. 1971. Technological change and caloric costs: Sisal agriculture. *American Anthropologist* 73(3):725–740.

Gross, Daniel R., et al. 1979. Ecology and acculturation among native peoples of Central Brazil. *Science* 206(4422):1043–1050.

Grossman, Lawrence S. 1983. Cattle and rural economic differentiation in the highlands of Papua New Guinea. *American Ethnologist* 10(1):59–76.

Hames, Raymond B. 1979. A comparison of the efficiencies of the shotgun and the bow in neotropical forest hunting. *Human Ecology* 7(3):219–252.

Hardenburg, Walter E. 1912. *The Putumayo, the Devil's Paradise: Travels in the Peruvian*

Amazon Region and an Account of the Atrocities Committed Upon the Indians Therein. London: T. F. Unwin.

Harding, Thomas G. 1960. Adaptation and stability. In *Evolution and Culture*, ed. Marshall Sahlins and Elman Service, pp. 45–68. Ann Arbor: University of Michigan Press.

Harrop, Angus J. 1937. *England and the Maori Wars.* New York: Books for Libraries Press.

Hart, John A., and Terese B. Hart. 1984. The Mbuti of Zaire. *Cultural Survival Quarterly* 8(3):18–20.

Hastings, Peter. 1968. West Irian—1969. *New Guinea* 3(3):12–22.

Heilbroner, Robert L. 1963. *The Great Ascent: The Struggle for Economic Development in Our Time.* New York: Harper Torchbooks.

Henry, Jules. 1941. *Jungle People.* New York: J. J. Augustin.

Hickey, Gerald C. 1967. Some aspects of hill tribe life in Vietnam. In *Southeast Asian Tribes, Minorities, and Nations*, ed. Peter Kunstadter, pp. 745–769. Princeton, N.J.: Princeton University Press.

Hippler, Arthur E. 1979. Comment on "Development in the non-Western world." *American Anthropologist* 81:348–349. (Reprinted in Bodley, 1988.)

Homewood, K. M., and W. A. Rodgers. 1984. Pastoralism and conservation. *Human Ecology* 12(4):431–441. (Reprinted in Bodley, 1988:310–320.)

Hooton, Earnest A. 1945. Introduction. In *Nutrition and Physical Degeneration: A Comparison of Primitive and Modern Diets and their Effects* by Weston A. Price. Redlands, Calif.: The author.

Huff, Lee W. 1967. The Thai Mobile Development Unit Program. In *Southeast Asian Tribes, Minorities, and Nations*, ed. Peter Kunstadter, pp. 425–486. Princeton, N.J.: Princeton University Press.

Hughes, Charles C., and John M. Hunter. 1972. The role of technological development in promoting disease in Africa. In *The Careless Technology: Ecology and International Development*, ed. M. T. Farvar and John P. Milton, pp. 69–101. Garden City, N.Y.: Natural History Press.

Hunter, Guy. 1967. *The Best of Both Worlds: A Challenge on Development Policies in Africa.* London: Oxford University Press.

Hurault, J. 1972. The "Francization" of the Indians. In *The Situation of the Indian in South America*, ed. W. Dostal, pp. 358–370. Geneva: World Council of Churches.

Hutt, W. H. 1934. The economic position of the Bantu in South Africa. In *Western Civilization and the Natives of South Africa*, ed. I. Schapera, pp. 195–237. London: George Routledge and Sons.

Huxley, Julian. 1931. *Africa View.* New York: Harper and Row.

Hvalkof, Søren, and Peter Aaby, eds. 1981. *Is God an American? An Anthropological Perspective on the Missionary Work of the Summer Institute of Linguistics.* IWGIA/Survival International Document no. 43.

Hyndman, David. 1988. Melanesian resistance to ecocide and ethnocide: Transnational mining projects and the Fourth World on the island of New Guinea. In *Tribal Peoples and Development Issues: A Global Overview*, ed. John H. Bodley, pp. 281–298. Mountain View, Calif.: Mayfield.

ICA (International Congress of Americanists). Proceedings. Various locations.

Illich, Ivan. 1970. *Deschooling Society.* Vol. 44, *World Perspectives.* New York: Harper and Row.

Independent Commission on International Humanitarian Issues. 1987. *Indigenous Peoples: A Global Quest for Justice.* London: Zed Press.

International Labour Office. 1953. *Indigenous Peoples: Living and Working Conditions of Aboriginal Populations in Independent Countries.* Studies and Reports, New Series no. 35. Geneva.

IUCN (International Union for the Conservation of Nature). 1977. *World Directory of National Parks and Other Protected Areas.* Morges, Switzerland: IUCN.

————. 1980. *World Conservation Strategy: Living Resource Conservation for Sustainable Development.* Gland, Switzerland: IUCN.

————. 1982. *United Nations List of National Parks and Protected Areas.* Gland, Switzerland: IUCN.

IWGIA (International Work Group for Indigenous Affairs) 1986. *The Naga Nation and its Struggle Against Genocide.* IWGIA Document no. 56. Copenhagen: IWGIA.

————. 1987. *IWGIA Yearbook 1986: Indigenous Peoples and Human Rights.* Copenhagen: IWGIA.

————. 1988. *IWGIA Yearbook 1987: Indigenous Peoples and Development.* Copenhagen: IWGIA.

Iyer, L. A. Krishna, and L. K. Bala Ratnam. 1961. *Anthropology in India.* Bombay: Bharatiya Vidya Bhavan.

Jabavu, D. D. T. 1934. Bantu grievances. In *Western Civilization and the Natives of South Africa*, ed. I. Schapera, pp. 285–299. London: George Routledge and Sons.

Jimenez, Nelly Arevalo de. 1972. An analysis of official Venezuelan policy in regard to the Indians. In *The Situation of the Indian in South America*, ed. W. Dostal, pp. 31–42. Geneva: World Council of Churches.

Jones, Garth N. 1965. Strategies and tactics of planned organizational change: Case examples in the modernization process of traditional societies. *Human Organization* 24(3): 192–200.

Jones, J. D. Rheinallt. 1934. Economic condition of the urban native. In *Western Civilization and the Natives of South Africa*, ed. I. Schapera, pp. 159–192. London: George Routledge and Sons.

Jull, Peter. 1982. Canada: A perspective on the Aboriginal Rights Coalition and the restoration of constitutional aboriginal rights. *IWGIA Newsletter* 30:82–98.

————. 1987. Canada: Aboriginal self-government—assessing the constitutional failure. *IWGIA Newsletter* 50:69–81.

Jungius, Hartmut. 1976. National parks and indigenous peoples—A Peruvian case study. *Survival International Review* 1(14):6–14.

Kaines, Joseph. 1873. Western anthropologists and extra-Western communities. *Report of the British Association for the Advancement of Science for 1872, Transactions of the Sections* 42:189–190.

Kaplan, David. 1960. The law of cultural dominance. In *Evolution and Culture*, ed. Marshall D. Sahlins and Elman R. Service, pp. 69–92. Ann Arbor: University of Michigan Press.

Kar, Parimal Chandra. 1967. A point of view on the Garos in transition. In *A Common Perspective for North-East India*, ed. Rathin Mittra and Barun Das Gupta, pp. 91–102. Calcutta: Pannalal Das Gupta.

Keesing, Felix M. 1941. *The South Seas in the Modern World*. Institute of Pacific Relations International Research Series. New York: John Day.

Keesing, Felix M., and Marie Keesing. 1934. *Taming Philippine Headhunters: A Study of Government and of Cultural Change in Northern Luzon*. London: George Allen and Unwin.

Kelm, Heinz. 1972. The present situation of the Indian populations in non-Andean Bolivia. In *The Present Situation of the Indian in South America*, ed. W. Dostal, pp. 158–172. Geneva: World Council of Churches.

Kietzman, Dale W. 1977. Factors favoring ethnic survival. *International Congress of Americanists, Proceedings* 42(4):527–536.

Kiste, Robert. 1974. *The Bikinians: A Study in Forced Migration*. Menlo Park, Calif.: Cummings Publishing Co.

Klee, Gary A. 1980. *World Systems of Traditional Resource Management*. New York: W. H. Winston, Halstead Press.

Klima, George J. 1970. *The Barabaig: East African Cattle Herders*. New York: Holt, Rinehart and Winston.

Kloos, Peter. 1972. Amerindians of Surinam. In *The Situation of the Indian in South America*, ed. W. Dostal, pp. 348–357. Geneva: World Council of Churches.

———. 1977. *The Akuriyo of Surinam: A Case of Emergence From Isolation*. IWGIA Document no. 27. Copenhagen: IWGIA.

Kohr, Leopold. 1978. *The Breakdown of Nations*. New York: Dutton.

Kolarz, Walter. 1954. *The Peoples of the Soviet Far East*. New York: Praegar.

Korwa, Fred. 1983. West Papua: The colonisation of West Papua. *IWGIA Newsletter*, nos. 35/36:192–197.

Kosokov, K. 1930. *Voprosu o Shamanstve v Severnoy Azii* [On the question of shamanism in northern Asia]. Moscow.

Kroeger, Axel, and Françoise Barbira-Freedman. 1982. *Culture Change and Health: The Case of South American Rainforest Indians*. Frankfurt am Main: Verlag Peter Lang. (Reprinted in Bodley, 1988:221–236.)

Kruyt, A. C. 1929. The influence of Western civilization on the inhabitants of Poso (Central Celebes). In *The Effect of Western Influence on Native Civilizations in the Malay Archipelago*, ed. B. Schrieke, pp. 1–9. Batavia: Java Royal Batavia Society of Arts and Sciences.

Kunstadter, Peter, ed. 1967. *Southeast Asian Tribes, Minorities, and Nations*. Princeton, N.J.: Princeton University Press.

Lambert, S. M. 1931. Health survey of Rennell and Bellona Islands. *Oceania* 2(2):136–173.

Lane Fox Pitt-Rivers, A. H. 1872. Address to the department of anthropology. *Report of the British Association for the Advancement of Science for 1871* 41:157–174.

———. 1882. Anniversary address to the Anthropological Institute of Great Britain and Ireland. *Journal of the Royal Anthropological Institute* 11(4):488–509.

La Raw, Maran. 1967. Toward a basis for understanding the minorities in Burma: The Kachin example. In *Southeast Asian Tribes, Minorities, and Nations*, ed. Peter Kunstadter, pp. 125–146. Princeton, N.J.: Princeton University Press.

Lehman, F. K. 1963. *The Structure of Chin Society: A Tribal People of Burma Adapted to a Non-Western Civilization*. Illinois Studies in Anthropology no. 3. Urbana, Ill.: University of Illinois Press.

Levin, M. G., and L. P. Potapov. 1964. *The Peoples of Siberia*. Chicago: University of Chicago Press.

Levi-Strauss, Claude. 1951. Social science in Pakistan. *International Social Science Bulletin* 3(4):825–831.

Lindley, M. F. 1926. *The Acquisition and Government of Backward Territory in International Law*. London: Longmans, Green.

Lipkind, William. 1948. The Carajá. In *Handbook of South American Indians*, ed. Julian Steward, pp. 179–191. Vol. III. Bureau of American Ethnology Bulletin 143. Washington, D.C.: Smithsonian Institution.

Lizot, Jacques. 1976. *The Yanomami in the Face of Ethnocide*. IWGIA Document No. 22. Copenhagen: IWGIA.

Loram, C. T. 1932. Native labor in Southern Africa. In *Pioneer Settlement*, ed. W. L. G. Joerg. American Geographical Society, Special Publication no. 14, pp. 169–177.

Louis, Roger, and Jean Stengers. 1968. *E. P. Morel's History of the Congo Reform Movement*. Oxford: Clarendon Press.

Lugard, Sir F. D. 1928. The International Institute of African Languages and Cultures. *Africa* 1(1):1–12.

––––––. 1965. *The Dual Mandate in British Tropical Africa*. London: Frank Cass.

Lurie, Nancy Oestreich. 1957. The Indian Claims Commission Act. In *American Indians and American Life*, ed. George E. Simpson and J. Milton Yinger, pp. 56–70. The Annals of the American Academy of Political and Social Science (May), vol. 311. Philadelphia.

Mair, Lucy Philip. 1970. *Australia in New Guinea*. Melbourne: Melbourne University Press.

Malinowski, Bronislaw. 1929. Practical anthropology. *Africa* 2(1):22–38.

Manners, Robert A. 1956. Functionalism, realpolitik, and anthropology in under-developed areas. *America Indigena* 16(1):7–33.

––––––. 1967. The Kipsigis of Kenya: Culture change in a "Model" East African tribe. In *Contemporary Change in Traditional Societies*, ed. Julian Steward, vol. 1, pp. 205–359. Urbana: University of Illinois Press.

Maunier, René. 1949. *The Sociology of Colonies*. Vol. 2. London: Routledge and Kegan Paul.

Maybury-Lewis, David. 1983. The Shavante struggle for their lands. *Cultural Survival Quarterly* 7(1):54–55.

Maybury-Lewis, David, and James Howe. 1980. *The Indian Peoples of Paraguay: Their Plight and Their Prospects*. Special Report no. 2, Cultural Survival, Cambridge, Massachusetts.

McCullum, Hugh, Karmel McCullum, and John Olthuis. 1977. *Moratorium: Justice, Energy, the North, and the Native People*. Toronto: Anglican Book Centre.

McIntyre, Loren. 1988. Last days of Eden: Rondonia's Urueu-Wau-Wau Indians. *National Geographic* 174(6): 800–817.

McNeely, Jeffrey A. 1982. The people of Siberut: Indonesia's original inhabitants. In *Culture and Conservation, IUCN/CEP* (International Union for the Conservation of Nature and the Commission on Environmental Planning), Work in Progress 13, Paper no. 3. Gland, Switzerland: IUCN/CEP.

McNeil, Mary. 1972. Lateritic soils in distinct tropical environments: Southern Sudan and Brazil. In *The Careless Technology: Ecology and International Development*, ed. M. T. Farvar and John P. Milton, pp. 591–608. Garden City, N.Y.: Natural History Press.

Mead, Margaret. 1961. *New Lives for Old*. New York: New American Library.

Meggers, Betty J. 1971. *Amazonia: Man and Culture in a Counterfeit Paradise*. Chicago: Aldine.

Merivale, Herman. 1861. *Lectures on Colonization and Colonies*. London: Green, Longman and Roberts.

Mey, Wolfgang E. 1983. Dammed for progress: About the perversity of state and nation-building in Bangladesh—The Chittagong Hill Tracts Case. Paper presented at symposium, The Fourth World: Relations Between Minority Peoples and Nation-States. XIth International Congress of Anthropological and Ethnological Sciences, Vancouver, Canada.

Miner, Horace M. 1955. Planning for the acculturation of isolated tribes. *International Congress of Americanists, Proceedings* 31(1): 441–446.

Mittra, Rathin, and Barun Das Gupta. 1967. *A Common Perspective for North-East India*. Calcutta: Pannalal Das Gupta.

Moasosang, P. 1967. The Naga search for self-identity. In *A Common Perspective for North-East India*, ed. Rathin Mittra and Barun Das Gupta, pp. 51–57. Calcutta: Pannalal Das Gupta.

Mönckeberg, F. 1968. Mental retardation from malnutrition. *Journal of the American Medical Association* 206: 30–31.

Montagu, Ashley. 1972. Sociogenic brain damage. *American Anthropologist* 74(5): 1045–1061.

Morauta, Louise, John Pernetta, and William Heaney. 1982. *Traditional Conservation in Papua New Guinea: Implications for Today*. Monograph no. 16, Institute of Applied Social and Economic Research. Boroka, Papua New Guinea.

Moreira Neto, Carlos de Araujo. 1972. Some data concerning the recent history of the Kaingang Indians. In *The Situation of the Indian in South America*, ed. W. Dostal, pp. 284–333. Geneva: World Council of Churches.

Morel, E. D. 1906. *Red Rubber*. New York: The Nassau Print.

———. 1969. *The Black Man's Burden*. Northbrook, Ill.: Metro Books. (Reprint of 1920 edition.)

Mosonyi, Esteban E. 1972. The situation of the Indian in Venezuela: Perspectives and solutions. In *The Situation of the Indian in South America*, ed. W. Dostal, pp. 43–55. Geneva: World Council of Churches.

Mountjoy, A. B. 1967. *Industrialization and Underdeveloped Countries*. Chicago: Aldine.

Münzel, Mark. 1973. *The Aché Indians: Genocide in Paraguay*. IWGIA Document no. 11. Copenhagen: IWGIA.

Murdock, George P. 1959. *Africa: Its Peoples and Their Culture History*. New York: McGraw-Hill.

Murphy, Robert, and Julian Steward. 1956. Trappers and trappers: Parallel processes in acculturation. *Economic Development and Culture Change* 4:335–355.

Nag, Amit Kumar. 1967. The society in transition in the Mizo District. In *A Common Perspective for North-East India*, ed. Rathin Mittra and Barun Das Gupta, pp. 80–90. Calcutta: Pannalal Das Gupta.

Nahanni, Phoebe. 1977. The mapping project. In *Dene Nation—Colony Within*, ed. Mel Watkins, pp. 21–27. Toronto: University of Toronto Press.

Nash, Roderick. 1968. *The American Environment: Readings in the History of Conservation*. Reading, Mass.: Addison-Wesley.

Nederlandsche Commissie voor Internationale Natuurbescherming. 1937. *Conservation of Primitives Still Living in the Stone Age, Especially in New Guinea*. Medeelingen no. 11, pp. 1–7. (See also abstract of report, Proceedings of the Seventh Pacific Science Congress 1953, pp. 148–149.)

Netting, Robert M. 1977. *Cultural Ecology*. Menlo Park, Calif.: Benjamin/Cummings.

New Zealand, Department of Statistics. 1960. *The New Zealand Official Year-Book*. Wellington: R. E. Owen, Government Printer.

Nietschmann, Bernard. 1984. Biosphere reserves and traditional societies. In *Conservation, Science and Society: Contributions to the First International Biosphere Reserve Congress, Minsk, Byelorussia/USSR*. Vol. 2, pp. 499–508. Paris: UNESCO–UNEP.

———. 1985. Indonesia, Bangladesh: Disguised invasion of indigenous nations. *Fourth World Journal* 1(2):89–126. (Reprinted in abridged form in Bodley, 1988:191–207.)

———. 1988. Miskito and Kuna struggle for nation autonomy. In *Tribal Peoples and Development Issues: A Global Overview*, ed. John H. Bodley, pp. 271–280. Mountain View, Calif.: Mayfield.

Niklaus, Phil. 1983. Land, power and yellowcake. *IWGIA Newsletter*, no. 34:6–15.

Nimuendaju, Curt. 1946. *The Eastern Timbira*. University of California Publications in American Archaeology and Ethnology, vol. 41. Berkeley: University of California Press.

Nishi, Midori. 1968. An evaluation of Japanese agricultural and fishery developments in Micronesia during the Japanese mandate 1914–1941. *Micronesia* 4(1):1–18.

Oliver, Douglas L. ed. 1951. *Planning Micronesia's Future: A Summary of the United States Commercial Company's Economic Survey of Micronesia*. Cambridge: Harvard University Press.

Otten, Mariël. 1986. Transmigrasi: Indonesian Resettlement Policy, 1965–1985. IWGIA Document No. 57. Copenhagen.

Palacios i Mendiburu, S. 1892. Conferencia sobre la colonizacion de Loreto. *Boletin de la Sociedad Geografica de Lima* 2:267–312.

Palmer, George. 1871. *Kidnapping in the South Seas*. Edinburgh: Edmonston and Douglas.

Patterson, Dennis. 1984. Canada: Inuit and Nunavut. *IWGIA Newsletter*, no. 37:39–52.

Peacock, Nadene. 1984. The Mbuti of Northeast Zaire. *Cultural Survival Quarterly* 8(2):15–17.

Peoples, James G. 1978. Dependence in a Micronesian economy. *American Ethnologist* 5(3):535–552.

Pitt, David. 1983. *Culture and Conservation: An Action/Research Plan.* Gland, Switzerland: IUCN.

Pittock, A. Barrie. 1972. *Aboriginal Land Rights.* IWGIA Document no. 3. Copenhagen: IWGIA.

———. 1975. *Beyond White Australia: A Short History of Race Relations in Australia.* Surrey Hills, New South Wales: Race Relations Committee of the Religious Society of Friends (Quakers) in Australia.

Pitt-Rivers, George H. 1927. *The Clash of Culture and the Contact of Races.* London: George Routledge and Sons.

Popenoe, Paul. 1915. One phase of man's modern evolution. *International Congress of Americanists* 19:617–620.

Portas, Julio Aníbal. 1967. *Malón Contra Malón: La Solucion Final del Problema del Indio en la Argentina.* Buenos Aires: Ediciones de la Flor.

Portugal, Pedro. 1980. Entrevista con Pedro Portugal. In *Primer Congreso de Movimientos Indios de Sudamerica,* pp. 169–180. Paris: Ediciones Mitka.

Powell, J. W. 1881. *First Annual Report of the Bureau of Ethnology to the Secretary of the Smithsonian Institution 1879–80.* Washington, D.C.: Government Printing Office.

Presland, Anna. 1979. An account of the contemporary fight for survival of the Amerindian peoples of Brazil. *Survival International Review* 4(1):14–40.

Price, A. G. 1950. *White Settlers and Native Peoples.* London: Cambridge University Press.

Price, Weston Andrew. 1945. *Nutrition and Physical Degeneration: A Comparison of Primitive and Modern Diets and Their Effects.* Redlands, Calif.: The author.

Prior, Ian A. M. 1971. The price of civilization. *Nutrition Today* 6(4):2–11.

Radcliffe-Brown, A. R. 1930. Editorial. *Oceania* 1(1):1–4.

Raglan, Lord Fitzroy R. S. 1940. The future of the savage races. *Man* 40:62.

Rambo, A. Terry. 1985. *Primitive Polluters: Semang Impact on the Malaysian Tropical Rain Forest Ecosystem.* Anthropological Papers no. 76, Museum of Anthropology, University of Michigan.

Razon, Felix. 1976. *Native Peoples Struggle Against U.S. Imperialism in the Philippines.* IWGIA Document no. 25, pp. 32–41. Copenhagen: IWGIA.

Redfield, Robert. 1953. *The Primitive World and its Transformations.* Ithaca, N.Y.: Cornell University Press.

———. 1962. *A Village that Chose Progress: Chan Kom Revisited.* Chicago: University of Chicago Press, Phoenix Books.

Redfield, Robert, Ralph Linton, and M. J. Herskovits. 1936. Memorandum on the study of acculturation. *American Anthropologist* 38:149–152.

Reed, Stephen W. 1943. *The Making of Modern New Guinea.* Philadelphia: American Philosophical Society.

Reinhard, K. R. 1976. Resource exploitation and the health of western arctic man. In *Circumpolar Health: Proceedings of the Third International Symposium, Yellowknife, Northwest Territories*, ed. Roy J. Shephard and S. Itoh, pp. 617–627. Toronto: University of Toronto Press. (Reprinted in Bodley, 1988.)

Reining, Conrad C. 1966. *The Zande Scheme: An Anthropological Case Study of Economic Development in Africa*. Evanston, Ill.: Northwestern University Press.

Ribeiro, Darcy. 1957. *Culturas e Linguas Indigenas do Brasil*. Separata de Educacão e Ciéncias Socais no. 6. Rio de Janeiro: Centro Brasileiro de Pesquisas Educacionais.

Rivers, W. H. R. 1922. *Essays on the Depopulation of Melanesia*. Cambridge: Cambridge University Press.

Roberts, Janine. 1978. *From Massacres to Mining: The Colonization of Aboriginal Australia*. London: War on Want.

Roberts, J. P., ed. 1975. *Mapoon—Book One: The Mapoon Story by the Mapoon People*. Victoria, Australia: IDA (International Development Action).

Roberts, J., and D. McLean. 1976. *Mapoon—Book Three: The Cape York Aluminum Companies and the Native Peoples*. Victoria, Australia: IDA (International Development Action).

Roberts, J., M. Parsons, and B. Russell. 1975. *Mapoon—Book Two: The Mapoon Story According to the Invaders*. Victoria, Australia: IDA (International Development Action).

Roberts, Stephen Henry. 1969. *Population Problems of the Pacific*. New York: AMS Press. (Reprint of 1927 edition.)

Rocamora, Joel. 1979a. Agribusiness, dams and counter-insurgency. *Southeast Asia Chronicle*, no. 67:2–10.

———. 1979b. The political uses of PANAMIN. *Southeast Asia Chronicle*, no. 67:11–21.

Rodman, Margaret, and Matthew Cooper, eds. 1979. *The Pacification of Melanesia*. Association for Social Anthropology in Oceania Monograph no. 7. Ann Arbor: University of Michigan Press.

Rossel, Pierre. 1988. *Tourism and Cultural Minorities: Double Marginalisation and Survival Strategies*. IWGIA Document no. 61. Copenhagen: IWGIA.

Rotberg, Robert, and Ali Mazrui, eds. 1970. *Protest and Power in Black Africa*. New York: Oxford University Press.

Rowley, Charles D. 1966. *The New Guinea Villager: The Impact of Colonial Rule on Primitive Society and Economy*. New York: Praeger.

———. 1967. The villager and the nomad: Aboriginals and New Guineans. *New Guinea* 2(1):70–81.

———. 1970. *The Destruction of Aboriginal Society*. Vol. 1, *Aboriginal Policy and Practice*. Canberra: Australian National University Press.

———. 1971. *The Remote Aborigines*. Vol. 3, *Aboriginal Policy and Practice*. Canberra: Australian National University Press.

Rushforth, Scott. 1977. Country food. In *Dene Nation—Colony Within*, ed. Mel Watkins, pp. 47–61. Toronto: University of Toronto Press.

Russell, Peter H. 1977. The Dene nation and confederation. In *Dene Nation—Colony Within*, ed. Mel Watkins, pp. 163–173. Toronto: University of Toronto Press.

Ryan, John. 1969. *The Hot Land: Focus on New Guinea*. New York: Macmillan.

Said, Beshir Mohammed. 1965. *The Sudan, Crossroads of Africa*. Chester Springs, Penn.: Dufour Editions.

Sanders, Douglas E. 1977. *The Formation of the World Council of Indigenous Peoples*. IWGIA Document no. 29. Copenhagen: IWGIA.

Saussol, Alain. 1971. New Caledonia: Colonization and reaction. In *Land Tenure in the Pacific*, ed. Ron Crocombe, pp. 227–245. Melbourne: Oxford University Press.

Scarr, Deryck. 1968. Introduction. In *A Cruise in a Queensland Labour Vessel to the South Seas*, by W. E. Giles. Canberra: Australian National University Press.

Schapera, I. 1934. *Western Civilization and the Natives of South Africa*. London: George Routledge and Sons.

Schneider, David. 1955. Abortion and depopulation on a Pacific island: Yap. In *Health, Culture, and Community*, ed. B. D. Paul, pp. 211–235. New York: Russel Sage.

Schoen, Ivan L. 1969. Contact with the Stone Age. *Natural History* 78(1):10–18, 66–67.

Seiler-Baldinger, Annemarie. 1988. Tourism in the upper Amazon and its effects on the indigenous population. In *Tourism: Manufacturing the Exotic*, ed. Pierre Rossel, pp. 177–193. IWGIA Document no. 61. Copenhagen: IWGIA.

Sinclair, Keith. 1961. *The Origins of the Maori Wars*. 2d ed. Wellington: New Zealand University Press.

Smith, Edwin W. 1934. Anthropology and the practical man. *Journal of the Royal Anthropological Institute* 64:xiii–xxxvii.

Smith, V. L., ed. 1977. *Hosts and Guests: The Anthropology of Tourism*. Philadelphia: University of Pennsylvania Press.

Smith, Wilberforce. 1894. The teeth of ten Sioux Indians. *Journal of the Royal Anthropological Institute* 24:109–116.

Snow, Alpheus Henry. 1921. *The Question of Aborigines: In the Law and Practice of Nations*. New York: G. P. Putnam's Sons.

Soja, Edward W. 1968. *The Geography of Modernization in Kenya*. Syracuse Geographical Series, no. 2. Syracuse, N.Y.: Syracuse University Press.

Spencer, Baldwin. 1913. *Preliminary Report on the Aboriginals of the Northern Territory*. The Parliament of the Commonwealth of Australia, Northern Territory of Australia, Report of the Administrator for the Year 1912, pp. 36–52.

Spooner, Brian. 1973. *The Cultural Ecology of Pastoral Nomads*. Modules in Anthropology. Reading, Mass.: Addison-Wesley.

Starr, Cecie, ed. 1971. *Anthropology Today*. Del Mar, Calif.: Communications Research Machines.

Steward, Julian H. 1948. The Witotoan tribes. In *Handbook of South American Indians*, ed. Julian H. Steward, pp. 749–762. Vol. III. Bureau of American Ethnology Bulletin 143. Washington, D.C.: Smithsonian Institution.

Steward, Julian H., ed. 1967. *Contemporary Change in Traditional Societies*. Urbana: University of Illinois Press.

Stoll, David. 1982. *Fishers of Men or Founders of Empire? The Wycliffe Bible Translators in Latin America*. London: Zed Press; Cambridge, Mass.: Cultural Survival.

Sturtevant, William C. 1967. Urgent anthropology: Smithsonian–Wenner–Gren Conference. *Current Anthropology* 8(4):355–361.

————. 1970. Resolution on forced acculturation. *Current Anthropology* 11(2):160.

Suess, Paulo. 1980. Tríplice Alianca na Luta Indígena. *Porantim* 3(17):8–9.

Sumardja, Effendy A. 1984. Siberut Reserve Impacts on Indigenous People in West Sumatra, Indonesia. Paper presented at the First World Conference on Cultural Parks, Mesa Verde, Colorado.

Suret-Canale, Jean. 1971. *French Colonialism in Tropical Africa 1900–1945.* New York: Pica Press.

Thiek, Hrilrokhum. 1967. An outlook for a better understanding of the tribal people. In *A Common Perspective for North-East India,* eds. Rathin Mittra and Barun Das Gupta, pp. 103–109. Calcutta: Pannalal Das Gupta.

Thomson, Donald F. 1938. Recommendations of Policy in Native Affairs in the Northern Territory of Australia. The Parliament of the Commonwealth of Australia No. 56.-F.2945.

Thornton, Russell. 1987. *American Indian Holocaust and Survival: A Population History Since 1492.* Norman and London: University of Oklahoma Press.

Townsend, G. 1933. The administration of the mandated territory of New Guinea. *Geographical Journal* 82:424–434.

TTR: *See under* United States.

Turnbull, Colin M. 1963. "The lesson of the Pygmies." *Scientific American* 208(1):28–37.

————. 1972. *The Mountain People.* New York: Simon and Schuster.

United States, Department of the Interior, Office of Territories. 1953. *Report on the Administration of the Trust Territory of the Pacific Islands* (by the United States to the United Nations) for the Period July 1, 1951, to June 30, 1952.

————. 1954. *Annual Report, High Commissioner of the Trust Territory of the Pacific Islands to the Secretary of the Interior* (for 1953).

United States, Department of State. 1955. *Seventh Annual Report to the United Nations on the Administration of the Trust Territory of the Pacific Islands* (July 1, 1953, to June 30, 1954).

————. 1959. *Eleventh Annual Report to the United Nations on the Administration of the Trust Territory of the Pacific Islands* (July 1, 1957, to June 30, 1958).

————. 1964. *Sixteenth Annual Report to the United Nations on the Administration of the Trust Territory of the Pacific Islands* (July 1, 1962, to June 30, 1963).

————. 1973. *Twenty-Fifth Annual Report to the United Nations on the Administration of the Trust Territory of the Pacific Islands* (July 1, 1971, to June 30, 1972).

Valcarcel, Carlos A. 1915. *El Proceso del Putumayo y sus Secretos Inauditos.* Lima, Peru: H. La Rosa.

Wagley, C. 1951. Cultural influences on population. *Revista do Museu Paulista* 5:95–104.

————. 1977. *Welcome of Tears: The Tapirape Indians of Central Brazil.* New York: Oxford University Press.

Watkins, Mel, ed. 1977. *Dene Nation—The Colony Within.* Toronto: University of Toronto Press.

WCIP (World Council of Indigenous Peoples). 1977. World Council of Indigenous Peoples Second General Assembly, Kiruna, Sweden, August 24–27, 1977 (report).

Webb, W. E. 1966. Land capacity classification and land use in the Chittagong hill tracts of East Pakistan. *Proceedings of the Sixth World Forestry Congress* 3:3229–3232.

Webb, Walter Prescott. 1952. *The Great Frontier.* Boston: Houghton Mifflin.

Weiss, Gerald. 1988. The tragedy of ethnocide: A reply to Hippler. In *Tribal Peoples and Development Issues: A Global Overview,* ed. John H. Bodley, pp. 124–133. Mountain View, Calif.: Mayfield.

Wellington, John H. 1967. *South West Africa and Its Human Issues.* Oxford: Clarendon Press/Oxford University Press.

Whitten, Norman E. 1976. *Ecuadorian Ethnocide and Indigenous Ethnogenesis: Amazonian Resurgence Amidst Andean Colonialism.* IWGIA Document no. 23. Copenhagen: IWGIA.

Winnacker, Martha. 1979. The battle to stop the Chico dams. *Southeast Asia Chronicle,* no. 67:22–29.

Wirsing, R. 1985. The health of traditional societies and the effects of acculturation. *Current Anthropology* 26:303–322.

Wise, Mary Ruth, Eugene E. Loos, and Patricia Davis. 1977. Filosofía y Métodos del Instituto Linguistico de Verano. Proceedings of the 42nd International Americanists Congress, Paris. Vol. 2:499–525.

Wollaston, A. F. R. 1920. Remarks on "The opening of new territories in Papua." *The Geographical Journal* (June):457–458.

Wood Jones, Frederic. 1928. *The Claims of the Australian Aborigine.* 18th ANZAAS, Perth, 1926, Report 18:497–519.

Woodruff, William. 1966. *Impact of Western Man.* London: Macmillan.

Wright, R. Michael, Brian Houseal, and Cebaldo de Leon. 1985. Kuna Yala: Indigenous biosphere reserve in the making? *Parks* 10(3):25–27. (Reprinted in Bodley, 1988:352–356.)

Zallez, Jaime, and Alfonso Gortaire. 1978. *Organizarse o Sucumbir: La Federacíon Shuar.* Mundo Shuar Serie "B," No. 14. Sucua, Ecuador: Centro de Documentacion e Investigacíon Cultural Shuar.

Zaman, M. Q. 1985. Tribal survival in the Chittagong hill tracts of Bangladesh. *Man in India* 65(1):58–74.

Index

RSV - Princ. of Anthropology